To: Immanuel
From: John Crowan

MW00597703

CHOOSE TO BE A DISCIPLE

Don't Turn Back

TESTIMONIES AND RAMBLINGS OF A REDNECK DISCIPLE OF JESUS CHRIST

ELLISON S KELLY JR

ISBN: 1499317360
ISBN: 9781499317367
Library of Congress Control Number: 2014908226
CreateSpace Independent Publishing Platform
North Charleston, South Carolina

DEDICATION

This book is dedicated to my daughter, Susan Elizabeth Kelly.

God used my unconditional love for my daughter to help me understand His unconditional love for someone like me.

Opening Statement

To God be all the praise, honor, and glory!

This book is not about me. It's about a *personal relationship.* It's about the personal relationship our God wants to have with each of His children. And this relationship will be different and specific for each one of us.

This nonfiction book reflects my experiences and those of close personal friends while walking with our Savior over the last twenty-five years. While I didn't keep a journal during this time, these testimonies were chosen by our Lord to recall to my imperfect memory. I've put them on paper as accurately as possible without trying to sensationalize or glorify the experiences. My intent is to glorify only my God: the Father, the Son, and the Holy Spirit.

My prayer is that these writings will encourage you to draw close to our Lord and have a personal relationship with Him. My prayer is that these writings will encourage you to step out in faith and share the good news of Jesus Christ with a dying world. My prayer is that these writings will encourage you to get out of the boat and get in the fight against Satan and his evil forces. My prayer is that you will choose to be a disciple. Don't turn back.

Something Else

Our God is still at work in our lives today. So is Satan.

Tomorrow I plan to send the final draft of this book to the publisher. Satan has really been hitting me hard to water down the testimonies, telling me, "Don't publish the book." He's hitting me hard with his mind games. He keeps telling me, "The readers won't believe you. They'll think you're crazy. You'll make a fool of yourself." I was really thinking of deleting some of the testimonies and watering down others. But God said no. And He confirmed this to me three times today, the day before the book goes to the publisher.

First, we were at the College of Charleston this morning giving out Gideon New Testaments to students. A young man walked up to me and asked, "Sir, have you ever seen anyone whose face was radiant? I mean, whose face actually glowed?"

I told him, "Yes, one time." He explained how a lady whose face was radiant came up to him and said, "Be careful. One day you may be entertaining angels." She then left. A short time later, she came back and gave him a Bible. He opened the Bible, and his eyes immediately went to a verse. He said this one verse somehow stood out from all the others on that page. It said, "Do not forget to show hospitality to strangers, for by so doing some people have shown hospitality to angels without knowing it" (Hebrews 13:2). He looked up, but the lady had disappeared. He asked if I thought she was an angel. I told him yes, because I've had a similar experience. (Satan had been telling me to delete the chapter on the vanishing hitchhiker and how Delores's face was radiant in the chapter "Go See Delores").

Second, later this same day, I had lunch with a good Christian friend who told me of a vision experience where God took his spirit out of his body. With tears in his eyes, he explained how he was engulfed in God's love. He explained much more. He said, "After that vision experience, I have no fear of death." (Satan had been telling me to delete the chapter "The Vision.")

Third, this evening at a meeting, we discussed dreams and visions. One of the men told of how he has a friend who just really doesn't believe in visions. As we discussed, Satan was telling me, "See, they won't believe you either." Then, after the meeting, one of the men called me aside and asked, "Could I tell you about two dreams I've just had? I had the same dream two nights in a row. I normally don't have dreams, so why did God show me the same dream two nights in a row?" I explained that God was confirming the dream. My friend did not realize it, but God also just used him to give me a third confirmation in one day to publish the book.

Later the same evening, God then told me, "Don't worry about the scoffers. There will always be scoffers. This book is for those who believe. This book is for those who have a relationship with Me. This book is for those who long to have a relationship with Me."

CONTENTS

Introduction

The name of this book comes from the Gospel of John. In addition to the twelve, Jesus had a large crowd of people who followed Him, and they too wanted to be His disciples. A disciple is a student who walks with a master and listens, learns, and obeys the master and his or her teachings. Throughout the gospels, Jesus explained the cost of being one of His disciples. He gives us a choice—to follow Him and be a disciple, or to turn back, as many did then and many do today.

Some of His teachings include:

> "I am the way and the truth and the life. No one comes to the Father except through me" (John 14:6).
>
> "If your right eye causes you to stumble, gouge it out and throw it away" (Matthew 5:29).
>
> "If anyone slaps you on the right cheek, turn to them the other cheek also" (Matthew 5:39).
>
> "Whoever acknowledges me before others, I will also acknowledge before my Father in heaven. But whoever disowns me before others, I will disown before my Father in heaven" (Matt 10:32–33).
>
> "Whoever is not with me is against me" (Matthew 12:30).
>
> "Whoever wants to be my disciple must deny themselves and take up their cross and follow me. For whoever wants to save their life will lose it, but whoever loses their life for me and for the gospel will save it" (Mark 8:34–35).

> "Anyone who wants to be first must be the very last, and the servant of all" (Mark 9:35).
>
> "No one who puts a hand to the plow and looks back is fit for service in the kingdom of God" (Luke 9:62).
>
> "You cannot serve both God and money" (Luke 16:13).
>
> "If the world hates you, keep in mind that it hated me first" (John 15:18).
>
> "If they persecuted me, they will persecute you also" (John 15:20).

Then, when Jesus was teaching in the synagogue in Capernaum, He really laid it out for His disciples. He said, "Whoever eats my flesh and drinks my blood remains in me, and I in them" (John 6:56). The Bible then tells us, "From this time many of his disciples turned back and no longer followed him" (John 6:66). These verses inspired the title of this book: *Choose to Be a Disciple—Don't Turn Back.*

God gives each of us a choice. We can choose to give up our lives and hold to the life of Christ and follow Him—or we can choose to sit on the sidelines and watch others who choose to follow our risen Savior.

I hesitate to call this a book. I would say it is more a group of testimonies that are bound in something that resembles a book. I love testimonies. One of my favorite Bible verses is:

> "They triumphed over him by the blood of the Lamb and by the word of their testimony; they did not love their lives so much as to shrink from death" (Revelation 12:11).

Satan hates testimonies that glorify our God; therefore, I love testimonies that glorify our God. When I pray, I often ask

God to help me love the things He loves and to hate the things He hates.

Most Christians have many testimonies. One might give a cup of hot coffee to a beggar. Another might lead a crusade. Both testimonies glorify God. Our testimonies are like DNA and fingerprints; they are unique.

As I put these testimonies on paper, my prayer is that all of what I write will glorify God, not me. These testimonies are my firsthand accounts of God's work in my life and in the lives of others He has placed in my path. They are about what God has done to me and through me, and to others and through others. All the glory belongs to God. Without God, there would be no testimonies, and there would be no book.

There are two major parts to this book: BC (before I became a Christian) and AC (after I became a Christian). In between the BC and the AC, there is a major "pivotal moment." It was when I came face-to-face with God and surrendered my life to Him. I would consider the other major events "defining moments."

"Pivotal moments" are huge events after which the directions of our lives change forever. These events spell out who and what we are. Each is a total change in direction after where we came from to where we are going, and life is never the same. It is a point of no return. Saul (Paul) heard the voice of Jesus and was blinded for three days. Moses had his "burning bush" experience. Noah built the ark. Esther risked death to save the Jews. Elisha slaughtered his yoke of oxen and burned the plowing equipment. The disciples left their nets, boats, and livelihood to follow Jesus. These changed lives glorified God.

"Defining moments," on the other hand, are refining moments where we learn, grow, or possibly accomplish a major goal. They may also be major setbacks, such as the loss of a loved one. A defining moment could be the pain after committing a sin. It is where we make course adjustments in the directions of our lives. We encounter many of these defining moments during the courses of our lives.

When I became a Christian in 1988, I often listened to Dr. Charles Stanley's television sermons. He helped me tremendously in my early walk with our Lord. In one of his sermons, he suggested that Christians should keep journals. I remember saying, "That's a good idea. I'll keep a journal."

Then I heard God's voice. He said, "No, I don't want you to live in the past; I want you to live in the today and in the tomorrow (the future)."

I said, "OK," even though I did not understand. But I knew it was God's voice, so no explanation was needed.

Twenty years later, in 2008, God said, "Write it down." He didn't need to explain what to write down, because I knew exactly what He was saying to me. He was telling me to put on paper these testimonies and ramblings. At that time and for the next four years, I gave God many excuses for not writing this book. There were so many testimonies, because so much had happened over twenty years. Which testimonies should I write down? The task was so huge for someone like me. I started writing and then quit many times. I simply did not want to write this book. Obviously, I lost the argument.

Since I kept no journal, I wrote this book from memory. I wrote only what God recalled to my imperfect mind. My desire is to keep events and details as accurate as possible. In the Bible, God tells us not to add or take away from His word, and I feel the same thing applies here. Most of the defining moments (testimonies) I share are uplifting and what I would call "good" experiences. However, a few are very, very painful. Throughout the book, I changed names, places, and other details to protect the identities of the innocent and, in some cases, the guilty. These changes do not alter the essence of the spiritual battle that occurred. I absolutely do not want anyone to be hurt by this book. I have seen God lift up some of his Christian children and glorify himself. I have also seen God allow the evil one to have his way with Christian men and women. After

Satan slaps them down, God gently restores them and glorifies Himself through their recovery and growth.

The central theme of this book can be found in the close, personal relationship our God wants to have with each one of us. Our God is right in the middle of each one of the testimonies shared throughout the book. He wants to be closer to each of us than a husband and wife on their fiftieth wedding anniversary. This relationship doesn't start when we get to Heaven; it starts now. He wants to be active in our daily lives. Our love relationship with Jesus Christ will hopefully cause each of us to step out in faith—get out of the boat—and choose to be a disciple. Jesus wants each of us to choose to join Him and to "get in the fight." That fight will be different for each one of us. Two thousand years ago, many of Jesus's followers chose to turn back. Today, many still choose to turn back, while others choose to be disciples and follow Christ.

The testimonies I share show how God is active in our lives today. In them, I discuss visions, dreams, angels, demons, healings, God's voice, the Rapture, the Holy Spirit, and more. If you are a Christian who does not believe God is still active in these ways today, you may want to just go ahead and toss this book in the trash. If you choose to read on, please know that I have prayed that the testimonies you read will strengthen your faith. I pray you will hunger and long for this personal relationship with our Savior. God says, "You will seek me and find me when you seek me with all your heart" (Jeremiah 29:13). I pray you will seek to follow Jesus with all your heart.

I have Christian friends who believe God stopped doing miracles two thousand years ago. Still others do not believe in the virgin birth, Jonah, or Job. Even though they do not believe that every word in the Bible is God's word, and that's their choice, they are still my friends. But there is one thing we must all agree on: *Jesus is the way and the only way*. If you don't believe that, the rest really does not matter.

Someone once said, "For those who believe in God, no explanation is necessary. For those who don't believe in God, no explanation is sufficient." I believe that "with God all things are possible" (Matthew 19:26). I may not understand what is happening at a given time, but I accept what is happening as a "God thing" and keep moving forward. I still live in the "today" and in the "tomorrow."

I truly hope you will recognize the love of our Savior through the pages in this book. I truly hope you will choose to be a disciple of Jesus Christ. Don't turn back.

Keep the faith, my friend, and share it with all who will listen. Jesus is coming "soon" (Revelation 22:20).

CHAPTER 1

BEFORE CHRIST

This chapter is about my family and me before I came face-to-face with God in 1988. I was born during World War II. After Dad returned home from Germany, our family moved to a cotton-mill town in the upper part of South Carolina. Dad worked in the engineering office at the mill, and Mom stayed home to raise my sister, Connie, and me. In our small community, we had two choices for church: a small Southern Baptist church on one corner and a Methodist church on the other.

We had a drug problem in that small community. It occurred every Sunday morning. Dad took my right hand, Mom took my left hand, and they "drug" me to church. I don't remember ever liking church in those early days.

One Sunday evening, my buddies and I were sitting in the back pew while the preacher preached. I had found a penny-box of Dad's matches. The other boys dared me to shoot a "match rocket" (put a match against the strike strip on the match box and thump the match). As a young boy, you never walk away from a dare. So I set the match against the box and flipped it with my finger. The match immediately struck and flew several feet in the air, leaving a beautiful, flaming trail of white smoke. The boys then double-dared me to do it again. This time, the preacher saw what I had done. He immediately came down from the pulpit, took the matches away, and scolded me. He said I could have burned down the church. I think he just didn't like me. Dad immediately got up, took me out in front of the church, and beat my tail unmercifully. When we got home that evening, I got another beating.

Somehow, I survived Bible school, Royal Ambassadors, and other youth programs. When I was about fourteen years old, I joined the Baptist church and was baptized. I had no clue that I was a sinner and needed a Savior. I just wanted to drink the glass of grape juice and eat the saltine cracker when they were passed in church. You had to be a member of the church to take communion.

I remember the Sunday evening when I was baptized (dunked and almost drowned). I remember the preacher leaning over and whispering in my ear, "Exhale." So I blew all the air out of my lungs. Then he put his hand over my mouth and nose, and under the water I went. Even though I was under the water, I could hear him preaching what seemed like a sermon. My lungs were screaming for air. I started kicking my feet, and they came up, splashing water out of the in-church baptismal pool. I was fighting the preacher with all my strength. And then, finally, he pulled me up, and I gasped for air.

Later that evening at home, Mom asked me why I kicked and fought the preacher. I told her, "Mom, the preacher tried to drown me." I told her that the preacher had told me to exhale, so I did.

Mom said, "No, son, surely he must have told you to inhale." Mom's wrong; that man tried to drown me.

I would classify our preacher as a "hellfire and brimstone preacher." It seemed like every Sunday he was calling men by name, telling them they were going to Hell. One Sunday evening, he came down from the pulpit and climbed up on the first pew, putting one foot on its backrest and the other on the backrest of the second pew. He called out, "Jo Lee, I saw you behind the church this evening before the service taking a sip of whisky. You're going to Hell." Jo Lee probably needed that sip of whisky just to get through the service. I don't ever remember hearing about the love and goodness of God, only about "going to Hell."

After my sister and I were baptized and became members of the church, Dad and Mom slacked off attending. I think Dad and Mom figured we all had our tickets to get into Heaven, so the pressure of attending church was gone. After I graduated from high school and went off to college, I completely dropped out of church for the next thirty years.

I never cared much about organized sports, church, or school. But I loved the outdoors—hunting, fishing, camping, and all that. I joined the Boy Scouts and was the first Eagle Scout in our troop.

School

Making good grades in school was tough for me. My sister, on the other hand, made A's. I was two grades behind her, and each time I was promoted to the next grade, my new teacher would always say something like, "Oh, you're Connie Kelly's brother. Are you as smart as Connie?" And my answer was always no.

Throughout our school years, Mom and Dad told us and others that "Connie got all the 'book sense' and Ellison got all the 'common sense.'" And they were right.

Throughout school, and even now, I am not able to concentrate on what I'm doing. In school, I would sit and doodle rather than listen to the teacher. When I was required to read, the words seemed to flip backward. Numbers would also flip backward. Mom always said I had two left feet. Today, we have names like "dyslexia" and "attention deficit disorder" for these problems, and doctors can often help kids adjust. But back then, they knew nothing about such conditions, and my teachers just assumed I was not too bright.

I remember when I was in the third grade, Mom, Dad, and my schoolteacher had a conference to discuss my repeating the grade because I could not read and write. I begged them to let me stay with my buddies in my class and move on to the fourth grade. They finally agreed. But I struggled each year just to keep up with my friends. Then, again, when it was time to be promoted to the twelfth grade, there was a problem. This time, I didn't make it. I failed the eleventh grade and had to retake it. My classmates moved on, and I fell one year behind them.

At that time, to be admitted to college, a student had to graduate from high school and make a good score on the Scholastic Aptitude Test (SAT). I remember driving to Spartanburg one Saturday to take the exam. It's a two-part exam, and each part carries a maximum score of eight hundred points.

The morning math session went well; however, the afternoon verbal session did not. The afternoon questions were multiple choice. I started reading the questions and thought, "Wow!" I didn't have a clue what this was all about. I skimmed through all the questions and did not recognize a single one of them. None! I looked around the room at the other students. They were just ripping through the test. I thought about getting up, turning in my paper, and leaving. But I was afraid the instructor would chastise me in front of the other students. Even though our high school teacher told us not to guess at the answers to the questions, I took the answer sheet, and without looking at a single question, I guessed at an answer for every question. Then I waited for some of the smart kids to turn in their papers. After several of them did and left, I did likewise.

So why am I telling you how poorly I did in school? It's just to tell you that I'm about the last person on the face of the earth who should be writing a book. I'm like Gideon. When the angel of the Lord called out to him, he referred to Gideon as "mighty warrior" (Judges 6:12). Gideon's reply was, "I am the least in my family" (Judges 6:15). I too am the "least in my family." My sister and her husband have their PhDs, and they write books. I hunt and fish. But our God has plans for each of us. He does not focus on what we are today; He looks ahead to how He will use us in the future.

After the SAT, Mom asked me how it went. I could tell by the look on her face that she knew I would never be admitted to college, but she did not put me down. She always encouraged me. Dad did likewise, most of the time. I still remember the expressions on their faces when the SAT letter came in the mail. I knew I had done well on the math section, but to my surprise, I actually scored 354 on the afternoon verbal exam (where I guessed at every question). The 354 guesswork score paid off. When added to the math score, I qualified for admission at Clemson University.

Money was always a problem. Connie was smart and received a scholarship to college. I worked. When I turned fifteen, I started working in a grocery store after school, bagging groceries, mopping floors, stocking shelves, and that sort of thing. I worked several evenings during the week after school and every weekend. When I turned sixteen, I was old enough to work in the cotton mill. For seven years, I worked during the summers, Christmas breaks, spring breaks, Thanksgiving breaks, and any other time school was not in session. I saved all the money I earned, except 10 percent for church, to pay for college. I didn't understand why Mom and Dad made me give that 10 percent to the church, because I needed that money to pay for college.

Working in the cotton mill was tough. I usually worked the afternoon shift (3:30 p.m. to 11:30 p.m.) or the "graveyard" shift (11:30 p.m. to 7:30 a.m.). I frequently worked double shifts to make extra money and managed to pay for five years of college.

The first day at Clemson, I remember the president of the university addressing the freshman class. He said, "Look at the young man seated on your left. Now look at the young man seated on your right. Four years from now, they won't be here." He was telling us that two out of three of us would fail. He was right, and I was almost one of those who flunked out.

My college books and I did not get along well at all. For example, I took English 101 my first semester and failed it. I took it over my second semester and failed it again. My second year at college, I failed English 101 for the third time. Then, the second semester of my sophomore year, I barely passed English 101. I was on scholastic probation at the end of each of my first four years at college, and my grade point average was too low for graduation.

Then something happened. During the summer after my fourth year at college, I was working the graveyard shift in the cotton mill. I was running a set of drawing frames. I stopped working and looked around. I looked at some of the old men and women who were my work friends. I realized that my friends would be working that graveyard shift until the day they died. I thought, *Boy, you too will be on this graveyard shift the rest of your life if you flunk out of college.* When I returned to Clemson that fall, my grades improved. I finally had a reason to graduate. I did not want to work on graveyard shift in a cotton mill the rest of my life. I was able to pull up my average enough to barely graduate after five years at Clemson. I would say that night in the cotton mill was a "defining moment" in my life.

After College

After graduating from Clemson, I worked at a textile plant for about two years. Then the army came calling for recruits. After basic training and advanced individual training, I spent six months at Officer Candidate School (OCS). After graduating from OCS, I was stationed for two years with the Army Corps of Engineers in Charleston, South Carolina, and then off to Vietnam. It was in Charleston that I met my first wife. When I returned home from Vietnam, I received an honorable discharge and began looking for a job.

There was one positive thing that came out of the army experience—the army made a man out of me. Until that time, I was definitely tied to Mom's apron strings. The army cut those strings for me. It helped me realize what I was capable of both physically and mentally. The army, especially OCS, was another defining moment in my life.

I learned of a job opening in the physical plant of the Medical University of South Carolina (MUSC) in Charleston. I went by for an interview, and I met the director of the physical plant. He discussed the job with me and mentioned a pay grade, which meant nothing to me, and then he offered me a job. I didn't even know what a "physical plant" was, and I didn't know how much the job paid. I needed a job and gladly, I accepted the offer. Twenty-eight years later, I retired from MUSC.

I had helped a friend build a house, and he moved in a few months later. I thought, *If he can do it, so can I*. I asked all my friends if they would help me build a house. Most said they would be glad to help. So I bought a chain saw and began clearing a lot. Then came digging foundation ditches, pouring concrete, framing, roofing, plumbing, electrical, and all the rest. Five years after driving the first nail, we moved into the house. I never saw most of my friends during construction. But after starting the work, I met Doug, a new friend. Doug was a "redneck" who lived down the street from the new house. He was a true friend and a huge help in framing the house.

It was a beautiful house built one nail at a time, one day at a time, for five years. I would work a nine-hour work day at MUSC, come home, and work until midnight on the house. Since I was not a Christian and did not worship on Sunday, I worked on the house seven days a week. A short time after moving in, my wife and I were divorced. This was another "defining moment" in my life.

I remember just before entering the courtroom for the divorce, my lawyer said, "We're going to discuss several separate issues: fault, money, property, and Susan, your daughter." He said I probably wouldn't get everything I wanted and asked which one of these was the most important to me. I told him that the only thing that I cared about was my daughter, who was eight years old at that time. Nothing else mattered to me more than getting custody of her. Then he broke the bad news to me. My lawyer was an old man, and he said that in all his years of practicing law, he had represented only two men who were awarded full custody of a daughter as young as Susan. He said that 99 percent of the time, the mother would be awarded custody. And then he gave me more bad news: the judge was a woman. I felt like the deck was stacked against me.

But the judge awarded me full custody of Susan. That day, I became a full-time single parent. Even though I was not a Christian then, I know now that the Lord worked this out for us. God says, "'For I know the plans I have for you,' declares the Lord, 'plans to prosper you and not to harm you, plans to give you hope and a future'" (Jeremiah 29:11).

Becoming a single parent was another defining moment in my life. Much of that time, I worked two jobs while raising my daughter. God knew how tough it would be, so he moved my mom to Mount Pleasant, where we now lived, to help me raise Susan. It was also during this time as a single parent that I started dating my second wife, Connie. There wasn't much time for dating, but we were grateful for the time we had. After dating about three years, we were engaged. Two years later, we were married.

Church

During the single-parent years, I thought it would be good to take Susan to church. I assumed that I was a Christian since I was a member of the church back home and had been baptized. If there really was a God and a Heaven, I wanted Susan to also go to Heaven. I would take Susan to her Sunday-school class, and I would attend an adult version. Since they did not have a "single again" class, I met with the young, married adult class. I knew only one of the men in the class of about twenty couples.

I did this for about three months. Since I was new to the class and also divorced, I did not feel very welcomed. I felt, and was treated, like I had the plague. The husbands and wives stood around chatting and having a good time while I just sat on the sidelines by myself. I felt like an outcast.

After Sunday school was over, I would walk around to the front of the church to enter the sanctuary for the preaching service. There were always several men in white shirts and ties standing on the church porch, greeting people. I rarely got a handshake or a "howdy-do" from the greeters. They were gladly greeting and shooting the breeze with the folks they knew. But when I walked up, they hardly ever spoke to me. They were supposed to hand out the church bulletins to everyone entering the service, but they hardly ever handed one to me. I would usually just walk past the greeters ("clique" would be a better name for the group), and pick up my bulletin off the table inside the church.

Susan and I attended church for about three months. Then, one Sunday after hardly being spoken to in Sunday school or at preaching, I said to myself, "If this is what church is all about, to Hell with it!"

Even though I stopped attending, I still felt the need to take Susan. I thought she needed to become a Christian so she could go to Heaven if there really was one. I became one of the world's biggest hypocrites. I would drive to church on Sunday, drop Susan off at the back door so she could attend Sunday school, and leave, usually to do my weekly grocery shopping. I would then pick Susan up to go home. When she asked why I was not attending church, I explained that I was working two jobs and did not have time for Sunday school; I needed to do our grocery shopping on Sundays. I guess that sounded like a reasonable explanation to her.

One major outcome resulted from Susan's continued attendance at church. Ann, Susan's Sunday school teacher, led her to Christ, which is something that I, her dad, should have done. But I did not know Christ myself, even though I was a member of a church.

I continued taking Susan to Sunday school for a while. Then, since I felt she had her ticket punched to get into Heaven, we stopped.

Turkeys and the Heart Attack

In April 1987, I was still a single parent and had not yet become a Christian. I went turkey hunting in the Hell Hole section of Francis Marion National Forest. It was a beautiful Friday morning, and I hunted a swamp that was long and wide. That morning, I had gobblers answering my call, but I could not bring them close enough for a shot. About 10:00 a.m., the wind picked up, so I decided to head home.

As I walked down a deer trail that led out of the swamp, I felt a huge fist hit me in the center of my chest. I immediately looked around to see who had hit me, but nobody was there. I thought maybe a tree limb had hit me, but no tree limbs were near me. Then I felt a burning pain shooting up the left side of my neck. The pain started shooting down through my left arm. I broke out in a cold sweat, and the intense pain began moving down through my entire body. As I stood there, I thought, *I can't believe this. I'm forty-three years old, and I'm having a heart attack.* I thought, *Don't panic. If you can live through Vietnam, you can live through anything. Just don't panic.* I knew I needed to get to help fast.

I was growing weaker by the second, and the pain was increasing. I tossed my brand-new, Browning automatic shotgun and my bag of turkey calls on the ground and was going to just leave them there in the swamp. I knew I was in serious trouble, and my truck was a mile away. The nearest house was about two miles away. I took one step and realized I could walk no further. I was so weak and the pain was so severe that I knew in a matter of seconds, I would pass out, fall on my face, and die right there in Hell Hole Swamp.

I've been told that a soldier who has been wounded and is about to die will cry out to either God or Mom. I knew Mom couldn't help me, so for the first time in my life, I prayed a "real" prayer to God. I can tell you the exact words I prayed. When you're about to die, you don't forget things like that. Looking up into the sky, I said,

> "God, I have never asked you for anything for myself before. But I'm asking you now, let me live long enough to raise my daughter. Then, when she's old enough to take care of herself, if you still want me dead, kill me, I don't give a xxxx."

I really didn't care about myself. I only cared about my daughter. My world for the last four years as a single parent had revolved around raising my daughter. Like most parents, I wanted the best for her. I wanted much more for my daughter than what life had dealt to me.

I will tell you that immediately—I say again, immediately—after I said that prayer, the heart attack went away. It was like it had never happened. All the severe pain was immediately gone. The weakness to the point of passing out immediately left, and my strength was totally back, just as if the heart attack had never happened. I was soaking wet in a cold sweat, but the heart attack was completely gone. I went from near death to life in a split second.

> *My good friend, Bryan, had served on the navy ship Lindsey during World War II. Bryan has shared his testimony with us many times. He and his fellow sailors were manning a gun when seven Japanese Kamikaze airplanes headed for them. Brian told me that one plane was so close that he could see the pilot's face. They kept firing at the plane when Bryan prayed, "Dear Lord, not now!" Their gun immediately shot a wing off of the airplane, and it flipped over and crashed into another area of the ship. Fifty-seven men lost their lives, and that many more were wounded in that one attack, but Bryan's life was spared. He said, "For some reason, our Lord saw fit to spare me that day." Bryan knows God heard his prayer and immediately answered it. Bryan said, "He had something here on earth for me to do."*

I picked up my shotgun and pack and walked out of the woods to my truck. I did not even bother to thank God for sparing my life. I stood there beside my truck for a half hour or so and drank a beer or two (I often carried a cooler and a six-pack in the back of the truck.) I was not so much concerned about myself. I just did not want to have another heart attack while driving home. I did not want my truck to hit a car and kill innocent people.

Over the weekend, I started thinking about going to a doctor to check out my heart. On Monday, I went to see Dr. Gazes, one of the top heart doctors in the United States. After Dr. Gazes examined me and completed all his tests, he sat with me and told me what had happened. He explained, "Yes, you had a heart attack, and it was a bad one." Then he started using big medical terms to describe it.

I stopped him and said, "Hey, doc, talk to me in English."

He said, "It's like someone put their hand inside your chest and squeezed your heart. It completely stopped working. You should be dead." Well, that was clear enough.

I asked, "Could it happen again?"

He said, "Yes, it could happen anytime."

I asked, "Will it kill me if it happens again?"

He said, "There's a high probability that it will."

Today they call it "sudden cardiac arrest," and I've since read that it happens mostly to young men. And 95 percent of these young men die on the spot. But even this did not get my attention and turn me to God. It doesn't even count as a "defining moment" in my life. To me, it was no big deal. Everybody dies.

Then it happened: my "pivotal moment."

The Holy Spirit Pays a Visit

On a hot Saturday morning in June 1988, I was in the backyard working on a small boat I was rebuilding. I came into the house to fix myself a cold drink (bourbon and Coke). I fixed the drink, sat in my recliner, and turned on the TV. To my surprise, the TV was on one of those "religious" channels. We absolutely never watched those religious channels in our house. How the TV got on that channel, I did not know (now I realize it was a "God thing," a work of the Holy Spirit).

There was an old man, a TV evangelist named John G. Hall, talking about how the stars were going to fall from the sky, millions of people would be killed, scorpions would sting people, and on and on. He said the Christians would be gone, that they would have been caught up in the Rapture (whatever that was) and would miss all this "Hell on earth." He said people would beg God to let them die, but God would not let them die. He was preaching from Revelation, although I did not know it at the time. What he preached made me very uncomfortable.

Then he pointed his finger at the TV camera, seemingly directly at me, and said, "And if you're not a Christian, judgment and Hell are waiting on you." I caught the last five minutes of his message, which made me even more uneasy. So I did what came natural. I fixed myself another drink and went back to work on the boat.

The next Saturday, I was again working on the boat. I came into the house and fixed myself a drink. I flipped on the TV, and again, the same preacher, the same message, and the same last five minutes of the program were on it. The TV preacher again said, "And if you're not a Christian, judgment and Hell are waiting on you." Well, he just about scared the Hell out of me this time. I turned off the TV, fixed myself another drink, sat down, and thought about what he had said. I thought, *Am I a Christian?*

I started thinking about all the "good things" I had done in my life. I was a good kid. I was an Eagle Scout. I helped old ladies across the street. I occasionally gave a little money to charity. I served my country in Vietnam. I was a good father to my daughter. And the list went on and on. Then I thought about things I was not so proud of. Even though I cursed fluently and was somewhat proud of my cursing vocabulary, I knew it was wrong. I looked at the drink in my hand and remembered the preacher who baptized me. He had pointed to men in the church and told them they were going to Hell for drinking alcohol. I remembered when I shortchanged the cashier in the grocery store and did not tell her. And the list goes on and on.

I wondered, *Just how do we get into Heaven? How much* good stuff *do we have to do to make up for all the* bad stuff*? Do we take a test or something?* I had almost flunked out of school. Was I now going to flunk out of getting into Heaven?

In the Gospel of John, Jesus told the disciples that He would send the Holy Spirit to them and that "When he comes, he will prove the world to be in the wrong about sin and righteousness and judgment" (John 16:8). Even though I did not have a clue, the Holy Spirit was convicting me to my core. Somehow, I knew I was roadkill. I knew I needed help, but I did not know who I could talk with. None of my friends were Christians. They were just like me. Then I thought of someone I could talk with: Mom was a strong Christian, and she usually came by the house on Sundays after church.

When she came by, I asked her, "How do you know if you're a Christian?"

Mom said, "Don't you remember joining the church and being baptized?"

I told her, "Yes, I remember. The preacher tried to drown me." I asked again, "But can you know, for certain, that you're a Christian?"

She said, "You know because you have Jesus in your heart."

I then asked, "Well, how does Jesus get into your heart? Through your mouth? Through your nose? How?" Mom once knew how to share the gospel, but she was now seventy-four years old and said she didn't remember how to explain it. Mom offered to have the preacher come by the house and I told her, "No way. All preachers want is your money, and I don't want him near me."

Mom then said, "Well, I guess you'll have to ask one of your Christian friends—someone who is younger and can explain it to you."

I said, "Mom, I don't have any Christian friends."

Mom said, "Then you'll have to find the answer for yourself. The answer will be in the Bible." She asked if I still had the Bible from my childhood, and I told her it was somewhere around the house. But I don't read well and did not want to read the whole Bible.

I asked, "Where is the answer in the Bible?"

She said, "You'll find the answer in the New Testament."

"Is that the front half of the Bible or the back?" I remembered from my childhood that there were two parts to the Bible. She told me to find the table of contents, look for Matthew, and start reading there.

After Mom left, I found the Bible from my childhood, wiped off the dust, found Matthew, and started reading. The Gospel of Matthew begins with the genealogy of Jesus Christ. Wow! It read like a jigsaw puzzle. The Bible made no sense to me, with all this crazy language. Out of frustration and the conviction of the Holy Spirit, I threw the Bible all the way across the room. I complained, "I don't need all this crap; all I want to know is if Heaven is real. And if it is, how do I get in?"

I really didn't want to, but I had no choice. I picked up the Bible, skipped all the names, and started reading about the birth of Jesus. The Bible I was reading was the King James Version (KJV), and since I did not read well, I truly had a difficult time. I understood very little of what I was reading, partly because of my reading problems, but more because, "The god of this age has blinded the minds of unbelievers, so that they cannot see the light of the gospel that displays the glory of Christ" (2 Corinthians 4:4).

During the next two weeks, I read the Bible every spare minute I had. I didn't know how to pray, so I would just say out loud, "God, if you are real, help me find the answers I need." I remember reading John 3:16 and saying to myself, "Hey, that's the Bible verse I memorized when I was a kid." I thought, *Why did we memorize that verse?* I read it over and over and could not for the life of me understand why God would give his Son for the "world." I did not understand that the "world" referred to the people on planet earth, not the planet. Satan definitely had me blinded.

I remembered the TV preacher saying the "Rapture" would happen and all the Christians would leave the earth "before" all these horrible things occurred. Then I started getting scared—really scared. What if that Rapture thing happened today and I'm still not a Christian? Now I needed to know when the Rapture was going to happen. So far, when reading the Bible, I had not seen the word Rapture (now I know it is because the word "Rapture" is not in the Bible). I needed to know, and needed to know "now," how much longer I had to find the answer about becoming a Christian (before the Rapture happened). Who could I go to and ask about the Rapture?

I thought of one man: Roy. I knew Roy was a Christian. He didn't lie, curse, steal, or cheat. He went to church on Sundays and could be trusted. On Sunday afternoon, I gathered up some courage and went to Roy's house. I rang the bell, and he came to the door. I said to Roy, "You're a Christian, aren't you?" He answered yes. I then asked him if he knew anything about the "Rapture."

He answered, "Yes. The word is not used in the Bible, but the Bible talks about when the Christians will be 'taken away.'"

"Roy, when is it going to happen?"

He said, "The Bible doesn't tell us. No one knows. The Bible only tells us to *be ready*."

That was not the answer I wanted to hear. I wanted to ask, "What does it take to become a Christian and know that you are going to Heaven?" But I was about to cry, and since rednecks don't cry, I just turned around, walked to my truck, and drove home.

I really didn't understand what was going on. Up until that point in my life, I was quite happy. I had my daughter, fiancée, job, house, guns, boats, ATV, and four-wheel drive truck. I thought, "What more could a man want?" I really didn't need God. So now I feel like I'm running in circles, chasing my tail and thinking, *Is Heaven real? If it is, then Hell must also be real.*

I was under the conviction of the Holy Spirit. I needed answers, and I needed them now. I again picked up the Bible and continued reading. Later that Sunday evening, the doorbell rang. It was Roy. He gave me a handful of tracts that he had picked up at church that evening. He said, "Ellison, maybe these will help you find some answers you're looking for." Then he left.

The tracts were a huge help because they were written in everyday English that I could understand. They even explained John 3:16. For the first time in two weeks, I started to understand what the Bible was telling me: I was a sinner, I needed a Savior, and Jesus Christ was the only Savior that was acceptable to God. Over the next few days, all the pieces of the puzzle began to fit together. For the first time in my forty-four years, I understood what those crosses on church buildings symbolized. I understood why Jesus was crucified; He went to the cross in my place.

On Wednesday afternoon, Roy called and asked if I wanted to attend the Wednesday evening church service with him. He offered to come by and give me a ride. I declined and said maybe some other time. By Thursday evening, I had it all together. Some of the Bible verses that rang my bell included:

> "For all have sinned and fall short of the glory of God" (Romans 3:23).
>
> "For the wages of sin is death" (Romans 6:23).
>
> "But God demonstrates his own love for us in this: while we were still sinners, Christ died for us" (Romans 5:8).
>
> "For God did not send his Son into the world to condemn the world, but to save the world through him" (John 3:17).
>
> "Whoever believes in him is not condemned, but whoever does not believe stands condemned already because they have not believed in the name of God's one and only Son" (John 3:18).

That Thursday evening, I put Susan to bed early. I recalled that when my sister and I were small kids, Mom would kneel with us beside our beds and pray the "Now I lay me down to sleep" prayer. I took my Bible to my bedroom and laid it in front of me on my bed. I turned out the lights. I got on my knees and looked up (I figured that if Heaven was up there somewhere, that was where God would be) and started talking. Since I didn't know how to pray like the people in church, I just talked to God.

I started by telling God why I was there. I told him, "God, I need your help. I need to get saved." I told God, "I don't know who I'm supposed to talk to about this." I asked, "Do I need to talk to you (God the Father), or to Jesus (God the Son)?" I said, "I'm going to try to do it right, but if I get it all screwed up, I'm asking you to straighten it out for me." I told God that I understood what sin was and that I knew I was the "world's worst sinner"—and I meant it.

Immediately, all my sins started flashing before my eyes: the marbles I stole as a child, the "white lies" I had told, and how I cheated on tests in school when I needed help (or when a friend needed mine). Everything was before me. As I talked with God, He moved from Heaven to right in front of me. Even though I could not see Him with my eyes, I somehow knew that He knelt down on his knees, right in front of me. I absolutely knew that I was in the presence of our holy God.

I kept reaching my hand out to touch Him, but I could not. His love engulfed me. Each time I told Him of another sin and told Him how sorry I was, I would hear God say two words out loud: "I know." I say again, I heard God's voice audibly, "out loud." He was on his knees right in front of me. I could not understand how God could be right in front of me, but I still could not see Him or touch Him. I could feel His presence, His love, and His warmth. I could clearly hear His voice. But when I reached out, no matter how hard I tried, I could not touch Him. At that time, I did not understand that God is Spirit. The Bible says, "God is spirit, and his worshipers must worship in the Spirit and in truth" (John 4:24).

Somehow, I knew what His words, "I know," meant. It's like when you're five and you hit a baseball, breaking a window. Dad comes out, looks at the window, and then looks at you. You run over, wrap your arms around his leg, and start crying. You say, "I'm sorry! I'm sorry! I didn't mean to break the window!" What does your dad do? He wraps his arms of love around you and says, "I know." With these two comforting words, "I know," dad tells you that it's OK. Everything is OK. That is what God was telling me: "It's OK."

The whole bedroom was filled with God's love. As I confessed my sins to God, I told him that I took full responsibility for all the sin in my life. No one had pressured me into sinning. I had chosen to do all the sinful things myself. I offered no excuses. I told God that I alone was guilty of my sins. In the eyes of humanity, I was a good man: a good father, a good friend, a good neighbor, and a good supervisor at work. But kneeling in the presence of our holy God, I felt like the lowest piece of trash on the face of the earth.

Some of you may laugh. God didn't laugh; He knew how serious I was. God also knew how broken I was. Even though I did not know who the Holy Spirit was, I had been under His conviction for two full weeks. He had cleaned my cage.

> *At that time, the only thing I knew about ghosts was the cartoon character, "Casper the Friendly Ghost." I kept reading in the KJV Bible about this Holy Ghost. I could only assume that this ghost was the ghost of Jesus. Jesus was holy, and they killed Him. So this must be His "Holy Ghost" floating around. I just could not figure out why the Bible kept talking about His ghost.*

By now, I realized two things. I still did not have Jesus "in my heart" as Mom had described, and I was lying face down, spread-eagled, on the floor. I lay prostrate before God for hours, shedding tears of sorrow and repentance. I had no strength left and nowhere to turn. I was completely on empty.

I got back on my knees and told God that I was simply too bad. I did not deserve for Jesus to be tortured to death to pay my sin debt so I could get into Heaven. I told God that Jesus died for the good people, not for a sinner like me. I told God there must be another way.

It is easy for us to just say, "Jesus died on the cross for our sins." He did die on the cross for our sins—but to me, there is much, much, more to that action. In the army, I learned about what happened to some of our soldiers who were captured. They were tortured before being put to death. I won't go into any graphic details, but Jesus did not just die on the cross—He was tortured to death. The Bible says:

> They "spit in his face and struck him with their fists" (Matthew 26:67).
>
> They "twisted together a crown of thorns and set it on his head" (Mathew 27:29).
>
> They took a staff and "struck him on the head again and again" (Matthew 27:30).
>
> Pilate "had Jesus flogged, and handed him over to be crucified" (Matthew 27:26).
>
> Those who passed by "hurled insults at him" (Matthew 27:39).
>
> They shouted at him, "Come down from the cross, if you are the Son of God!" (Matthew 27:40).
>
> "the chief priests, the teachers of the law and the elders mocked him" (Matthew 27:41).

The soldiers drove huge spikes into His hands and feet and hung Him on the cross.

Even God the Father turned away from Jesus when my sins and your sins were placed on Jesus. The Bible says of God the Father, "Your eyes are too pure to look on evil" (Habakkuk 1:13). It was then that Jesus cried out "My God, my God, why have you forsaken me?" (Matthew 27:46). God judged Jesus for our sins. When all of our garbage was piled on Jesus, God the Father turned away from His Son because of me and because of you. That is what this Jesus did for me and what Jesus did for you.

Now you may be thinking, because of my sinful life, what a horrible person I must be. Yes, in the presence of our holy God, I was simply a pile of filthy garbage. But let me explain just how horrible I am in the world's eyes. If you put me in line with ten godly deacons and elders from your church and you knew everything about each one of us, would you be able to pick out which one is the most horrible sinner? I doubt it. (By the way, I've been both a deacon and an elder in the church.) We're all sinners. My sins, in the eyes of the world, are no worse than those of the other deacons and elders. My sins are no worse than your sins. Your sins may even be worse than mine, in the eyes of the world.

But I will tell you this: if you are not a Christian and you are ever in the presence of our holy God, you will do exactly the same thing I did. You will fall flat on your face before our holy God and weep tears of sorrow for your sinful life. Our God is that holy and that pure. If you are a Christian, when God looks on you today, He now sees your blood-washed body and the righteousness of His Christ. He no longer sees the filth of your sinful life. Your sin debt has been paid in full.

Several years after I became a Christian, I went on a men's retreat. We broke into small groups and Curtis asked, "Could I ask you men a question? I have a problem, and it's bothering me." We all listened as he explained, "I've been trying to read through the Bible, and the more I read, the filthier I feel. Sometimes I feel so filthy that I want to just

> *quit reading the Bible. Do you men have that problem?" Curtis was on the right track, and God had his hand on him. The closer we get to God, the more we realize that He is holy and righteous, and we are sinful and unrighteous. That's why we have a Savior.*

It was probably around 3:00 a.m. when I crawled into bed, knowing that I was not a Christian. I knew for a fact that if I died in my sleep, the next event in my life would be judgment and Hell. I turned on the lamp beside the bed and sat up in bed all night to avoid going to sleep. I had a heart attack a year earlier, and I wanted to make sure that if I had a heart attack that night, I could quickly call for help and hopefully live. I even laid four nitroglycerine pills on the table beside the bed, just in case they were needed.

I thought about how horrible Hell would be. I thought about the fires in Hell that never burn out. I even took a cigarette lighter, lit it, and held it to the palm of my hand to see how long I could stand the pain. That, of course, lasted for only a few seconds. As I took the cigarette lighter away from my hand, I realized I had control and could remove the fire from my hand. However, in Hell, I would have no control over the fire and pain. I was scared—I was almost scared to death.

I was a nervous wreck that Friday at work. I kept talking with God about finding another way to be saved. I just did not deserve for Jesus, God's holy Son, to die for me. He died for the "good" people.

Friday night, I was on my knees again. As soon as I started talking with God, He was again on his knees, right there in front of me. I again told God that I did not deserve to go to Heaven. I knew I had earned and deserved Hell. It's not so much that I wanted to go to Heaven. Quite frankly, I didn't even care about Heaven. I just didn't want to go to Hell for eternity. I fully understood what the Bible meant by "where 'the worms that eat them do not die, and the fire is not quenched' " (Mark 9:48). People don't just die, go to Hell, burn up, and then their ashes just blow away. The Bible explains that Hell is pure torture and that it lasts forever. I have heard preachers say that Jesus talked more about Hell than he did about Heaven. God does not want any of us to go there. The Bible describes "God our Savior, who wants all people to be saved and to come to a knowledge of the truth" (1Timothy 2:3–4).

I finally broke. I told God, "I know there is no other way to avoid going to Hell except through Jesus and His death on the cross to pay for my sins." I told God, "I want to ask Jesus to be my Savior and save me from Hell." I don't think that I ever asked Jesus to "come into my heart," as Mom had explained to me. Instead, I totally surrendered ownership of my life to God. I gave up everything.

Once you've come to the cross of Christ, you'll never be the same. It's at the cross of Christ that we experience the depth of God's love for each one of us. There is no turning back. The old life is gone, and the new life with our Risen Savior lies ahead. It's like God has a huge computer with lists of all of our sin and garbage. When we surrender our lives to Christ, God hits the "delete" key and our sins are gone. Jesus paid our sin debt for us. We are born again. We begin our new life in Christ.

I became God's servant. I committed my life to Him. I told God that every minute of every day of the rest of my life belonged to Him. I told God, "I will go anywhere you send me and do anything you tell me to do. I belong to you." I had no idea where He would take me or what He would ask of me. All I knew was that I would live out my days serving my Savior. I had wasted forty-four years of my life, and I now wanted to live all the remaining days of my life for my God. Jesus died for me, and now I would live my life for Him.

I was so ashamed of my sinful life that I told God I would never sin again, and I meant it, but that lasted about two weeks—and then I blew it and sinned again. I had also read in the gospels about a sin called "blasphemy against the Spirit" (Matthew 12:31). The Bible said this sin would not be forgiven in this age or in the age to come.

I did not know what blasphemy meant. I told God that I knew He could not forgive me of the "blasphemy" sin, if I had in fact done that one. I really did not know what it meant, but since I had done so much else wrong, I had probably done that too. If I had committed the blasphemy sin, I knew He had no choice but to send me to Hell. I told God to "just go ahead and send me to Hell—it's not your fault, it's my own fault. Just do it! Hell is what I deserve—I did it to myself." Even if I had to go to Hell when I die, I would still live every minute of every day of the rest of my life for Him. I was absolutely serious.

I got off my knees and went to bed. I did not feel the weight of the world lift off my shoulders, as many say they do, because I still did not know what "blasphemy against the Spirit" meant. I figured there was still a high probability that I'd be spending eternity in Hell. But I fully intended to live the rest of my life, one day at a time, for God.

That Friday night when I surrendered my life to God, I experienced the one and only "pivotal moment" in my life. The entire focus of my life changed from being centered on me to being totally committed to God my Father and to Jesus Christ, my Savior and the Lord of my life. This change in purpose and direction was so profound that it far outweighs all the other events in my life combined. Once you've been to the blood-stained cross of Christ and encountered God the Father face-to-face, you'll never again be the same. This pivotal moment is so great that I simply do not have words in my vocabulary to describe it.

Billy Graham said, "Perhaps you do not know the power of the resurrected Christ. You have never knelt at the foot of the cross and had your sins forgiven."[1] If you've knelt at the cross, if you've been there, then you understand. If you've never been there, then I encourage you to get on your knees right now.

I sometimes wonder how many others have "been there." We had a conference at work where between fifty and sixty management and supervisory employees met. The man who led the conference said, "We're going to start the meeting with an icebreaker to help you get to know one another." He gave his definition of a "pivotal moment" and said, "Now let's go around the room, and each of you briefly tell us of the most important pivotal moment in your life." I thought, *OK, we're about to find out how many people in the room know Jesus.* As they went around the room, we heard answers about marriage, babies being born, Vietnam, divorce, car wrecks, and so on. No one mentioned God. Then, finally, one lady said something about God. She was so brief and she spoke so low that no one really even seemed to hear what she said. But I did just barely hear her mention the name "God."

When it was my turn, I said, "In 1988, I came face-to-face with God. I asked Jesus Christ to be my Savior and Lord of my life. God changed my life forever. I've never looked back, and I'll never go back to what I was before I came to know God. Two thousand years ago, Jesus died for me, and today I live my life for Him." My answer was also brief, but I didn't whisper when I shared my pivotal moment.

The others in the room stared at me. Some snickered. A few just downright laughed. My question is this: how could only two out of fifty or sixty people mention the name "God"? That amounts to only 4 percent. This is not a third-world country where people still worship the moon. This is America. America is supposed to be a "Christian" nation.

My friend, the question today is, what is the greatest pivotal moment in your life? Have you ever "knelt at the foot of the cross"? Do you have an ongoing *relationship* with our God of creation, or do you know only what people have told you about Him?

Your eternal destiny depends on your answer.

CHAPTER 2

After Christ

When I woke up Saturday morning, I had a feeling that things were different. I couldn't explain it, but I felt different. I walked down the hallway into the den. On the wall in the den, I had gun racks with my fine rifles and shotguns hanging there to be admired. I even had a rack with huge offshore fishing rods and reels. I looked at those gold-colored reels and the fine shotguns and rifles. I had been so proud of my toys. But that day, as I looked at them, I wanted to vomit. They made me sick. I walked over to the kitchen and looked out the bay window into the backyard. There were my three boats. Again, I wanted to vomit. Then I thought about (well, God brought to my mind) all the drinking I had been doing. I felt ashamed. (I was not an alcoholic; I just drank a lot). I went to the liquor cabinet and took out all the liquor bottles. I remembered from my youth a preacher telling men in the church they were going to Hell (although you don't) because they drank liquor.

I thought, *What will I do with all this liquor?* I thought about giving it to friends, but then realized that if it was wrong for me to do all that drinking, it would also be wrong for them. So I poured it down the kitchen sink drain. That day, I had the most sterile pipes in Mount Pleasant! A lot of booze and a lot of money went down the drain that morning.

I thought about a friend who loved hunting but he did not have a deer rifle. I took one of my fine rifles off one of the gun racks, gathered up some camouflage hunting clothes, drove to a friend's house and gave them to him. I also gave some of my offshore rods and reels to friends. I had another friend who loved hunting as much as I did, as did his three sons. A burglar had broken into his house, and all his guns had been stolen. I took down a shotgun, a deer rifle, and a .22 rifle and gave them to him. A year later, Hurricane Hugo washed his house away, and he lost everything, including the guns I had given him. So I gave him more guns. I continued giving away. I even gave away one of the boats. I sold most of my remaining toys since they no longer had an appeal to me.

At that time, I did not understand why all the guns, fishing equipment, boats, and such were so repulsive to me, but today I understand. These things were my "gods." These things had now been replaced by my Lord and Savior. There is a song that we sometimes sing in church: "Turn Your Eyes upon Jesus." The words are, "Turn your eyes to Jesus, look full in His wonderful face, and the things of earth will grow strangely dim in the light of His glory and grace." That song explains what had happened to me.

The Bible says, "Do not love the world or anything in the world. If anyone loves the world, love for the Father is not in them. For everything in the world—the lust of the flesh, the lust of the eyes, and the pride of life—comes not from the Father but from the world. The world and its desires pass away, but whoever does the will of God lives forever" (1 John 2:15–17).

Jesus told Nicodemus, "Very truly I tell you, no one can see the kingdom of God unless they are born again" (John 3:3). That night in 1988, I had been "born again." I had a new heart. In 1987, I had a heart attack and almost died, but in June 1988, I had a heart "transplant." God gave me a new heart that will last for eternity. I now had the Spirit of God in me. Jesus said, "On that day you will realize that

I am in my Father, and you are in me, and I am in you" (John 14:20). The Bible says, "For the life of a creature is in the blood" (Leviticus 17:11). Today, I not only have a new heart, I have the heart of Christ. I not only have His heart, I have the blood of my Lord and Savior flowing through my veins. I've been washed inside and out by the blood of Christ.

Jesus told His disciples, "Then you will know the truth, and the truth will set you free" (John 8:32). Jesus is that "truth." That Friday night, God set me free. The old is gone, and all things are new. Today, twenty-five years later, the desire of my heart is still to live every minute of every day of the rest of my life for my Savior. I've learned that we don't need to worry about all the "stuff" in our lives. When we are "sold out" to Jesus Christ, everything else in life just seems to fall right into place.

Unconditional Love

There was another huge change that had taken place. I had been a very judgmental person. I could meet a person and form an opinion right there on the spot. I was judgmental of my friends as well as the people I worked with. Quite frankly, I had very little use for most Christians that I knew because I felt most of them were hypocrites. They talked one story but lived another. Overnight, God put a new, unconditional love in my heart. I learned that when we stand before the cross of our Savior, we no longer see the shortcomings of our friends. We see only our own shortcomings.

Jesus put His unconditional love in my heart. Saturday morning, I loved everyone-yes, everyone, even the hypocritical Christians I knew. And furthermore, I loved them unconditionally, just as my God loves me. God says, "We love because he first loved us. Whoever claims to love God yet hates a brother or sister is a liar. For whoever does not love their brother and sister, whom they have seen, cannot love God, whom they have not seen. And he has given us this command: Anyone who loves God must also love their brother and sister" (1 John 4:19–21). This unconditional love is not something we have to muster up ourselves. It's something God does to us and for us.

God was talking to the nation of Israel and told them, "I will give you a new heart and put a new spirit in you; I will remove from you your heart of stone and give you a heart of flesh. And I will put my Spirit in you" (Ezekiel 36:26–27). He did that not only for Israel, He did that for me, and He will do it for you. He not only gives us a new heart and a new spirit, He gives us His heart and His Spirit.

A week later, I started attending church. I wanted to walk in and hug everyone and tell them, "I'm one of you now." But when I went to church, things had not changed from a few years earlier when I had "tried" church. There was still no greeting at the front door, and hardly anyone spoke to me. But that didn't matter, because I still loved every one of them unconditionally. Today, this church has a new heart that warmly welcomes everyone.

At that time, Connie and I were engaged, and we planned to marry in July. Over the two years we had been engaged, I would often tell Connie that she would always be number one in my life. But now that I was a Christian, I told Connie that she will always be number two in my life; Jesus will always be number one. Needless to say, Connie was not happy about being number two in my life. Connie looked at what I had become. I no longer told dirty jokes. I quit drinking and cursing. All I wanted to do was read the Bible, go to church, and tell people about Jesus. Connie said, "I don't know if I like you this way. I think I liked the 'old you' better." She called off the July wedding. But later, in October, we were married.

Connie joined an Episcopal church in Charlotte, North Carolina as a child, went through a confirmation program, and was "sprinkled." I tried to explain to her that there is a difference between being a member of a church and having a relationship with Jesus Christ. I told her that church membership and baptism do not necessarily mean a person is a Christian, but she would not listen to me. However, the Holy Spirit had been working on Connie, and I did not know it.

A year or two later, Connie, Mom, and I went to Atlanta, Georgia, to visit Dr. Charles Stanley's church. Dr. Stanley preached a good sermon and then had an altar call. Connie was sitting next to Mom. We were all standing when Dr. Stanley made the call. Connie, without saying a word, pushed Mom back into her seat and moved across in front of her. She then pushed me back into my seat and stepped out into the aisle. I held her arm and said, "What are you doing?" She didn't say a word. She just went down that aisle and right up to Dr. Stanley. Yes, there is a difference between being a member of a church and being a Christian.

Dr. Stanley handed Connie off to a deacon who was standing nearby, and they went through a door to a back room to talk and pray. To this day, I've never asked what she said to Dr. Stanley, and she has never told me. There is a difference between knowing what someone told you about Jesus and knowing Jesus personally. Today, Connie is not only a member of a church, but she knows her Savior and has an ongoing relationship with Him.

When Connie and I were dating, we sometimes discussed our past failed marriages, but Connie found it difficult to talk about her first marriage. When she spoke of her first husband, she would usually say, "I'll kill that man if I ever see him again." The first few times I heard her say that, I thought she was kidding, but I soon realized that she was serious. He had left her, an eighteen-year-old girl, with their baby son, Richard, and moved to California. He never contacted Connie, helped financially, or did anything for Connie or their son. Connie had to write bad checks just to buy a few groceries. Then she had to remember which grocery stores not to return to because they might recognize her. Connie and her son did not live; they just existed day to day. She never forgave her husband for abandoning her and their son. She hated this man with a passion. I am positive she would have killed him if he had ever shown up. But when Connie surrendered her life to Christ at

Dr. Stanley's church, something inside her changed. God gave her His heart, and she now had the love of Christ in her heart. She too had been born again, and she loved everyone unconditionally, even her ex-husband.

A short time later, Connie searched through various records to find her ex-husband. She wanted desperately for her thirty-three-year-old son to meet and get to know his dad. Connie found him and wrote him a letter. He drove to South Carolina from California and spent a weekend with their son. About a year later, Richard's dad had a heart attack and died. Richard flew to California for the funeral. He would have never known his dad if Connie had not surrendered her life to Christ and been born again. Jesus removed her heart of stone and gave her a new heart filled with His unconditional love.

The New Man

After being saved on Friday evening and the events of Saturday, I did not go to church on Sunday. Things were still spinning around in my head. I stayed home and watched several preachers on TV and continued reading the Bible. It was like I was starving for God's word. I could not get enough. For the next year, every spare minute I could find, I would read the Bible. I would even take my Bible to work, where I would arrive an hour early and read first. It was like I had been in the desert without water for weeks. I was craving God's "living water" (John 4:10).

A friend at work called me into his office, and we talked for an hour about what had happened to me. I tried to explain to him about Jesus and the cross, but he didn't really want to listen. He was a member of a church, and that was good enough for him. I told him that I had been a member of a church, but knowing about Jesus and knowing Jesus are two entirely different things. God is looking for a relationship, not to see who drives the nicest car on Sunday or who wears the finest clothes.

My friend Pete and I were asked to visit a couple who were members of a nearby church. When we made the visit, the husband was not home, so we talked with the wife. I told her, "Before leaving, I'd like to ask you a question. What do you understand it takes for a person to get into Heaven?"

Her answer included things like, "You need to be a good person, do kind things for others, believe in Jesus, go on a mission trip or two, and give some money to the church. Oh, and I teach Sunday school too." Most of her answer was about works. We talked with her about her answer, and we explained that Jesus, without the works, is the correct answer.

Then her husband came home. We made small talk, and then I asked him the same question. His answer was, "I believe in God, and I've been a member of that church for twenty-two years! Are you telling me that I am not good enough to get into Heaven?"

I answered, "Believing there is a God does not get you into Heaven. Neither does being a member of a church." I told him that the Bible says, "You believe that there is one God. Good! Even the demons believe that—and shudder" (James 2:19).

When Billy Graham was preparing to write his book *The Reason for My Hope*, he said in an interview, "I want the book to speak to the unchurched as well as those in the church who think they are saved but are deceived, claiming to belong to Him without knowing the change that is brought about when the Holy Spirit of the living God dwells within."[2]

I'm certainly not being critical of this couple, as that is how I was for thirty years. At age fourteen, I joined the church and was baptized. I thought that made me a Christian and gave me a ticket to Heaven. All during those thirty years, I was headed straight for

Hell and didn't even realize it. I was one of those Billy Graham referred to as being in church and "deceived."

If someone answers such questions and never mentions the name Jesus as their Lord and Savior, I'd say there is a good chance they don't know our Savior. All people believe in God, including atheists. If there were no God, there would be no atheists. An atheist's god is their unbelief, and most of them are quite proud of their unbelief.

Our God is not looking to see how much "stuff" we do on Sunday at church. Yes, the stuff needs to be done. But our God is looking for a relationship with us. Satan loves it when we get sidetracked and focus on the stuff rather than on worship and the relationship. Once we have that relationship, everything else falls right into place, including all the stuff.

The correct answer is, "I know that I'm a sinner and I need a Savior. Jesus died on that cross to pay for my sins. God raised Him from the dead, assuring me my sins have been forgiven. God has opened the door of eternal life to me through the blood of Jesus. I have chosen to love Him, surrender my life to Him, and follow Him as my personal Lord and Savior." You don't need to use those exact words, but the correct answer is "Jesus." When we *surrender* our all and commit our lives to Jesus, that personal relationship with Him begins.

Let me share another example. We were preparing for a "Walk to Emmaus" weekend. A pastor of a large church here in the Lowcountry met with us and shared some of his testimony. He said he had been a member of a church all his life. He said he graduated from seminary and preached great sermons in his church. He led others to Christ and baptized them. He knew a great deal of theology. He knew all about Jesus, but he never knew Jesus. He did not know Jesus and have a personal relationship with Him until after he had been in the pulpit preaching for five years. He too tried to emphasize the difference between knowing about Jesus and having a personal relationship with Jesus.

The Preacher Man

The following week after I surrendered my life to Christ, I went by the church to see the preacher and tell him I had been "saved." He was excited when I explained to him what had been happening over the last few weeks. I asked him if I needed to be baptized again. He basically said, "I'll leave that up to you and God." I was already a member of this church because Mom and I had transferred our membership a few years earlier. It was not necessary to do anything.

I told the preacher that I had been "dunked" when I was a kid, but I never knew Christ. I told him that I now knew the difference between knowing about Jesus and knowing Jesus. He suggested that if I wanted to, I could walk down the aisle at church Sunday, and I told him that I planned to do that.

Sunday, when the preacher gave the altar call, I walked down the aisle. As the preacher and I stood before the congregation, he said, "This is Ellison Kelly. He is already a member of our church, but today he wants to rededicate his life to Jesus Christ." Wrong! I did not come to "rededicate my life," because my life had never been dedicated to Christ in the first place. I was a member of the church, but that was all. I was also a member of a deer-hunting club, but what does that have to do with having a relationship with Jesus Christ? I didn't say anything because I knew the preacher meant well. A few weeks later, I was baptized for the second time. When I was fourteen years old and joined the church, being baptized meant nothing to me. This time, it meant everything. Jesus said, "Whoever believes and is baptized will be saved" (Mark 16:16).

The night that I was saved, one of the things I told God was that I would never sin again. I was so ashamed of my sinful life. I truly thought that if I could choose to sin, then certainly I could choose not to sin. I fully intended to live the remainder of my life without sinning.

About two weeks later, I was barefooted and mowing the grass in the backyard. There was a short, wooden board lying in the yard near the azalea bushes that had a sixteen-penny nail sticking out of it. I knew the board with the nail was there, but I had not yet picked it up. As I pulled the lawn mower backward, zap! I stepped on the nail. It went deep into my foot. I just stood there on the nail, looking at my foot and the blood running out, and I didn't say anything. Then I started praising God, because I had not said a single curse word. In the past, I would have had quite a bit to say about the nail in my foot (cursing). Now, I knew I had defeated sin in my life.

I Sinned Again

About a week later, on a Friday afternoon, I stopped to buy gas. I was pumping my gas and minding my own business when a car pulled up to the pump behind me. I could hear the other pump pumping gas, and I turned and glanced behind me. There was a young lady with blond hair, wearing what I've always called "hot pants." They were so short that there was not much left to the imagination. She had a skimpy halter around her well-built chest. It only took me about three seconds to gather in all that information about her body. I didn't want to stare, even though she was beautiful, so I turned back and continued pumping my gas. I remembered what Jesus said about adultery: "But I tell you that anyone who looks at a woman lustfully has already committed adultery with her in his heart. If your right eye causes you to stumble, gouge it out and throw it away. It is better for you to lose one part of your body than for your whole body to be thrown into hell" (Matthew 5:28–29). I continued pumping my gas, knowing that even though this was a beautiful woman, I would not take another look, because that would definitely be what the Bible calls "lust." I absolutely did not want to commit adultery, which is one of the "big ten."

Then, as I pumped my gas, it was like I had absolutely no control over my own head. It just slowly turned to the left, and there she was, pumping and smiling at me. I immediately turned my head back. The damage was done. I had just committed adultery. I felt Satan's dagger jab into my heart. I had just sinned against my Savior! I was so unbearably ashamed. I had told God I'd never sin again, and I just blew it; I sinned.

> *A few years ago, my good Christian friend, Hal, and I leased a piece of property for deer hunting. We both agreed that we would only shoot eight-point bucks or larger and let the younger bucks walk. I had already seen a couple of small bucks and let them walk. I even let a young eight-pointer walk. Then Hal shared a story with me and apologized. He said he saw a small four-point buck headed his way, and even though he knew he was not to shoot it, he said, "My arm just started moving, and my bow just came up and I drew it. It was like my brain was telling me, 'Don't do it,' but my arms were not listening. I lifted my bow, and as I was aiming at the deer, my brain was telling me, 'Don't do it.' But I aimed anyhow. Then I was ready to shoot, and again my brain said, 'Don't do it.' Then I shot, and my arrow missed the deer." Hal said he had never experienced anything like that before in his life. He said that his arms just seemed to move on their own. He had no control over them.*

That's the way I felt when my head just moved on its own. I finished pumping gas and immediately drove to our church. I knew that the Bible said it was better to gouge out an eye than to go to Hell, and I fully intended to do just that. I just didn't know which eye to gouge out—my right eye, which is my shooting eye (for aiming a rifle) or my left eye. And I did not know how to go about gouging out my eye. In the army, I learned how to gouge out the eyes of an enemy soldier, but this was a little different. Now we're talking about gouging out *my* eye.

> *Stop right here and listen. When Jesus was telling us to gouge out an eye and cut off a hand, He was not speaking* literally. *He was speaking* allegorically. ***Don't gouge out your eye or cut off your hand.*** *Jesus was telling us to hate sin that much. He was making a strong point about hating sin in our lives. Jesus is not telling us to actually gouge out an eye or cut off a hand.*

Thank God the preacher was working late that Friday. He invited me in, and he could tell I was upset. I explained what had happened. He then explained that Jesus was telling us to hate sin so much that it could be compared to an extreme of gouging out our eye or cutting off our hand. I told the preacher that I did hate sin that much, and that is what I fully intended to do. He said, "But Jesus is not telling you to do that. He is telling us to hate sin that much." I remember him asking me, "If you gouge out one eye today, and next week you mess up and sin again, what will you do? Will you gouge out your other eye?"

I told him, "Yes, I'd rather enter Heaven blind than to go to Hell with two eyes."

He then told me, "Close your eyes. And in your mind, can you see that young lady?"

I closed my eyes, and said, "Yes, there she is."

The preacher said, "Now, if you've gouged out both of your eyes and you still see her in your mind, what are you going to do next? Are you going to blow your brains out?"

I told him, "Yes, if I have to."

By now, you must think I was crazy. I was crazy, and I still am today. I'm crazy about my Lord and Savior. I truly want to obey my Lord. Jesus said, "If you love me, keep my commands" (John 14:15). It took the preacher the better part of an hour to help me understand what Jesus was telling us in the Bible. He explained other Scriptures that helped me understand about sin and what had just happened at the gas station. He explained that God made women beautiful so that men would look at them. He made men handsome so that women would look at them. Then, Satan will try to take that God-given gift, twist it around, and turn it into the sin of adultery. Satan is trying to destroy us.

The preacher suggested I buy a study Bible. I was still using my childhood King James Version Bible, and using it with great difficulty because of my reading problems. I went to the Christian bookstore and showed the lady the Bible I was using. She asked how long I had been a Christian, and I told her a few weeks. She knew what I needed and showed me a NIV Study Bible. She explained how to use all the footnotes, the concordance, and other features. Reading from the NIV was like a breath of fresh air.

Sunday School

I started attending Sunday school again. While we were sitting in class, I looked at the Bibles others were holding and noticed the covers were well worn. Here I was with a brand-new Bible. I felt like the kid at school with a new pair of tennis shoes. I was embarrassed that I was forty-four years old and had just now become a Christian. Then I silently began questioning things.

The Sunday school teacher asked, "How many of you read the lesson for today?" I boldly held up my hand because I not only read the lesson, but I also looked up all the reference Scriptures as well. I actually studied the lesson because I was hungry to learn. One other person raised a hand. The teacher said, "That's about what I expected." I thought, *What's wrong with this picture? I thought everyone wanted to learn about God.* The next Sunday, there was the same question and the same answer.

Then I noticed, when we opened our Bibles to look up a Scripture, the pages in my Bible were already worn and marked up with my notes and questions. The pages in some of my new friends' Bibles still looked brand new, even though the covers on their Bibles were completely worn. Either they already knew all of the

Scriptures—and some did have a great deal of Bible knowledge—or they had not been studying God's word.

Those first months as a new Christian were filled with talking with God and studying His Bible. I would often stop by the preacher's office with questions. He was very kind and patient with me. He never asked me to make an appointment, and he would always stop what he was doing and take time with me. I have never forgotten his help.

The next few months, I didn't say much in church because I didn't want the others to realize how little I knew about the Scriptures. Many of my new church friends were way ahead of me on the life journey with our Savior. They knew the Lord well and certainly had a personal relationship with Him. But other new friends, even though they were members of our church, still struggled with faith, healing, hearing God's voice, Heaven and Hell, and more. I remember one lady saying, "How are we supposed to believe all this stuff in the Bible?" Another said, "I think the 'fish story' and other stories are just made-up stories for us." I expect some of these church members may be among those Billy Graham was concerned about when he talked about those in our churches who "think they are saved but are deceived."

One thing I did not realize at the time is that I was having a "mountaintop experience." In the chapter on the Gideons, I'll explain what happened when the preacher told me I was having this kind of experience. I was on the mountain with God for four months. At the time, I thought it was that way for all Christians. I didn't realize that I was on a mountain while all the folks around me were in the valley, struggling with daily life. Then, four months later, I joined my friends in the valley, but my hunger for God's word grew even stronger.

I remember one of my friends questioning the "healings" in the New Testament. At that time, my mom had been very sick for well over a year. She was so sick that she looked like she would have to die just to get better. One Thursday night in July 1988, I knelt and asked Jesus to heal my mom. Jesus healed her before I even got up off my knees. (Read about God healing my mom in the chapter "Healing Prayer/Spiritual Warfare.") I knew healing was real. I doubted nothing the Bible said. There was a lot that I did not understand, but I knew in time that God would explain the Scriptures to me.

I did not understand it, but some things were happening with me that were not happening with my friends at church. I was telling people I met about Jesus, and many were surrendering their lives to Christ. Mom had been healed. I had a vision experience. I was always hungry for more of the Bible. I actually thought something might be wrong with me. I remember one day asking the preacher, "What's wrong with me?" He told me there was nothing wrong, but there was still so much that I did not understand.

One day at church, the preacher said, "Ellison, I want you to give your testimony before the church."

I really wasn't sure what "giving your testimony" meant, but I had a good idea. I told him, "Preacher, right now, I'm really not sure about all that's going on."

He said, "I know. Maybe I'll ask you again a little later on." I came home and looked up the word "testimony" in my new Bible dictionary. Sure enough, it was exactly what I thought he was talking about.

A month or so passed. The preacher came to me and again said, "Ellison, I need for you to give your testimony to the congregation."

This time I told him, "Preacher, I don't think they will believe me."

He said, "I know they won't," and he walked away.

Even today, as I share testimonies about Jesus with Christian friends, some believe me and others, even close friends, do not. I think for many, if they have not personally experienced it, they don't believe such things can happen.

A few months later, Connie and I went to a weekend work conference at Myrtle Beach. We both wanted to worship at a church Sunday morning rather than just hang out at the motel. There were several large churches on the main street, but we chose to drive out into the country to find a small church for worship. We were driving toward Conway and saw a sign that read "The Christian Church." We turned left and drove until we came to this small, country church. We had hardly pulled into the parking lot when a young man came over, opened the car door, and greeted us. Shortly thereafter, we learned that he was the preacher. He made both of us feel genuinely welcome. As we walked into the church, we were greeted again and again by members of the congregation. And, most important of all, we were greeted by the Holy Spirit. He was there—in full force—pouring out His love on everyone. We both were overcome with the presence of the Holy Spirit. In that church, I felt the same love and warmth that I had felt the nights when I was on my knees in the presence of our God.

The people at the church had skin colors of white, black, yellow, and brown. They were all hugging each other, and they were hugging us. They were not dressed in fine clothes and competing with each other. There was no "put-on" here, just pure and simple, unconditional love. Even after the service, the people continued to greet us and invite us to come back. They were in no hurry to leave. They did not turn and storm out the front door. These people were there to worship our God and to love each other.

Christ in the Workplace

The first sixteen years I worked at MUSC, I was not a Christian; however, the last twelve years there, I was. During those twelve years, I had many well-meaning Christian friends tell me that we could not witness for Christ in our workplace because we were a state agency. There seemed to be a fear that an employee might file a grievance if you discussed your faith in Jesus, but I thought that was a bunch of garbage. I personally talked with many, many people at work about Christ. Many of those asked Jesus to be their Savior and Lord.

I've learned that you can't just throw caution to the wind. I never tried to shove Jesus down anyone's throat. Listen to the Holy Spirit. The Bible says, "But when he, the Spirit of truth, comes, he will guide you into all the truth" (John 16:13). Since I was a supervisor, I often had employees come to me with their problems, and I would listen and try to help. If the Lord gave me an opening, I would tell the employee that I too had similar problems. I would ask if the employee wanted to know how I handled my problem. If he or she said yes, I would explain, "Before I became a Christian, I used to beat myself up over problems like that. Now that I'm a Christian, I go to Jesus for help. He has never let me down." I would then "ask for permission" to discuss how Jesus and I handle my problems. If the person agreed, I proceeded to share a Christian perspective on working through the problem. I would share the gospel with the employee and I would ask, "Would you like to give Jesus a try at helping with your situation? Would you like to surrender your life to Christ right now?"

If employees said that they didn't want to hear about Jesus, I honored their right to struggle through life on their own. Even though an employee might not want to hear about Jesus at that time, I continued praying for him or her. I sometimes got a return visit and a second chance to share the gospel. Our God is a God of second chances. "Then the word of the Lord came to Jonah a second time" (Jonah 3:1).

At Christmas, I sent a "Jesus Christmas card" to each of our three-hundred employees. A "Jesus" card is about celebrating the birth of Christ—it's not about Santa and the reindeer. There were several Jehovah's Witnesses (JWs) in our department, and I knew they would have a problem with the Christmas card. JWs don't believe in accepting gifts, even Christmas cards. I also knew that if I singled them out and did not send each of them a card, they might complain about being discriminated against. So, either way, I lose. They are simply going to complain. So I sent the Jesus cards to everyone.

Sure enough, the JWs complained. One of my JW supervisors came to me and politely said he was not permitted to receive a card, a gift, like this from me. He didn't like receiving the card from me because it offended him. I asked him if he ever received any "junk mail" at home. He said, "Yes, sir, all the time." I asked what he did with the junk mail, and he said he threw it in the trash. I lifted my trash can in front of him, he tossed the card in the trash, and that was the end of the discussion.

Another Christmas, I included a Gideon New Testament inside the card sent to all of my foremen and supervisors. I knew three of the foremen were JWs, so I got ready. Sure enough, Ken came to me with the New Testament in his hand and said, "Mr. Kelly, you know I'm a JW and I can't accept this gift."

I said, "I know you are, Ken. I just didn't want you to feel left out. I know you can't accept the New Testament. But, Ken, do you know someone who needs to know the Lord? Maybe you could give them that New Testament."

Ken thought about it and said, "Yes, sir, I know someone I can give it to." Then he left the office. I hope whoever he gave that New Testament to came to know Jesus through that New Testament at the hand of a JW.

Twenty-Five Years

Looking back over the past twenty-five years, I've had many learning experiences. A disciple is a student who walks with a master and listens, learns, and obeys the master and his or her teachings. When I first became a Christian, I did not understand about discipleship. All I knew was that I wanted to walk with God for the rest of my life. Over the years, I have learned what it means to be a disciple of Jesus Christ and that there is a cost to it. Most of us in America have never suffered for our faith as did the twelve disciples and as missionaries and Christians in other countries suffer today. But we must still give up our lives to take hold of the life of Christ. We must completely surrender to God all aspects of our lives to be completely filled with the Holy Spirit. If we choose to surrender only certain parts of our lives, then I believe we will be filled with only some of the Holy Spirit. The jar must be completely empty before it can be completely filled. It is sometimes not as easy as it sounds. God knows our hearts, and if it is truly our desire to be completely filled with the Holy Spirit and follow Christ, our God will help us.

I "sold out" to Jesus Christ twenty-five years ago and have never looked back. Each day is an adventure. I live in the today and look forward to tomorrow. I have no idea what God will place in my path tomorrow, but I know my God will be there with me. I have only one claim to fame: I am a disciple of Jesus Christ.

In the following chapters, I share events that occurred during my walk with our Savior. I'm not bragging, and I'm not complaining; I'm just sharing some of my experiences. I also share testimonies from others that were given to me firsthand, which I know are true. As you read through the testimonies, I pray you will see the love of our God in each testimony. As you read, I also pray that you will "choose to be a disciple. Don't turn back."

CHAPTER 3

THE VISION

Some of my Christian friends today don't believe in dreams and visions. That's their choice. They are still my friends. God is, in fact, still at work in our lives today, just as He always has been. I personally can give firsthand testimony of that, and some of my friends can as well.

Don't assume that just because you have never experienced something others have experienced that their experience is not real. God deals with each of His children as individuals, and He has a personal plan for each of us.

In the Bible, God uses Joel to tell us about "the Day of the Lord," which is coming and has come. God said, "And afterward, I will pour out my Spirit on all people. Your sons and daughters will prophesy, your old men will dream dreams, your young men will see visions. Even on my servants, both men and women, I will pour out my Spirit in those days" (Joel 2:28–29).

Then, at Pentecost, Peter quoted this same Scripture. Peter told those who were present regarding this outpouring of the Spirit, "No, this is what was spoken by the prophet Joel" (Acts 2:16). Pentecost was only the beginning of the fulfillment of this prophecy. This outpouring of the Spirit is not a one-time event. What happened as Peter spoke was only the beginning. It's still happening today.

As far as I know, I've never had a dream from God. My dreams are usually somewhat weird. I'll dream that I'm back in college and I'm going to class to take an exam, but I can't remember where the classroom is located. As I start to panic, I wake up. Sometimes I dream that I'm on a magic carpet flying through the air, and the carpet starts to roll up under me. Just as I'm about to fall off, I wake up. I don't think these dreams are what Joel is talking about.

Mr. George was an old man when I first met him. He was one of those old men in the church that you look up to and learn from. He often told me of dreams he had. Almost all of his dreams dealt with sharing the gospel and leading people to Christ. His dreams always exalted Jesus, never himself.

I have other friends who say they have dreams, but their dreams seem to glorify themselves rather than God. In the Bible, God talks about lying prophets who say they had a dream but only prophesy "the delusions of their own minds" (Jeremiah 23:26). Their dreams are not from God. We are told to "test the spirits to see whether they are from God" (1 John 4:1). If people share dreams or visions with you, listen and see if they glorify God or themselves. See if they acknowledge Jesus Christ. See if they agree with or contradict the Bible.

One Sunday afternoon, I was home by myself. I had been to church, come home, and had been sitting quietly, reading the Bible. I felt very close to God. I felt His love, and I knew I was in the presence of God. I laid the open Bible against my chest, leaned back in the chair, and said out loud, "Boy, this is great, being a Christian. All I have to do now is go to church on Sunday, read the Bible every day, and wait on Jesus to come" (i.e., for the Rapture). I truly thought doing these three things summed up what being a Christian is all about. I leaned back in the chair and shut my eyes for a moment. I was not sleepy, and I was not going to take a nap. I just wanted to savor the moment.

The second that I closed my eyes, I was immediately "in the Spirit." Today I can explain what happened, but in 1988, I had been a Christian for only a few weeks and did not have a clue what was happening. All I knew was that this was from God. This was the beginning of a huge, full-blown vision. I believe the vision lasted about fifteen minutes. At that time, I had never heard of a vision from God. All I knew was that God was showing me something. In the twenty-five years that I have been a Christian, I have only personally met one other Christian who had a similar experience. I'll share his story at the end of this chapter.

When I closed my eyes, immediately my spirit left my body, traveled fifteen miles, and was now about two hundred feet in the air above Bulls Bay, near Awendaw, South Carolina. My body continued to sit in that chair and breathe air, and blood continued flowing through my veins, but my spirit was in the air above Bulls Bay.

Two Scriptures in the Bible help me understand what happened. They are found in Ezekiel and in Revelation. In Ezekiel, chapters 8 through 10, God took Ezekiel, in a vision, to the temple. God took Ezekiel's spirit and showed him various areas of the temple and all the detestable idol worship. In Revelation, God said to John, "'Come up here, and I will show you what must take place after this.' At once I was in the Spirit, and there before me was a throne in heaven with someone sitting on it" (Revelation 4:1–2). John said, "At once I was in the spirit," and God took his spirit to the throne in Heaven. "At once I was in the spirit," and God took my spirit to Bulls Bay. John's body stayed in that prison on the island of Patmos, and his spirit "at once" was at the throne in Heaven. My body stayed in the chair, and my spirit "at once" was in the air above Bulls Bay.

Some great theologians may disagree with my interpretation of Ezekiel 8–10 and Revelation 4, but they cannot say I'm wrong about my spirit leaving my body. I know for a fact it happened, because it happened to me.

We need to stop for a minute. Make sure you understand that I'm not comparing myself to Ezekiel or John. That would be like comparing a sand gnat to an elephant. All I'm doing in using this Scripture is attempting to help the reader understand what happened. It was several years later before I completely understood the vision experience.

In 2 Corinthians 12, the Apostle Paul mentions a friend who had a similar experience. Paul said his friend was caught up to the third Heaven, but he wasn't sure if his body went with him or not. This man went to the third Heaven (paradise). My spirit went only as far as the second Heaven (outer space).

As I looked down from two hundred feet in the sky, I saw Bulls Bay. I saw the Intracoastal Waterway and the hill (the mainland). I recognized this place. I used to live here. I looked over at Romain Retreat, the area where I previously lived. The vision shifted to the left, and I recognized the long, concrete "government dock" at Moore's Landing (now renamed Garris Landing).

The vision shifted, and I was looking out toward the ocean. All of a sudden, the water burst open, and people were rising up from under the water into the air. There were men, women, and children. Many of them were dressed like the early settlers (like those who were on the ships when Columbus came to America). Some were even dressed like pirates that I had seen in pictures. There were also others who were wearing more modern clothes. As the vision shifted back over to the hill, I realized I had no control over what I was seeing. God was in control.

The vision shifted to a cemetery that was near the coast. I thought, *I didn't know that cemetery was there.* I had never been there before, even though it was only a few miles from where I used to live. As I watched, tombstones fell over, graves burst open, and people rose out of the graves. Their arms and legs were floundering around, and all these people were ascending into the sky.

> *Years later, I was thinking about the vision and decided to drive to Awendaw and see if I could find the cemetery. I remembered in the vision the cemetery was further north*

> *of where I used to live. I drove to Doar Road, the first paved road past where I had lived. As I drove down Doar Road toward Bulls Bay, I saw a sign that read "Wilson's Cemetery." I drove down the road, and sure enough, there was the cemetery. The tombstones were still standing.*

The vision then shifted over to a wooded area. The ground burst open, and people rose from their graves and were caught up in the air with the others. These were people who had died and were buried in the woods with no grave markers. I looked up the coastline toward McClellanville. All around me, men, women, and children were rising into the air.

Suddenly, my spirit rose up into the sky with all the others. We gained altitude fast. The vision looked up the coast to McClellanville and down the coast to Charleston. I looked out over all of the Francis Marion Forest, where I often hunted deer. Then, as we climbed higher in the sky, I saw the coast to North Carolina and the coast to Georgia. I clearly saw Lake Marion and Lake Moultrie in the middle of the state. We continued climbing. I saw all of South Carolina, and a few seconds later, all of the eastern United States. We continued climbing. I saw the United States, Canada, and Mexico. As we moved swiftly through space, I saw the entire Planet Earth. As we moved further into space, the earth grew smaller and smaller.

We all moved together in one large mass, and when Planet Earth appeared smaller than a golf ball (I've been told this would be about 250,000 miles out in space), my brain started functioning again. I was thinking, *What in the world is going on here? Is this a dream? Are you crazy?* Then I thought, *No, this is not a dream. I'm not asleep. I'm wide awake.* I then thought, *Well, dummy, open your eyes and see if you are asleep.* I opened my eyes. Immediately, my spirit was back in my body.

I thought, *I'm awake. I'm not asleep. What was that all about?* I opened the back door, and the dogs were running around and barking. I went out and spoke to the dogs. I was awake. I had not been sleeping, and that was not a dream. Then I realized that it was God showing me the Rapture that John G. Hall preached about. I remembered reading in the Bible something about how we would all look up and see Jesus coming in the sky. I wondered if I sat in the chair, closed my eyes again, and looked up, whether I'd be able to see Jesus. I wasn't sure I wanted to see Jesus. I was still scared to death of God, because I knew how close I had come to dying and going to Hell. I was afraid God might strike me dead and just send me to Hell anyway. I made my decision: I wanted to take my chances and try to see Jesus.

I gathered some courage, sat in the chair, and gripped the armrests as tightly as possible. I slowly raised my head and closed my eyes. As soon as my eyelids closed, I was immediately in the spirit again. Did I see Jesus? No, but I was back in space where the vision left off. My spirit instantly traveled 250,000 miles. The Planet Earth was still smaller than a golf ball.

> *We think in terms of minutes, hours, and days. We think in terms of fifty-five miles per hour. Based on this vision experience, I'd say that in the spirit realm, travel is immediate. There is absolutely no "time of flight." The spirit is immediately either here or immediately there. Do I understand this? No. But I've been there and experienced it; so have a few of my friends. It's a "God thing."*

I looked around, and I was alone. While I had my eyes open, all the people I had been with had left. My spirit was alone in outer space, and fear came over me. All of a sudden, my spirit started falling back toward Earth at what must have been thousands of miles per hour. The earth was growing larger and larger, and fast. I thought, *Oh, no. I should have never opened my eyes. Now God is mad, and He's going to slam me into the earth and kill me.* When I was about a mile above the earth, God slowed the vision down to a very low speed. As I was getting close to Earth, I saw something that looked like fire ants swarming. They were swarming in a state of panic. I wondered, *Why is God showing me fire ants?* As I drew closer, I realized they were not fire ants; they were people. They were the people who were not taken up in the Rapture and were "left behind." There was total panic everywhere.

Sometimes today when we discuss the coming Rapture, we talk of how airplanes will fall pilotless from the sky, drivers will disappear from moving cars, and people will vanish into thin air. I did not see any of this. I only saw those taken in the Rapture and the panic of those left behind.

I still had my eyes closed. I thought, *OK, boy, let's just ride this one out and see what happens next.* I was a little braver now that I realized God was not going to kill me.

The vision shifted from those left behind to the north end of Bull Island. I thought, *OK, I recognize this place. It's the north end of Bull Island.* Then the vision shifted, and I saw Jack's Creek, where I had been before. I knew the place well, but I had never seen it from the air. The vision shifted to "the fingers," as we called them. The fingers are strips of land that run out into the marsh from the main island. They are maybe ten to thirty yards wide and a quarter mile long. This is where we hunted deer. We camped at the center of the island and hunted deer with a bow and arrow on these fingers. I even saw the tree I hunted from when I shot my first deer on the island.

The vision then shifted to the center of the island, where I saw the camping area and the Dominick House. It was like the Lord was showing me around. I recognized everything, because I had been there many times. Then the vision moved toward the south end of the island, where I had never hunted. I always hunted the north end. I remember thinking, as the vision moved south, that the trees and brush were just too thick for deer hunting on the south end.

Then I came to the end of the island and looked over Price Inlet. I recognized it because I often fished here. It seemed God was reading my mind. Each time He showed me a new scene, He would wait until I recognized the area and then move to the next scene.

As I moved over Capers Island, I recognized Schooner Creek, my favorite fishing spot. There was Santee Pass, a short-cut creek that led though the marsh to Bull Island. I knew this creek well. I could even run the creek in the dark when I traveled back and forth to Bull Island deer hunting.

Then I moved over Capers Inlet and slowly crossed over Dewees Island. I crossed over Dewees Inlet and came upon some land with huge buildings. I did not recognize this place, and I had never seen buildings this large so near the ocean. I could not figure out where these large buildings were located. Then the vision shifted to the boat ramp on the back side of the Isle of Palms, and I recognized where I was. The vision then shifted back to those buildings, and I realized that I was looking at the new Wild Dunes development on the north end of the Isle of Palms. The only time I had been to the north end of the Isle of Palms was in the early 1970s, when the area was just sand dunes. We would drive on a sand road to the north end of the island and surf fish. Then the developers moved in and closed off the area to develop the Wild Dunes resort.

> *I had never seen Wild Dunes before. Now I was seeing it for the first time from the air. About twenty years after the vision, friends who live in Wild Dunes invited Connie and me over for dinner. As we were driving around, looking for their house, we happened to drive to the area where these huge houses and buildings were. I remembered seeing them from the air in the vision twenty years earlier.*

The vision turned and headed down Palm Boulevard on the Isle of Palms. As the vision started down the street, I was now only about twenty feet above the road.

(God made many stops and showed me many detailed locations along the way. I'll discuss a few of the stops but omit most of the others and get on with the purpose of the vision. The purpose of the vision was not God giving me a scenic tour of the area. The purpose was what happened at the end of the vision.)

As I traveled down the highway, I passed Sea Island Shopping Center, proceeded down Coleman Boulevard, and stopped over another bridge. I did not know where I was. Then the vision looked to the right. I saw a creek and marsh but did not recognize it from the air. I had been in this creek in my boat hundreds of times, but it did not look the same from the air. Then I looked to the left and saw all the shrimp boats and knew this was the Shem Creek Bridge.

As I continued down Coleman Boulevard, I could see the OK Tire Store on the left. I remember thinking, *If I take a right turn here, I'll enter Cooper Estates. That's where my friends Doug and Kathy live.* Sure enough, I turned and worked my way to Doug's house. I could see the front of his house and his front yard. Then the vision slowly moved over into the backyard. There was Doug's above-ground swimming pool, but no one was in the pool. Then the vision shifted over to the left, to a small deck. I had never seen the deck before, and I remember thinking, *Doug just built a new deck.* Then the vision shifted over to their screened-in back porch; no one was on it. Then the vision made its last move.

The vision shifted to a grassy area between the pool and the house. There stood Doug, his wife, Kathy, and their children, Dale and Deirdre. All four of them were standing in a straight line, wildly waving their arms in the air at me with their hands in tight fists. Their fists were gripped so tightly that I could see the white on their knuckles. They were all four screaming at me in unison, "Ellison, why didn't you tell us? Ellison, why didn't you tell us? Ellison, why didn't you tell us?" They were hysterical, and tears were streaming down their faces as they screamed at me.

Somehow, I knew the next scene would be of my best friends being cast into Hell because they were not Christians. I knew I would be going to Heaven because I was a Christian. Now, for the first time, I realized that my best friends were doomed to Hell. I opened my eyes and hoped the vision would stop as it had earlier. I did not want to see what came next. When I opened my eyes, the vision was over. My spirit was immediately back inside my body.

I did not know what to do. I had never heard of "leading someone to Christ" or "sharing the gospel." I didn't even know what the gospel was at that time. I knew God (the Father). I knew Jesus (the Son). I had no idea who the Holy Ghost was. I knew about sin, Heaven, and Hell. I knew we all need a Savior to get into Heaven and that Jesus is the only Savior that is acceptable to God. That was just about the extent of my Bible knowledge.

I came out of the chair, fell to my knees, and cried out to God. I felt helpless because of what I had just seen, and I could do nothing about it. I begged God to save my friends. I told God, "They are just like me. They don't know any better either." I begged and begged, but God did not answer. I did not understand why He would not answer, because I knew He was in the room with me.

Between that Sunday afternoon and the next Thursday, I prayed and prayed and begged and begged. I even tried to cut a deal with God. I said, "God, if you can't save all four of them right now, how about just Doug and Kathy? We'll worry about the kids later." There was still no answer. Then I tried another deal. I asked "God, how about just saving Doug right now? We'll get to Kathy and the kids later." There was still no answer. I did not understand why God would not answer me.

No one had ever come to my house and shared the gospel with me. No one came to lead me to Christ, because God took care of all that Himself. He used a TV evangelist to get my attention. I absolutely believe there is a real place called Hell where those who are not Christians will spend eternity. How would you like for your very best friends to spend eternity in Hell? If it doesn't bother you, then either you really don't believe the Bible or you're not much of a friend. Jesus tells us that as we near the end of the age, "Because of the increase of wickedness, the love of most will grow cold" (Matthew 24:12).

All my prayers from Sunday until Thursday were focused on keeping my friends out of Hell. Thursday afternoon at work, I was sitting at my desk, talking with God, begging God to save my friends. Then I heard God's voice, the same audible voice I heard when I was on my knees getting saved. This time, God said five words: "Go tell Doug about Jesus." He did not need to repeat Himself. His voice was loud and clear. The voice came from my right side, and I immediately turned to my right to see God, but no one was there. I looked out the window of my second-floor office, but no one was there. I looked out into the hallway, but no one was there either.

I closed the door to my office and knelt on the floor. I looked up and said, "God, I clearly heard you. I'll go tell Doug about Jesus, but what do I tell him?" I expected to hear an answer, but there was none. There was only silence. I waited and waited. I probably stayed on my knees ten minutes, waiting on God to tell me what I was supposed to tell Doug. I expect God had a good laugh as He watched me on my knees waiting for an answer. I expect He was thinking, *How long will this guy stay there on his knees?*

I finally said to God, "Well, I guess you'll tell me what to say when you're good and ready." I got up, locked my office door, and headed to my truck and Doug's house.

As I walked down the hallway that leads out of our office, I told God, "OK, God, I'm headed to Doug's house. What do you want me to tell him about Jesus?" There was no answer. As I walked down the stairs out of the building, I again asked God, but there was no answer. As I was getting into my truck, I said, "OK, God, I'm getting into my truck and heading to Doug's house. What is it I'm supposed to tell him about Jesus?" Again, there was no answer. As I drove on the crosstown highway, over the Cooper River Bridge, down Coleman Boulevard, and on Pelzer Drive, there still was no answer. I was getting desperate. I had no idea what to tell Doug about Jesus. I pulled into Doug's driveway and sat in the truck and prayed one last time. Then God brought a Scripture to mind. God often brings Scriptures to mind to give us answers. It was the Scripture where

Jesus said, "Do not worry about what to say or how to say it. At that time you will be given what to say" (Matthew 10:19).

I took my Bible and walked to the front door. Doug is a "red-neck," and proud of it. I was one too, but not quite as "red" as Doug. I expected there was at least a 99 percent chance that when Doug saw me with a Bible in my hand, he would laugh at me, curse at me, and tell me to get out of his house. But I had to do it because Doug was my best friend, and you do things like this for your friends. His eternal destiny in Heaven or Hell was at stake. Furthermore, God told me to tell him about Jesus.

When the door opened, I remember my exact words. I said, "Doug, I have something to tell you. I don't know what I'm going to say yet, but when I say it, if you don't want to hear it, just tell me and I'll leave. Just don't curse me out and don't throw me out. Just tell me and I'll leave."

Doug said, "OK, come on in." We went in and sat in his living room. This was strange, because we never sat in the living room. Of the hundreds of times I've been in his house, we always sat in the den.

Doug sat in a chair, and I sat at the end of the couch. I looked at him and said, "Doug, something happened to me a few weeks ago. I got saved. I'm a Christian. When I die, I'm going to Heaven to be with Jesus forever. I want you to get saved too, so you can spend eternity in Heaven with me. I want to tell you about Jesus Christ."

Doug did not say a word. As soon as I mentioned the name "Jesus Christ," I saw tears well up in his eyes, but the tears never ran down his face. You see, real men don't cry, and rednecks absolutely never cry.

A few years earlier, Doug and I were going to cut down a large oak tree for firewood. Doug parked his new truck about thirty feet from the tree. I told Doug he had better park his truck further away from the tree; the tree might fall on it. Doug said, "I know what I'm doing. I've cut many trees for firewood. It will fall in that direction."

Doug proceeded to cut a wedge out of the base of the tree, and then he cut through the tree. It fell and crushed his new pickup truck. Doug started laughing. I said, "Man, what are you laughing about? You just destroyed your new truck."

Doug said, "I have to laugh to keep from crying." You see, rednecks never cry.

We were looking at each other eye to eye. Then something happened. My mouth opened, and I started sharing the gospel with Doug, even though I didn't even know what the gospel was. I was even quoting Bible verses. It for sure sounded like my voice, but it was not me speaking. I knew God was doing this thing. God was speaking through my mouth and sharing the gospel for me.

After Matthew 10:19 where Jesus said, "Don't worry about what to say," the next verse explains what was happening. Jesus says, "For it will not be you speaking, but the Spirit of your Father speaking through you" (Matthew 10:20). Over the twenty-five years that I've been a Christian, God has spoken through my mouth on several occasions. Several of my friends have also had this experience.

Some of you may be thinking, now I know he's crazy. *If that's the case, you need to stop right now and read Numbers, chapter 22. That's where the Holy Spirit spoke through the mouth of a donkey. If God can speak through the mouth of a donkey, He can certainly speak through my mouth. He can also speak through your mouth, if He so chooses. He is God; and "with God all things are possible" (Matthew 19:26).*

Doug looked me in the eyes the whole time we were talking. He never blinked. As I shared with him about God and his love, Jesus and his death on the cross, our sin and need of a Savior, Doug would just nod his head. He never spoke a single word, because he knew if he tried to talk, the tears would roll out of his eyes. The Holy Spirit had "cleaned his cage," just as he had cleaned my cage a few weeks earlier.

Then I heard a car drive up and park in the driveway. I knew it was Kathy. I thought, *Kathy will for sure laugh at me and maybe even toss a curse word or two at me.* I silently prayed, "God, when Kathy comes in the house, keep her in the kitchen. Keep that woman out of here. Don't let her come in here with us." I heard the side door open and heard Kathy's purse and a bag of groceries hit the kitchen counter. She then walked right in the room with Doug and me. She said, "Well, what are you boys talking about?" As she said that, she sat on the couch beside me.

I did not look at her. I knew Doug couldn't speak because he was too choked up. I just kept looking at Doug, even though I was talking to Kathy. I started over. "Kathy, something happened to me a few weeks ago. I got saved. I'm a Christian." Then the Holy Spirit repeated to Kathy what He had just spoken to Doug.

After a few minutes, I noticed that Kathy had not said anything either. I thought maybe she had left the room. I turned to look, and she was sitting there with her head hanging down. Tears were flowing down her cheeks, and she said, "Ellison, my daughter is thirteen years old, and I need to be taking her to church. Tell me again what I need to do to get saved. I want to make sure I get it right the first time. I don't want to have to go through this again." She too had been under the conviction of the Holy Spirit.

We then talked about being baptized and church membership. Kathy laughed and said, "We don't even go to a church. Do you think your preacher would baptize people like us?" I told Kathy our preacher would love to baptize them and we'd love to have them join our church. I told Kathy to go by the church and talk with the pastor.

Kathy looked at my Bible. As she thumbed through the pages, she asked about all the footnotes. I explained that I had just bought the new NIV Study Bible. The footnotes helped me understand the Scriptures, since I was a new Christian. The next day, Friday, Kathy went by the Christian bookstore and bought a NIV Study Bible. She read the Bible cover to cover that weekend. She said she just couldn't put it down.

The next week, Kathy took off work early one day and went by the church to see the preacher about being baptized. When she got home late, Doug asked where she had been. Kathy said she had gone to the church to talk with the preacher. Doug asked her, "Why didn't you wait on me? I want to be baptized too."

Kathy told Doug, "Son, there are just some things every man has to do for himself. If you want to get baptized, then you go see the preacher."

A few weeks later, Doug, Kathy, Dale, and Deirdre joined the church, and all four stepped into the pool and were baptized together. They attended our church for only a few weeks. When they did not come back, I called Doug and asked him why they were not coming to church. He said a friend of Kathy's at work invited them to visit their church on Dorchester Road. Doug asked me, "What you all do at your church on Sunday? Is that it?" I told him that was it. He said, "No, there has to be more than that." At that time, I didn't understand what he was talking about, but later, I did understand.

Doug and his family had gone to what I would call a "Spirit-filled church." For example, at the first Sunday-evening service, a lady stood in the aisle and "jabbered." Doug and Kathy didn't think too much about it and didn't even discuss it. The next Sunday evening, the same thing happened again. On the way home, Doug asked Kathy, "What was that lady jabbering about?" Kathy didn't understand, and Doug again explained, "You know, when that lady stood in the aisle and jabbered on and on. You couldn't understand a thing she said."

Kathy said, "Doug, I understood every word she said." Kathy then told Doug what the lady said. The lady had been speaking in "tongues," but Doug did not have the spiritual gift of interpreting tongues as Kathy did.

> *A similar thing happened with my wife when we were at a Christian conference. The leader asked everyone to split up into groups of three and for one person in each group to pray over a member of their group. Connie, Janice, and Rhonda got together. Janice asked for prayer, and Rhonda prayed over her. After praying, everyone returned to their seats. Connie was sitting next to Janice and said to her, "Wasn't that the most beautiful prayer you've ever heard?"*
> *Janice laughed and said, "No. I couldn't understand a word she said. She prayed the entire prayer in tongues." Connie had understood every word.*

Doug and Kathy were like Connie and me at the time: none of us had a clue about spiritual gifts. Doug had been given the gift of evangelism and started handing out Jesus tracts at work and telling people about Jesus. Kathy had the gift of interpreting tongues. Dale spoke in tongues. Dale was so on fire for the Lord that he bought two large "I Love Jesus" bumper stickers and put them across the back window of his pickup truck. Doug and his family continued worshiping at the small church on Dorchester Road.

Our two families usually got together for a dinner around Christmas. This year after dinner, Doug and I sat in the den talking about the Lord. I remember saying, "Doug, I've never told you about the vision and how God told me to come tell you about Jesus." I then shared the story of the vision with him.

Doug said, "That's a good story, but that's only half of the story."

I told Doug, "No, that's it. That's the whole story."

Doug again told me, "No, that's only half of the story."

Again, I told Doug, "Hey, it's my story. That's all of it."

He said, "That's only your half. You haven't heard my half of the story." He then proceeded to share his story with me.

Doug said that it started two weeks before I came to visit him. He got up on Sunday morning, put his fishing rods in the boat, and headed up the highway to Maybelline Lodge to fish, just like he did every Sunday morning. He said that as he drove up the highway, he was flipping through the radio stations and came across one where people were singing Christian songs. He said they were the old-time Christian songs, like they sang in church when he was a kid. He said when he heard the songs, he started crying. He kept crying but didn't know why. He was able to hold it back while he launched his boat. He ran his boat across the lake, and as he sat there fishing, he started crying again, and he couldn't stop. He got frustrated and said, "If I'm just going to sit here and cry, I may as well go home." He quit fishing, took his boat out, and drove home.

The next Sunday, he did the same thing. He loaded his boat and headed up the highway. Then he heard those old-time Christian songs on the radio again, and he started crying again. He said, "Well, there's no need in going fishing today. I may as well go home right now." He turned around and drove home.

On Monday at work, Doug and a coworker were talking, and the coworker told Doug that he needed to get right with God. The same thing happened Tuesday with another coworker. Doug said he started thinking, *Where is all this God stuff coming from?* Then on Wednesday, Doug was at home sitting on his back porch. He looked at his four-bedroom house, his car, his truck, his boat, and his swimming pool. Then he said out loud, "For a poor farm boy, you have really done well for yourself."

As soon as Doug said those words, he heard God speak out loud. God said, "I gave it all to you, and I can take it all away." Doug said it scared him so bad that tears welled up in his eyes. He didn't want his wife and daughter to see him crying, so he ran out into the backyard and hid behind a large fig tree. After he regained his composure, he came back over to his chair on the porch.

Thursday at work, Doug started having chest pains. The doctor at work sent him to his family doctor, who told Doug his heart was

OK. He then told Doug, "You just need to take a little time off and go out into the woods by yourself and talk to God." Doug said he thought, *Who does that punk think he is, telling me to go out in the woods and talk to God?* Then Doug drove home.

Doug said that a short time later, he heard a pickup truck pull into his driveway. He went to the window and saw me sitting in the truck, "talking to myself." I was actually praying. He said he saw me get out of the truck and walk up the sidewalk. When he saw that I was carrying a Bible, he threw his hands up and said, "God, I give up. I can't take it anymore." Doug said, "I couldn't believe what I was seeing. You, of all people, were carrying a Bible!" Doug told me that when he saw me with a Bible in my hand, he surrendered to God right then, before I even set foot in the house. Doug said, "All I needed then was to know how to get saved, and you came in and told me how to do that."

Over the years, I've learned that God's timing is important and that it's perfect. The second Sunday that Doug tried to go fishing was the Sunday that God showed me the vision. However, God was not yet ready for me to make the visit. Doug and Kathy were not ready either. Then, every day that week, I prayed and cried out to God to save Doug and Kathy. Every day that week, the Holy Spirit continued convicting Doug and Kathy. The Holy Spirit put someone in Doug's face each day to mention the name "God." By Thursday afternoon, Doug was ready. It was then that God told me to "Go tell Doug about Jesus." God went with me, and the Holy Spirit had already done His convicting work. When I showed up, it was already a "done deal." All that was needed was for a friend to deliver the good news of Jesus Christ.

The next Monday, Doug had three painters painting his house. When he got home from work, he found they had dropped two gallons of paint on the front brick steps. The painters told Doug, "We'll leave if you want us to." They thought they were going to get fired.

Doug said, "Don't worry about it. Go buy some more paint and get on with the painting."

A few minutes later, Kathy said, "Doug, we have a problem. The liner in the pool has split, and we've already lost half the water from the pool."

Doug said, "No problem. That's why they make replacement liners. We'll get another one."

Doug told me if these two problems had happened a few weeks earlier, before he became a Christian, he would have pitched a fit using a great deal of profanity. God had already changed his heart. Doug had been born again, and now he had the peace of Christ in his heart. The Bible says, "And the peace of God, which transcends all understanding, will guard your hearts and your minds in Christ Jesus" (Philippians 4:7).

Good friends are hard to come by. Best friends are rare. Do your friends have a personal relationship with our Savior? Will your friends spend eternity in Heaven or in Hell?

Another Man, Another Vision

In my twenty-five years as a Christian, I have personally come across only one person who had a similar vision and experience. I met the man a short time after I became a Christian. My good friend, Pete, and I were doing our Tuesday night visitation. We visited a young man in an apartment complex. We told him we were from First Baptist Church and were visiting people in the community. We wanted to invite him to worship with us, and when we started talking about our church, the young man stopped us. He said, "I appreciate your coming, but you're wasting your time. You need to go visit someone else." He said, "I know Jesus, and I'm getting my affairs in order. I'm leaving in a couple of days to be a missionary." The word "missionary" rang my bell. I felt that God was also calling me to be a missionary, so I asked him to tell us about his call to be a missionary. He said, "God took me and showed me where I am to serve in Africa, and I'm packing and getting ready to leave."

I asked him, "How did God show you this?"

He said, "God took my spirit out of my body and took me to Africa, and he showed me where I would serve him. I saw the area from the air." He told us, "I'm out of here. You need to go visit someone who needs to know the Lord."

Pete, of course, didn't understand any of this and continued trying to invite this young man to come worship at our church. I told Pete, "Let's go. This man is way ahead of us." I knew exactly what that young man was talking about. God had taken my spirit and shown me where my mission field would be: right here in the Lowcountry. This young man's mission field was to be in Africa.

In the past twenty-five years, this young man is the only person I have personally come in contact with who also had an out-of-body vision experience. I expect there are others, but like me, they simply don't talk about the experience. They know their Christian friends won't believe them. I wish now I had stayed and listened to this man's full testimony of "being taken in the spirit to Africa."

Many books have been written and testimonies shared on "life, death, and back-to-life" experiences. I personally believe God uses those who have these "near-death" experiences to testify to us of the Heaven or Hell that awaits each one of us. My experience was not a "near-death" experience, but my spirit sure did some traveling.

Another Vision Trip

A few months ago, a friend loaned me a book about several powerful evangelists that God used around the 1900s. One was a woman named Maria Woodworth-Etter. I'll share what was said in the book about her spirit trip:

> Then Maria had a great vision. Angels came into her room. They took her to the West, over prairies, lakes, forests, and

> rivers where she saw a long, wide field of waving golden grain. As the view unfolded she began to preach and saw the grains begin to fall like sheaves. Then Jesus told her that, "just as the grain fell, so people would fall" as she preached.[3]

Maria began preaching the Word all over America, just as she had been shown in the vision. When she preached, people fell under the power of the Holy Spirit.

CHAPTER 4

Go See Delores

During the early 1980s, I was divorced and a single parent of my eight-year-old daughter. I truly understand what it means to be a single parent, because I was one for five years. I also understand what it means to be a "soccer mom," because I often was one. My daughter, Susan, had eight or ten close friends her age. Their moms and I took turns taking the girls to softball practice, Girl Scouts, horseback riding, cheerleading, school field trips, and anything else the girls could come up with. I even went on a camping trip with the Girl Scouts because I wanted to do my part.

Jennifer is one of Susan's friends. One day in the summer of 1987 (a year before I became a Christian), I went to see Jennifer's dad, Danny. I wanted to talk with Danny about fishing. I rang the doorbell, and Jennifer's mom, Delores, came to the door. Delores had a smile on her face that went coast to coast. Her face literally glowed. I actually saw a radiance coming from her face. That radiance scared the daylights out of me. I had never seen anything like that before. The Bible says, "Those who look to him are radiant; their faces are never covered with shame" (Psalm 34:5).

Delores said something like, "Ellison, I just want to tell you that God is so good. I truly love the Lord. God is so good," and so on. It seemed like every other word out of her mouth was "God" or "Jesus." Between the radiance coming off her face and all the God stuff coming out of her mouth, I started backing up and immediately got out of there.

Later, I went by June's house. June was one of the moms in our group. I asked her, "What happened to Delores?"

She asked, "What do you mean?"

I said, "What's all this God and Jesus stuff about?"

June laughed and said, "Oh, didn't you hear? Delores went and got religion."

My comment was, "Oh great, another one of those religious freaks!"

Over the past few years, Delores, her husband, Danny, and I had been friends, mainly because of working together with the girls. Now I totally avoided Delores. I had my fill of Christians at work. Many employees who worked in our department were not Christians, and most of them were excellent employees. Others let everyone know they were Christians, and it was as if they thought they were a cut above everyone else. However, many of these Christians were some of our worst employees. They would lie, steal, loaf on the job, and all that. For example, one of man tried to get some plumbing supplies out of our stock room. He and his friends were doing some renovation work at their church. He was going to take plumbing supplies from work and use the materials at his church. I really knew only a handful of men and women at work who claimed to be Christians and actually acted the way I thought Christians were supposed to act.

During the next year, I stayed away from Delores and Danny. Whenever I saw June, I would ask her, "How's the holy roller doing?" June would just laugh and say that Delores was still about the same. I knew June and the other moms would probably tell Delores that I was calling her a religious freak and a holy roller behind her back, but I really didn't care.

Then it happened. In June 1988, I came face-to-face with God. Jesus told Nicodemus, "You must be born again" (John 3:7), and that's what happened to me. As my neighbor June would probably say, "Ellison went and got religion." I had been born again, even though I did not have a clue what that meant.

A few weeks passed, and then it started. Every morning as I drove to work, God would speak to me. Sometimes He spoke out loud, and sometimes He spoke silently (God often speaks silently). Either way, I would hear His voice as clear as a bell. He would always say those same three words: "Go see Delores." But He would never tell me why. The subdivision where Delores lived was adjacent to the one where I lived. I drove past her subdivision every day going to and from work. When God said, "Go see Delores," I would always make an excuse such as, "God, you know I'm the boss at work, and I need to get to work early and set the example for others to follow. I don't have time to go see Delores." God would not argue. Then on the way home, as I approached Delores's subdivision, God would again say those same three words: "Go see Delores." My response was always the same. "God, I don't have time. I need to get on home and make sure Susan is OK and doing her homework. I'll go see Delores some other time." This went on day after day for several weeks.

Why didn't I just go see Delores? I wouldn't go because I did not want to face her. I knew that she was aware that I had been calling her a religious freak and a holy roller behind her back for the last year. I figured God was calling me to account for my actions. I assumed He was going to make me apologize to Delores. I absolutely did not want to face her. I guess I still had some of the old redneck left in me.

Then one day at work, I received word from the president of the university that the director of the hospital in Kingstree had asked him to send his physical plant employees to look at the Kingstree hospital's HVAC systems and make recommendations for improvements. I was the "boss," but I didn't have the technical knowledge needed. I supervised those who did have this knowledge. I asked Don, our maintenance supervisor, to go with me to Kingstree.

Don and I met at the Texaco station at Highway 41. He parked his truck there, and we drove to Kingstree in my truck. We looked over their plant, discussed what we saw, and headed home. It was midafternoon when we arrived back at the Texaco station. We normally get off work at 4:00 p.m., so I assumed Don would say, "I think I'll just head on home." I certainly did not plan to go in to work that late in the day. But Don was more dedicated than me. He said, "I'm heading in to work to check and make sure everything is OK." But since I was the boss, how could I not go in to work and check on my areas of responsibility?

I told Don, "I'll be about ten minutes behind you. I need to stop by the house and make sure Susan is OK." Don drove to work without a problem.

I went home to check on Susan, and she was fine. I told her I was going to work for an hour or two and would be home shortly. As I passed Delores's subdivision, I heard God's voice again: "Go see Delores." It was as if God was always standing on that street corner. I could not pass by that subdivision without hearing God say those three words. Again I gave God the same excuse. "God, you know I'm the boss, and I need to set the example for my employees to follow. I'll go see Delores some other time."

In 1988, there were two bridges that crossed over the Cooper River from Mount Pleasant into Charleston; the old bridge (John P. Grace Bridge) and the new bridge (Silas N. Pearman Bridge). As I approached the old bridge, I saw thick, black smoke rising from its first span. A truck appeared to be on fire, and traffic began backing up as the bridge shut down. I cut across a few medians and headed over to the new bridge. As I approached the ramp onto the new bridge, I saw traffic begin to back up. Apparently, a car had broken down. Either way, I had no intention of sitting in traffic an hour or two waiting on the bridges to be cleared and reopened. I decided to just go home, wait an hour, and then see if one of the bridges reopened.

(Later, I found out a truck loaded with pine straw had caught on fire and shut down the old bridge. A car broke down on the new bridge, blocking traffic. Don, who was only ten minutes ahead of me, drove in to work with no problem. God then closed both bridges.)

As I headed home and approached Delores's subdivision, I heard God's voice again. He was right there with those same three words: "Go see Delores." I started to tell God that I needed to go home and check on Susan, but I realized I had just checked on Susan, and she was OK. I had no excuse this time. In frustration I shouted back at God, "OK, OK, I'll go see Delores! Just leave me alone! I can't take it anymore!"

As I drove into Delores's subdivision, I started thinking about how I'd apologize for making fun of her and her religion. As I drove by her house, I saw no cars in the driveway, so I thought Delores was not home. I drove around the cul-de-sac and looked again at her house, and there were no cars there. Now I boldly told God, "OK, God, I've done what you told me to do. I'm here. Both cars are gone, so no one is home. That's your problem. Now leave me alone!"

Then, as I started to drive home, I was oh, so bold. I said, "God, I tell you what I'll do. I'll even go knock on the door. If Delores isn't home, that's your problem. I've done what you told me to do." I drove over to her house, parked in their driveway, and walked to the side door. I boldly knocked on the door. Boldly, I say, because I knew no one was home. Then my heart sank to the ground as I heard footsteps inside the house. I could tell they were a woman's footsteps walking across the hardwood floor. I knew it was Delores.

The door opened, and Delores's exact words were, "Hi, Ellison, I've been expecting you. Come on in." I immediately thought, *How could she be expecting me?* I had just chosen to come to her house. There was no way for her to know I was coming. I had not been to her house in over a year.

The side door of their house led into their game room, and there was a pool table in the middle of it. I remember we walked around the right side of pool table, with Delores in front of me. I followed behind her like a little puppy dog. As we walked, she looked over her shoulder at me and said, "Ellison, what can I do for you?"

I was about to tell her I had come to apologize. But before I could say anything, my mouth opened, and words came out. It was my voice, but it was not me speaking. It was the Holy Spirit speaking through my mouth. The Holy Spirit said, "Delores, I'm scared to death of God."

This is the second time the Holy Spirit had spoken through my mouth. The first time was when I was telling Doug and Kathy about Jesus. Remember, if God can speak through a donkey's mouth (Numbers 22:28), He can speak through my mouth, and He can also speak through your mouth if He so chooses.

I was, quite frankly, shocked to hear the words the Holy Spirit spoke out of my mouth. When the Holy Spirit said, "Delores, I'm scared to death of God," I thought, *Where did that come from?* I was, in fact, "scared to death of God," but I thought all Christians were. I knew that on that Thursday night in June 1988, if I had had another heart attack and died, God would have thrown me into Hell for eternity. You're mighty right, I'm afraid of God, but why did God say this to Delores? I thought, *Aren't we all supposed to be God-fearing? Aren't all Christians afraid of God?*

As we walked past the pool table, Delores again looked over her shoulder at me and said, "Come on into the kitchen. My Bible is on the counter. I've got it marked." As we walked into her kitchen, there on the counter beside the range was her Bible. It was full of white paper bookmarks. She said, "Sit at the table, and let's talk." She followed with, "Ellison, you don't have to be afraid of God. He loves you. Your sins have been forgiven, and they are gone." I asked about the blasphemy sin. She said, "Don't worry about that one. That's not you. You belong to Jesus." She went bookmark by bookmark, sharing with me Scriptures of how much God loves me. She explained to me that I would not be going to Hell, because Jesus had paid for *all of my sins*. My sins were gone, and I was a new creation. I was free. I felt the fear of Hell lifting off my shoulders. Jesus took the fear and set me free.

What Delores said made sense to me. The radiance on her face I had seen a year earlier was gone, but she still had the joy of the Lord pouring out of her. Delores truly loves our Savior, and she was now being used by God to help a new Christian, me, start on the journey we call sanctification. She is a disciple of Jesus Christ, and she was now doing that work.

After she finished her mission of telling me how much God loves me, that I did not need to be afraid of God, and that I was not going to Hell, she began to laugh. She said, "Ellison, I know that for the last year, you have been making fun of me. You've been calling me a 'holy roller' and a 'Jesus freak' and other names, but I took all those names as compliments. I remember a year ago, when you came to see Danny. I truly loved the Lord, and I came to the door and was talking about Jesus. I remember how you backed away and left in a hurry." Delores said, "I want you to know that every day since that happened, I have prayed for your soul. I have prayed that you too would be saved. I have not missed praying for you one single day. Then, when I heard you found Jesus, I just praised God. I was so excited for you."

Over the years, I've learned that when someone puts you on their "holy hit list," you better watch out!

My head was spinning. I thought, *How did she know all this? How did she know I was coming? How did she already have bookmarks in her Bible on all those Scriptures about God's love?*

Today I can tell you how all that can happen. God has a tremendous love for us. That's how. He truly must have a huge computer up there in Heaven to keep track of all of us, all the time. He loves each one of us that much. The Bible says, in fact, that "God is love" (1 John 4:16).

Over the next few years, I realized that there were others in our churches that were just like me. They were members of a church, but they were not Christians. They had joined the church and been baptized for whatever reason but did not know our Savior. I thought about my kinfolk and gathered all of the addresses I could find and sent Jesus Christmas cards to them. Inside the cards, I enclosed a letter explaining that there is a difference between knowing about Jesus and knowing Jesus. I explained that even though I joined the church and was baptized at age fourteen, I was not a Christian then. I wanted all of them to examine their own hearts and see if Jesus was there. I tried to explain the difference between head knowledge and heart knowledge. I wanted to make sure that when I got to Heaven and looked around, they would all be there.

The first response to the letter came from my sister. Mom told me that she called and asked, "What happened to Ellison? I think he's fallen off the deep end."

I asked Mom, "What do you think?"

Mom said, "Well, son, I worry about you. All you do is read the Bible and go church. You don't even go deer hunting anymore." She said, "I'm afraid you're going to turn into one of those religious fanatics."

I thought about that for a few seconds and responded, "I'm not going to turn into one of those religious fanatics; I'm already one. I'm a fanatic about Jesus."

Mom thought about that a few seconds and responded, "Yes, you are, son, and I'm proud of you."

In 2013, I met Delores for lunch. We had not seen each other for twenty-five years. She has many testimonies of her own that glorify God. I'll share with you one of her testimonies that involved me. It happened four years after I became a Christian. However, I did not know of my involvement in her testimony until we met for lunch.

Danny and Delores

Delores and her husband, Danny, moved to Romain Retreat. In 1992, Danny was driving a tractor and bush-hogging some of the property at the subdivision. He got off the tractor, unhooked the Bush Hog, and got back on the tractor. When he put the tractor in gear, his foot slipped off the clutch, and the tractor flipped over. The tractor pinned Danny to the ground, completely crushing his chest. Death was knocking at Danny's door. He could not move or breathe, and he was losing blood. He was going to die right there under the weight of the tractor.

Delores said Danny later told her that "someone" lifted the tractor off of him. She said Danny felt hands under his arms, and they quickly slid Danny out from under the tractor. That "someone" laid the tractor back down on the ground. There was no one near the tractor and Danny, except the angels whom God had sent to save his life.

Several other men working nearby saw the tractor crushing Danny. One of the men told Delores that he saw the tractor "just lift up off Danny," and then he saw Danny "shoot out from under the tractor." He did not see the angels, but they were there.

A neighbor who worked in a local hospital emergency room was home and came to help. Danny's condition was so critical that a helicopter was dispatched to transport him to the MUSC hospital. He was placed in the intensive care unit. His condition was so grave that the doctors told Delores that Danny would not live. They told her that she should prepare their three children for his passing.

Delores spent that night at her sister's house, and she slept in an upstairs bedroom. The Lord woke Delores at 5:00 a.m. and told her, "Go read Jeremiah 30:17 out of your sister's Bible," which was downstairs. Delores didn't understand this, because Danny's Bible was right there beside her bed in the upstairs bedroom. She started to pick up Danny's Bible, and the Holy Spirit again told her to get her sister's Bible, which was downstairs. This time she did as she had been told. Delores went downstairs and read the Scripture God had sent her to: "But I will restore you to health and heal your wounds, declares the Lord" (Jeremiah 30:17).

God speaks to us in many ways, and this is one of them. The day I learned of Danny's accident just happened to be my day in the prayer room at church. After I prayed for Danny and others, I decided to mail Delores a prayer-gram (similar to a get-well card) from our church prayer room. In our prayer-grams we usually write notes and try to encourage people who are hurting. We often quote a Bible verse in the prayer-gram. Since I had been a Christian for only a short time, I would always pray for the person in need and then ask God what I should write on the prayer-gram and which Bible verse I should use. There are over thirty thousand verses in the Bible. And out of these thirty thousand verses, the verse God sent me to was "Jeremiah 30:17."

About two days after Delores was awakened by God in the middle of the night and sent to her sister's Bible, she received the prayer-gram in the mail. When she saw I had used the identical Bible verse God had given to her, she knew God was confirming that Danny would recover. She claimed God's word, even though the doctors kept telling her Danny was going to die.

Why did God send Delores downstairs at 5:00 a.m. to read the Scripture from her sister's Bible when Danny's Bible was right beside her? Today, there are many versions of the Bible. The wording in Danny's Bible was a little different from the wording in her sister's Bible and my Bible. The wording of Jeremiah 30:17 in her sister's Bible was identical to the wording that I used in the prayer-gram. God confirmed to Delores, word for word, that "you" (Danny) will be restored to health and "your" (Danny's) wounds will be healed.

Delores told the doctors that Danny was not going to die because God had told her that he would be healed. The day Danny was released from the hospital, his primary doctor stood at the door with tears on his face. He told Danny that he was not supposed to live, that he was supposed to die there in that hospital bed.

I did not know about God sending both Delores and me to the same Bible verse until the day we had lunch together. God used Delores to help me in my time of need (when I was scared to death of God), and He used me to deliver God's confirming message, Jeremiah 30:17, to Delores when she was in a time of need.

I think we would all be blown away if we knew how often God uses one Christian to lift up another Christian who is in need. God gives us "a word," and then we have a choice. We may say, "Yes, Lord" and obey, or we may give God an excuse and fail to obey. Or worse yet, we may be so caught up in the things of the world that we do not even hear God's voice at all.

CHAPTER 5

DISCIPLESHIP

After reading some of the Scriptures in the Introduction, one might ask, "Who, then, would want to be a disciple?" Jesus made it clear to everyone that there would be a huge cost associated with being a disciple. He said, "In the same way, those of you who do not give up everything you have cannot be my disciples" (Luke 14:33). The number-one cost for discipleship is crystal clear: we must give up "everything." The Apostles who walked with Jesus gave up everything, including their lives, as have thousands of Christians all over the world.

Spiritual Gifts

There is work to be done for our Savior. There are many calls to discipleship. If we choose to answer the call and follow Jesus, He may send us to Africa, as He did the young man described in the chapter "The Vision." He may call us to be a preacher, a teacher, or an evangelist. Some are called to serve and encourage, while others are called to lead. The Holy Spirit chooses which spiritual gifts to give to each of us and how we will be used to build up the body of

Christ. Some of these gifts are mentioned in Romans 12, Ephesians 4, and 1 Corinthians 12. I personally believe there are additional gifts that are not mentioned in the Bible, but there still remains the choice. We each must choose to be a disciple and use these God-given gifts to glorify Jesus. "For we are God's handiwork, created in Christ Jesus to do good works, which God prepared in advance for us to do" (Ephesians 2:10).

When I surrendered my life to God, I told Him I would go anywhere and do anything He told me to do. I had never heard of discipleship. I only knew that Jesus had given His life (His all) for me, and now I would live my life (my all) for Him. Shortly after I became a Christian, I thought God was calling me to be a missionary. I was ready to leave my family, my job, and my all. The Bible says, "God knows your hearts" (Luke 16:15). The Lord knew my heart, and He knew I was serious about leaving everything to go to another country to tell them about Jesus. Then the Lord stopped me. He showed me where He wanted me to be a disciple of Christ. He wanted me to reach the world for Christ through the Gideon Ministry and to also reach people for Christ right here in the Lowcountry.

Being a disciple of Jesus Christ does not necessarily mean we must pack up and go to Africa. It means we must be *willing* to pick up and go, if God calls us to do so. We truly must be willing to give up everything and serve Jesus wherever He places us. For most of us, our mission field is right where we live and work. He does not ask us to give up our home and our country. When you read the chapter "America," you will understand why God has given so many of us a mission field right here in America.

Spiritual Gifts and the Nursing Home

A few months after I became a Christian, one of the men in the church asked if I'd like to help with a nursing-home ministry on Sunday afternoons. He said they would gather the residents into a large room, and then have a thirty-minute church service. He said they were shorthanded and really needed the help. I thought about it and agreed to help because it seemed like the Christian thing to do.

The next Sunday, we met at the nursing home. We helped the residents get into their wheelchairs and rolled them to the meeting room. We sang a couple of Christian songs, had a short message, prayed with them, and rolled them back to their rooms.

After shooting guns most of my life, I'm very hard of hearing. Most of the folks in the nursing home have difficulty speaking, so they mumble. When the residents tried to talk with me, I could not understand them, and they would often become frustrated and shout at me. I also became frustrated but didn't say anything to anyone. I remember one Sunday I was rolling a lady to the church service, and she was screaming at me. By the time we were close to the meeting room, she began cursing me. Since I used to curse fluently, I recognized some of the names she was calling me, and she called me quite a few choice names.

Jehue walked over, laughing at me, and said, "What's the matter, Ellison?"

I told him, "I don't have a clue." I asked Jehue if he knew what I was doing wrong.

Jehue laughed and said, "Ellison, she's a Jew. She doesn't want to be here with us at a Christian church service." Jehue, still laughing, rolled the lady back to her room.

I did the nursing-home church ministry for about a year and a half. I looked forward to going to my church on Sunday morning but dreaded with a passion going to the nursing home Sunday afternoon. Connie kept telling me I needed to just quit. I told her there were not enough men willing to do this work, so I needed to continue helping. I was not a quitter, and I was not going to let God and my friends down. I knew I would feel horribly guilty if I quit.

One Sunday afternoon as we were leaving the nursing home, Mr. Herman put his arm around me. He looked at me eye to eye, and with a huge grin on his face, he said, "Ellison, didn't you get a blessing out of that service today?" He meant it. He loved it.

Before I could answer, my mouth opened and words came out, but it was not me speaking. The Holy Spirit again spoke through my mouth and said, "No, Mr. Herman, I hate doing this."

I would never say anything like that in my early walk with the Lord. We're supposed to love doing things like the nursing-home ministry for the Lord and for other Christians. Furthermore, I don't like the word *hate*. The only time I use the word is when I pray and ask God to "Help me love the things you love, and to hate the things you hate." I knew it was God speaking through my mouth again.

Before I could say anything else, Mr. Herman said, "Ellison, you don't need to come back. We'll take care of the nursing home. God has something else for you to do. I don't know what it is, but you will know it when you find it, because you'll love doing it for the Lord."

"You will know it when you find it, because you'll love doing it for the Lord."

We Christians mean well, but we sometimes place burdens on each other. During my first few years as a Christian, different people at church would come up to me and say, "Ellison, you need to come join us and help us with this ministry. You and I both know God wants you to help us. You're not going to say no to God and to this ministry, are you?" I didn't know how to say no, and before long, I was involved in over a dozen ministries. I was working full time, taking care of my family, taking care of my mom, and helping take care of Connie's parents. Then I completely burned out on God. I did not hear God's voice, but He clearly showed me what to do. I quit everything. I stepped back and took a long, hard look at what I was doing at church.

I remembered what Mr. Herman told me: "You will know it when you find it, because you'll love doing it for the Lord." The things I truly loved doing were telling others about Jesus, praying, and studying the Bible so I could share God's word with others. I refocused and started doing ministries that involved these three things. I also learned how to say no to my well-meaning friends.

A year or so later, we did a study on spiritual gifts at church. Gifts such as helps, mercy, and service were not on my plate. But for Mr. Herman, these were among his many spiritual gifts. That's why he loved serving in the nursing-home ministry.

If you're not sure what your spiritual gifts are, there are many good "spiritual gifts inventories" on the Internet. One such site is www.spiritualgiftstest.com. It is important to know where our God is calling us to serve and also where He is not calling us to serve. God's plan is different for each of us.

Take Up Your Cross

Jesus opens the door with a choice. He said, "Whoever wants to be my disciple must deny themselves and take up their cross and follow me. For whoever wants to save their life will lose it, but whoever loses their life for me and for the gospel will save it" (Mark 8:34–35). I don't think Jesus is telling us to walk around with our hands together, chanting prayers all day. Neither is He telling us to carry our big, leather-bound Bible everywhere we go to impress others. He's telling us to "be Christ" to others.

I once heard a preacher explain Matthew 28. He explained the meaning of the words, "Go and make disciples of all nations" (Matthew 28:19). Jesus is not telling us *to go* but *as you go*. It's already understood that we will be going. The Scripture says "as you go into the world." It's telling us: as we go into the supermarket, look for opportunities to be Christ to others. As we go into our schools, our workplaces, our ladies' clubs, our hunting clubs, our ball games, to be Christ to those around us. We are to let others see Christ in us. We are to be Christ to others at each opportunity God lays before us. The "as you go" becomes our lifestyle. Telling others the "good news" of the gospel becomes a lifestyle. It's like breathing—it just comes naturally.

Jesus said, "Whoever acknowledges me before others, I will also acknowledge before my Father in heaven. But whoever disowns me before others, I will disown before my Father in heaven" (Matthew 10:32–33).

I'm not ashamed of Jesus. He saved my life and my soul. He is the Lord of my life, so it is an honor for me to tell others about my Savior and Lord.

Sometimes when I'm in the supermarket, I'll smile and speak to the lady at the cash register. If she smiles and seems happy, we'll chat and I'll be on my way. If she looks like the world has caved in on her, I'll say to her, "Ma'am, it looks like you're having a rough day, like things are really piling up on you." Her response may be personal, or about a problem or long hours at the store. I'll tell her I'm a Christian and ask if I can pray for her. I've never had anyone say no. I simply reach over and place my hand on her shoulder and pray for her need. I watch as Jesus restores her smile. I'll give her a Gideon New Testament and invite her to our church. I've never had another customer come up while we're praying and ask us to hurry up; they normally just stand there silently and smile.

I've even stopped people in Walmart and asked if I could pray for them. I once stopped a woman who was shopping and asked if I could pray for her. She told me yes. She told me her name and what her problems were. As I was about to start praying for her, two of my Christian friends walked up. I told them I was about to pray for the woman. We all three laid hands on her and prayed for her as other customers walked by and stared at the four of us. She left with a smile on her face and the joy of the Lord in her heart. God took her burdens and replaced them with His peace.

Before Connie and I eat a meal at home or at a restaurant, we always pray and give thanks. Whenever we're out to lunch with friends, we ask, "Would you mind if we give thanks to God for this meal?" In twenty-five years, we've never had anyone say no.

The Journey

Life is a journey. On this journey we are either growing in Christ or dying in Christ. We either hunger for the things of God or for the things of the world.

I can easily relate the journey of a disciple with walking down a deer trail in the woods. Even though I try to stay on the main trail, I sometimes make a wrong turn and end up on a side trail. I have to back up, get back on the main trail, and continue on to the area I'll be hunting. Sometimes I trip over a root and fall. Occasionally, I take a wrong trail and get completely lost and need a compass to find my way out of the woods. That is what discipleship is all about. We do our best to follow Jesus down the trail of life, but sometimes we get sidetracked. The sidetrack may come as a result of sin in our lives, or we may get lost because we tried to get ahead of God and we make a wrong turn. We sometimes get sidetracked because we just don't want to listen to God and we want to do things our way.

When we mess up and fall, Jesus, our Master and Teacher, is always there to pick us up. When Peter got out of the boat, he walked on water for a short distance. Then when he took his eyes off Jesus, he started sinking. Jesus reached out his hand and caught Peter, the same as He will catch us (cf. Matthew 14:27–31).

My early days as a deer hunter were mostly trial and error. My dad was not a hunter, and I did not have anyone to teach me how to hunt, so I made a lot of mistakes. Later on in life, I made friends with some older men who were deer hunters, and they taught me a great deal. They shared their experiences (testimonies) with me, and I learned from their experiences and advice. I would follow some of these older, experienced deer hunters as I walked the deer trails. They would explain the signs to look for, like buck rubs and scrapes. They explained the best ways to place a deer stand and the importance of wind direction in deer hunting. I learned a lot from those older men, but now, most of these older men are gone. I find myself at the hunting club, sitting with young boys and explaining to them about deer rubs and scrapes, about wind direction, and about deer stand placement. They call me "Mr. Ellison," the old man. They want to learn, and I'm grateful for the opportunity to share what I have experienced with them.

Being a disciple is like being that "Mr. Ellison." When I first became a Christian, I was on my own. There was so much I did not understand, and I think that's one reason God told me to join the Gideons. There I met several older men who had walked with the Lord most of their lives. I listened to them and learned from them. In some of our earlier Bible studies, I just listened to the older men. Today, most of those older men have gone home to be with our Lord, and I am now one of the older men.

In my early years as a Christian, I heard a lot about discipleship, but I never intended to be a disciple. I thought a disciple was a person who sat around a table and just coached younger Christians. I would tell others at our church, "I'll go out and share the gospel with the heathen and then point them in the direction of the church. When they come to our church, it's up to you to disciple them." I really didn't want to waste my time discipling others, because I was so overwhelmed with the burden of helping others get their ticket to Heaven. I had a huge fire in my gut that was compelling me to warn others of the coming judgment and Hell. The Bible says, "Anyone whose name was not found written in the book of life was thrown into the lake of fire" (Revelation 20:15). It's real. It's going to happen. God says so.

As a young Christian, when I prayed, I would ask God for wisdom, knowledge, understanding, and for a portion of common sense so that I could help others. I really didn't want all this wisdom and knowledge for myself. I already had my Heaven ticket. I wanted to help others come to know the Jesus I knew, and I wanted to take every ounce of what God gave to me and to share it with others. Without realizing it, the things I asked for now help me be a disciple and help guide others who are just starting on that path of discipleship. When I was younger, I learned from older men as we walked together down this path. Now I'm the older man reaching out to others and helping them walk the journey with our Savior. Being a disciple is a 365-day-a-year journey with our Lord. It is a lifestyle. It is also a choice.

Family

In Genesis, God created everything with a "created order." It was not haphazard. Every time I sit in a deer stand, I look out over what God created. In the fall, when the rut sets in, the deer mate. The bucks are chasing and mating with the does, and the remainder of the year, the bucks and does don't really associate with each other. That's God's created order for deer.

I have a bluebird nesting box in my backyard. One day, I sat on the porch and watched as the female flew back and forth, picking up pine straw and moss. She was hard at work, building her nest. While all this work was going on, the male stood guard over his mate and the nesting box. Then the male flew down and picked up a piece of pine straw. He lit on top of the box and sat there, quite proud of the fact that he had a piece of pine straw in his beak. The female just ignored him and continued building her nest. The male finally flew into the nesting box with his piece of pine straw. After a minute or two, he came back out of the box with the straw still in his mouth. It was obvious that he knew nothing about building a nest. He again lit on top of the box with the pine straw in his beak. Then he spit it out and went back to his role of guarding his mate and the nest. Again, that's God's created order.

Men and women also have roles in both the home and the church. I once went to the concordance in my Bible and looked up every reference to "man and woman" and to "husband and wife." I wanted to see what God's role was for me as a husband and as a man in our church. Men and women are both created equal in the eyes of God, but we each have different roles. The Father, the Son, and the Holy Spirit are all God and all equal, but they each have different roles. The Father always relates to the Son as Father. He has a leadership role. The Son does only what he sees the Father doing. The Son is obedient to the Father, even to death on the cross. The Holy Spirit does not glorify Himself but glorifies Jesus, and in doing so, He also glorifies the Father.

God put together His created order for men, women, and children, both in the family and in the church. We each have important but different roles. In our homes, we are one family, we are one body. In our church, we are one family, we are one body. God says, "So in Christ we, though many, form one body, and each member belongs to all the others" (Romans 12:5). We are there to build up the family, the body of Christ. We're there in times of plenty and in times of lean. God called for a man and woman to marry and to be fruitful and have children. God calls us to be a family at home and also in the church. All of the animals, fish, and birds I see when I'm out in the woods are still living within God's created order. But what has happened to our families?

What is the opposite of family? That would be Satan's plan for us. Satan's plan is divorce. I understand that about 50 percent of the couples who married in recent years have already divorced. This percentage includes both Christians and non-Christians.

Satan wants us to forget about the children. Divorce not only affects the husband and wife, but the children catch the brunt of the divorce. They often grow up without a dad or a mom role model. God tells us that when a man and woman are married, they are supposed to be so close together that they become "one flesh" (Genesis 2:24). A child in a single-parent home misses out on this closeness.

God draws us together as family and friends. Satan divides us and then attacks us when we're vulnerable. In Africa, a pack of lions will chase a large herd of wildebeests. Eventually, one of the wildebeests will split away from the herd. The pack of lions will attack the singled-out animal and kill it. That's what Satan tries to do to us. He tries to separate us from our own home family. He tries to even separate us from our church family. Then he attacks.

> *My good friend, Brent, was in the prayer room at church, praying one evening. He often hears God's voice while praying, but this day, he heard Satan's voice. Satan told Brent, "I may not be able to get you, but I've got your*

> *children." In the power of Jesus's Name and the Word, Brent rebuked Satan and continued praying. He recognizes Satan's tactics and his power, but Satan must submit to the Lord. Jesus is King of kings and Lord of lords.*

Yes, Satan wants your children too. You say, "That isn't fair." Who ever said Satan was fair? Satan does not know the meaning of the word. Husbands and wives, pray for each other, and pray for your children. Children, pray for your parents. Every day I pray for my family. In Job, the Bible says God has put a "hedge of protection" around Job, his family, and his possessions (cf. Job 1:10). Every day I pray for that same hedge of God's protection for my family.

God draws us closer together in Christ. When Jesus was training the disciples, He sent them out in pairs. I can testify that I would much rather go out visiting and sharing the gospel with another Christian than go out by myself. When I'm out there by myself, Satan always attacks. He tries to draw me away from my mission of introducing others to Christ. Jesus said, "For where two or three gather in my name, there am I with them" (Matthew 18:20). In the good old days, Pete and I would go out together, knocking on doors and sharing Christ with anyone who would listen to us. Pete was serious about prayer, and he prayed the entire time we were out sharing. I know his prayers kept Satan and his demons at bay. But when I go out by myself, I can tell you that every single time, for twenty-five years, I have had to fight the evil one in addition to sharing the gospel.

Unfortunately, some churches have become social clubs. People come to do their duty once a week. They come to be seen and show off their new clothes, their new car, and other toys. They come to make social ties and business contacts. Some even come because they feel they have to just to please God. They miss the point. God is looking for a relationship with us individually and as a family.

Just how close does God want to be with us? God wants to be closer than you and your spouse on your fiftieth wedding anniversary. If twenty-five years ago someone had told me I could be that close with the God of the universe, I would have told them they were crazy. I was scared to death of God twenty-five years ago, and I mostly wanted to just hide from Him. Today, I look for Him; I long to be with Him, and, I love being with Him. I'm so glad He said, "I will never leave you nor forsake you" (Joshua 1:5).

Preachers and Preachers

There are preachers, and then there are preachers. I love listening to good, Holy-Spirit-filled preachers preaching the word of God. My wife and I currently worship at four churches that we refer to as our home churches, and we frequently worship at several others as well. In some churches, we are overwhelmed with the love of God and the presence of the Holy Spirit. In other churches we visit, there seems to be a great void. Some preachers and churches are so filled with the Holy Spirit that we don't want to leave the church. In others, there is a stampede out the door when the service ends. If you've been a Christian for a while and visited other churches, you've probably come across both types.

Oswald Chambers, in his daily devotional book, *My Utmost for His Highest*, talks about preaching the gospel and preachers trying to impress people with their excellence of speech. Oswald says,

> The real fasting of the preacher is not from food, but rather from eloquence, from impressiveness and exquisite diction, from everything that might hinder the gospel of God being presented. The preacher is there as the representative of God-"as though God did beseech you by us." He is there to present the Gospel of God. If it is only because of my preaching that people desire to be better, they will never get anywhere near Jesus Christ. Anything that flatters me in my preaching of the Gospel will end in making me a traitor to

> Jesus; I prevent the creative power of His Redemption from doing its work.[4]

My interpretation of what Oswald said is that if we are focused on what a great preacher we have standing before us and how well he speaks and preaches, then it's a bad day in the pulpit. If the preacher causes us to focus on Jesus and He is exalted, then it's a good day in the pulpit. Paul said that when he preached the gospel, he did so "not with wisdom and eloquence, lest the cross of Christ be emptied of its power" (1 Corinthians 1:17). The same applies to lay leaders. Some seem to be focused on glorifying God, while others seem to seek the praise of their fellow man (cf. John 12:43).

The Professional Speaker

Preparing for a Saturday conference, we previewed the seven presentations that were to be given. The information in the presentations overlapped and tied together. The teachings were to be given by both pastors and laymen. One layman happened to be a professional speaker. When he presented his teaching for preview, he walked around the room, waved his hands and arms, raised and lowered his voice, and did all he could do to impress us with his ability as a professional speaker. He was, indeed, an excellent speaker.

When the group critiqued his presentation, we tried to politely explain to him that we knew he was an excellent speaker, but the conference was not about him. The whole purpose of his being there was to present the information to those attending the conference. We wanted the attendees to focus on Christ when they listened to his message, not on the speaker. We asked him to just stand behind the podium like the other presenters and to clearly present the information. He said he understood and agreed.

At the conference, when he presented his message, he blew it. He ignored what we said and again walked around the room, swinging his arms and making hand signals. He kept raising and lowering his voice, trying to impress everyone with his great speaking abilities. He was truly a good speaker. Several of the other speakers were preachers, and I think he may have wanted to show that he could speak better than they could. His focus was not on helping the audience gain an understanding of the material being presented. He wanted to impress the audience with his professional speaking abilities.

Unfortunately, he was so focused on himself that he lost track of the material he was presenting. He failed to present over half of the major points in the training—points that tied into the next speaker's message. The next speaker had to quickly rewrite his presentation to pick up all the main points that had been left out.

Those who made the best presentations caused the audience to focus on the material presented and on the love of Jesus Christ. They called no attention to themselves.

The Humble Speaker

Years ago, we drove to Atlanta to worship at First Baptist Church and to listen to Dr. Charles Stanley preach. We were seated and waiting on the service to start. There was another man sitting on the platform with Dr. Stanley. As Dr. Stanley stood to introduce his guest speaker, my heart sank. We had driven over 200 miles to hear Dr. Stanley preach. He said the guest speaker's name was Junior Hill. I was a new Christian and had never heard of Junior Hill, who is a very well-known evangelist.

As Mr. Hill sat there on the platform, I sensed that he was a very humble man. His head was bowed as though he was praying the entire time he was seated and waiting to speak. When he stood to preach, he was very soft-spoken and presented a simple gospel message. He did not raise his voice. He did not walk around on the platform. He did not use hand and arm signals. He was just a humble man presenting the gospel of Jesus Christ. At the end of his message, when he gave the altar call, I thought that maybe two or three people might come forward to accept Christ. Wrong! A crowd came forward. I couldn't believe what I was seeing. We were later told that over 150 people had come forward that morning to accept Christ.

In the world's view, I'd say that the professional speaker was a much better speaker than Junior Hill. So what was the difference? The answer is: the Holy Spirit and pride. Mr. Hill was filled with the Holy Spirit, and his message had the power of God behind his words. The professional speaker was filled with himself. "Pride brings a person low, but the lowly in spirit gain honor" (Proverbs 29:23).

You've Lost Your First Love

Several years ago, God told me, "You've lost your first love." I prayed and prayed about the loss. I kept questioning God, but He would not explain this statement. He never explains when he speaks to me. I knew that the Scripture came from Revelation 2, but I could not figure out what God was talking about. I studied and studied the verses in the Revelation Scriptures, but to no avail.

I asked God if He was talking about sharing the gospel with others. I was still sharing Christ with others, and I loved doing it. That was not the answer. I asked if it was the love of God, but I knew that when I first got saved, I did not love God. I was actually scared to death of God. I asked God if it was the church, the Gideons, the preachers, or what? I could not figure it out. From time to time over the next two years, I would clearly hear God repeat those same words to me: "You've lost your first love."

God gave me a clue one day at church. Several of us were "prayer-walking" around our church. As we walked, we silently prayed for our church and whatever else the Lord placed on our hearts. As we walked, I started thinking about a few people I knew (and being judgmental of them). As I silently talked with the Lord about these folks, I clearly heard the Lord speak to me. He said, "That's none of your business! You follow me!"

My response was, "Yes, Lord." That should have been a clue about my first love, but I just didn't get the message.

Finally, one day in October, I was sitting high up in a tree in a deer stand. As I waited for a deer to come by, I was reading a book about Mother Teresa of Calcutta. She was a special lady. She truly loved the Lord and knew Him well. I read of how she loved and helped everyone: Christians, Muslims, Hindus, Buddhists, atheists, and anyone that crossed her path. She loved them all unconditionally. Then it hit me. I realized that my first love was, as was Mother Teresa's love, the unconditional love of everyone. The day before I was saved, I was very judgmental of others, Christian and heathen alike. The day after I was saved, I truly unconditionally loved everyone.

The love in my heart for others was not something I conjured up. It was something that was done for me by God. The day I was saved, God gave me His heart. His heart is filled with unconditional love. For years, I truly loved everyone unconditionally. Somehow, as I walked the trail of discipleship, I had become sidetracked. Satan found an opening in my armor and got his hook into me. I began being judgmental of others. My God reached out His hand and corrected me. I repented and am again moving forward on the trail of discipleship. Today, I just accept people as they are. I love everyone unconditionally.

Study

A disciple is a student of the master, who in this case is Jesus Christ. Jesus told the disciples over and over to "follow me." He taught by example. There is a saying: "Cowboys herd and push cattle; shepherds lead sheep." We are the sheep, and Jesus is our Shepherd. Early in my walk with the Lord, I was listening to one of Dr. Charles Stanley's sermons. He cautioned new Christians to read only the Bible. He said that as new Christians, we should not read any other books. His concern was that we might pick up a book that looks good on the outside but misleads us on the inside. There are many cult books on the bookshelves. These books will take some of God's word and then add other non-Christian doctrine and call the end product a "Christian" book. That turned out to be good advice for me. For the next three years, I would not pick up another book. I read only the Bible, and I read it over and over.

Three years later, some good friends gave me *My Utmost for His Highest* by Oswald Chambers. At first I argued with them and told them what Dr. Stanley had said. I would not take the book, but they assured me this daily devotional book was OK to read. Today, I can tell you that this one book, in addition to the Bible, has helped me more in my walk with the Lord than any of the hundreds of other Christian books I have read. Oswald was definitely a disciple of Jesus Christ.

Dr. Stanley also explained that there is a great deal of wisdom in Proverbs. He recommended reading a chapter of Proverbs every day. If we do that, by the end of the year we will have read Proverbs twelve times. Then we should start over the next year. That was excellent advice for me. The wisdom in Proverbs helped me more in my job as a manager and supervisor than all the supervisory training classes I attended over the years.

Thanks to Dr. Stanley, I developed a work routine. I arrived at work at least an hour early, made a pot of coffee, prayed, read a chapter or two of Proverbs, read *My Utmost for His Highest*, read a section of the Bible, prayed again, and then started the workday. I kept this routine until I retired twelve years later. In the evenings at home, I would study different passages in the Bible. I found that by beginning and ending the day with the Lord, He would be my priority and my focus throughout the day.

Mrs. Accuser

Many years ago, Dr. Stanley mentioned arguments and criticism in one of his sermons. He said that when people criticize you and you know they are wrong, just let the criticism go over your head. Don't argue with them. Then say, "Thank you. I didn't realize I had done that." He said that once we apologize, the criticism or the argument is over. The other person has nowhere else to go. He said that it really doesn't matter who was right or wrong. We just don't want to damage a friendship over a trivial nothing.

The very next day at work, one of our foremen called me about a problem. There was a glitch in the electrical system, and some equipment was affected. Our foreman gave me all the details, and even though our employees did not cause the problem, he said, "You'll be getting a call from Mrs. Accuser." (Not her real name.)

Sure enough, the call came, and Mrs. Accuser ranted and raved over the telephone about the problem. She blamed everything on my men, saying, "I want you to come over to my office right now."

I went to her office and, in front of several of her employees, she chewed me out. I remembered that Dr. Stanley said, "It doesn't matter who was right or wrong. Just say 'I'm sorry,' and the argument goes away." I bit my tongue so hard I could taste the blood. When she stopped talking for a moment to catch her breath, I told her how sorry I was for the problem. I did not take blame for the problem, because that would have been a lie. I just gave her a generic apology and left. For the rest of the day, that chewing out she gave me really stuck in my craw.

The first thing the next morning, my telephone rang. It was Mrs. Accuser. She said, "Mr. Kelly, I need to apologize to you. I made a terrible mistake yesterday, and I hope you'll forgive me." She continued, "I knew the problem was not caused by your employees. But you stood there and just took all the comments I threw at you. You even apologized when it was not your fault. I don't know how you could take it like that and just walk away." I told her it was because I was a Christian. Jesus took a beating for me, so I took a beating for Jesus. She said, "Mr. Kelly, if you will come back over here, I'll apologize to you in front of my employees." I told her that would not be necessary, that we could put this behind us.

As Dr. Stanley said, "Just apologize. It doesn't really matter who's right or wrong. With an apology, the argument or criticism will go away."

Worry

Do you worry? If you do, you sin, and so do I. Jesus said, "So do not worry, saying, 'What shall we eat?' Or 'What shall we drink?' Or 'What shall we wear?' For the pagans run after all these things, and your heavenly Father knows that you need them. But seek first his kingdom and his righteousness, and all these things will be given to you as well. Therefore do not worry about tomorrow, for tomorrow will worry about itself. Each day has enough trouble of its own" (Matthew 6:31–34).

Mom was worried. The economy was sour, and she was worried about having enough money to live on until she died. She actually had no need to worry, because she lived with us, and we planned to take care of her until she went home to be with our Lord. But she worried anyway. I asked her, "Mom, what's the worst thing that could happen to you?"

She thought about it and then said, "I don't know."

I said, "How about if you lost what little money you have, I was not here to take care of you, and you just sat on the side of the road and starved to death?"

She said, "That would be about as bad as it gets."

Then I said, "Mom, when you die, what happens next?"

She smiled and said, "I'll go be with Jesus in Heaven."

I said, "You're right. You will go to Heaven and be with Jesus, with Dad, and with your parents. I know you're looking forward to that."

She smiled and said, "You're right. I do look forward to being with Jesus and my family." The worry left her.

Since worry is a sin, where do you think it comes from? It's certainly not of God; it's of Satan. Satan's playground is inside our heads.

Learn to Listen

For fifteen years, I worked with the Southern Baptist volunteers doing disaster-relief work. Our Baptist Association has a "mass-feeding unit," and we help people after disasters, such as hurricanes, major floods, tornados, ice storms, major power outages, and so on. Our unit would prepare several thousand hot meals each day for the disaster victims.

Training is a big part of this work. We not only learned how to safely prepare hot meals; we also learned how to talk with the disaster victims. I hope I never forget this one particular training class. I've used this training not only at disasters, but when I visit friends who are hurting.

A psychologist was the instructor for this class. He spoke for about three hours on helping disaster victims. At the end of his class, he told us, "I don't care if you forget everything I've told you over the last three hours. I want you to remember this one thing as you leave here today." He said we will be asked, "Why did God allow this tragedy to happen?" He said we should then turn the question around and ask, "Why do you think God allowed this to happen?" He continued, "You should then take two fingers, reach into your mouth, grab hold of your tongue, pull it out, and sit on your tongue." He told us that none of us in our great wisdom can satisfactorily answer that question for the hurting victims. He said we should just shut up, listen, and let them talk out their hurts.

Our instructor said, "They won't remember what you said anyhow, but they will never forget that you came, you cared, and you sat beside them and you listened."

Tithing

Tithing seems to be a touchy subject today. What does tithing have to do with discipleship? If we agree that everything we have belongs to God, why would we not want to let Him keep 10 percent and allow Him to give us 90 percent? My friend, Doug, clearly heard God tell him (out loud), "I gave it all to you, and I can take it all away."

Even though our money has been tight at times, we always tithe. It's like breathing: we don't think about breathing, we just do it.

When I was born again and began attending church, our church was going through a spiritual battle and a church split. Some members of the church were mad and stopped giving their tithes and offerings. The church was struggling financially and in other ways. I prayed about the financial problems and asked God, "What can we do to help?" Let me tell you right now, be careful what you pray for.

I clearly heard God say, "Why don't you double tithe to make up part of what the others stopped giving?"

I told Connie what God told me about giving 20 percent of our gross pay to the church, and she simply said, "OK. If God told you to do it, we'll do it."

We started double tithing and were also giving money to other ministries as the Lord directed. We were giving roughly 25 percent of our combined gross pay back to the Lord. After all the deductions came out of our paychecks, we barely had enough to live on. But during those years, the car never broke down, we were able to pay all our bills, and we never missed a meal.

Then it was time to buy a new car. I wanted a Jeep Cherokee with four-wheel drive. I also wanted twenty-two specific options on the car. I met with the dealer and looked over the numbers, and there was no way we could afford to buy that new car. Connie suggested maybe we should reduce our tithing to 10 percent so we could afford to buy the car. I told her, "No, God will tell us when to stop double tithing." Connie agreed that we could do without a new car.

We were driving to Columbia to a Gideon meeting a few weeks later, and Connie suggested stopping at a gas station to pick up a used-car magazine. I told her it would do no good, because I had been burned before buying used cars and trucks. Connie was driving, so she pulled into a gas station anyway. I went in and picked up one of the used-car magazines. I flipped through a few pages, and there was the exact car I was looking for: a Jeep Cherokee with four-wheel drive. It was two years old and had very low mileage. I looked at the options listed, and most of what I wanted was listed in the advertisement. The car was a one-owner, and the price was reasonable.

When I called the owner, he ran down the list of all the options on the car. It had all twenty-two that I wanted. The owner said it looked and ran like brand new, but there was a problem. Someone else had looked at his car and wanted to buy it. The owner had told the potential buyer he had until noon Friday to come up with the money. "But I'll sell it to you right now if you have the money."

I told him, "No. I'm a Christian. If you gave the other man your word that he had until noon Friday, then you stick to your word. After that, if he hasn't bought the car, call me." The seller called Friday afternoon, and we bought the used car. It was two years old, but it looked and drove just like the new one.

The Lord expects all of us to be wise in how we use the money He gives to each of us. Connie and I have always lived a very simple lifestyle. We always spend less than we make. Mom used to tell me, "If you don't have the cash to buy it, you don't need it." For over twenty-five years, we were caregivers for our parents. Mom was the last to leave us. She lived her last twenty years in our home. I believe that because we chose to "Honor your father and your mother" (Exodus 20:12), and because we have always honored God with our time, tithes, and offerings, God has greatly blessed us in return. "Honor the Lord with your wealth, with the first fruits of all your crops; then your barns will be filled to overflowing, and your vats will brim over with new wine" (Proverbs 3:9–10).

Connie and I love to fish the fresh waters of the Black River near Kingstree. We discussed the possibility of buying a fishing cabin that we could use on weekends. A short time later, a hunting buddy who owned such a place on the Black River called and told us he was selling his "river house" (cabin). Since we had saved our money, we were able to buy it. It's off the beaten path, and we drive down two miles of dirt roads just to get to the place. Now we sit on the porch and watch the river gently flow by. We fish when we feel like fishing. We mostly enjoy watching the beaver, otter, deer, turkey, songbirds, and other wildlife the Lord sends our way. It's so beautiful that we often pinch ourselves to make sure we're not dreaming. I will tell you this: you can't out give God. Jesus tells us, "Give and it will be given to you. A good measure, pressed down, shaken together and running over, will be poured into your lap. For with the measure you use, it will be measured to you" (Luke 6:38).

"Our Dock on the Black River"

Sometimes when we're in a small group or a Bible study, the subject of tithing comes up. The comment I hear most often is,

"Tithing is an Old Testament thing, and we no longer live under the law. We live under grace and no longer have to tithe." When Jesus was talking with the teachers of the law and Pharisees, He said, "Woe to you, teachers of the law and Pharisees, you hypocrites! You give a tenth of your spices—mint, dill and cumin. But you have neglected the more important matters of the law—justice, mercy and faithfulness. You should have practiced the latter, without neglecting the former. You blind guides! You strain out a gnat but swallow a camel" (Matthew 23:23–24).

These teachers of the law and Pharisees had a religion, but they did not have a relationship.

Jesus was telling them to practice the latter (justice, mercy and faithfulness) "without neglecting" the former (tithing a tenth of their spices—mint, dill, and cumin). If you want to hang on to your money, don't read Acts 4:32–37. That's where the New Testament Christians shared everything, because they were of one heart and mind. Tithing is not something we have to do; it's something we get to do because we have Jesus in our hearts. Jesus said, "These people honor me with their lips, but their hearts are far from me" (Mark 7:6).

The choice is ours. "Whoever sows sparingly will also reap sparingly, and whoever sows generously will also reap generously" (2 Corinthians 9:6).

Where Did the Money Come From?

Sandi is a good Christian friend. We are "like-minded." When she was a single parent raising her daughter, she, like many of us, had financial problems. She was $15,000 in debt.

Sandi wanted to tithe but just didn't have the money. One day, Sandi was in the kitchen, singing and praising God. Then she heard the Lord's voice. He said, "I want you to start tithing." Sandi responded, "Lord, how can I tithe when I can't even pay my bills?" The Lord answered, "When it hits your hand, ten percent is mine." Sandi said, "OK, Lord, I will, but you'll have to show me your word is true."

God's word says, "'Bring the whole tithe into the storehouse, that there may be food in my house. Test me in this,' says the Lord Almighty, 'and see if I will not throw open the floodgates of heaven and pour out so much blessing that there will not be room enough to store it'" (Malachi 3:10).

A short time later, Sandi needed some cash, so she went to the bank to cash a check. She asked the teller, "Is there enough money in the account to cover this check?"

The teller looked at the account and then asked Sandi, "How much money do you think you have in this account?" Sandi said she didn't know, but it couldn't be very much. The teller showed Sandi the balance. There was over $17,000 there.

Sandi asked, "Where did it come from? I don't have any money." The bankers could not explain where the money came from. Even the vice president of the bank could not find where the money came from. There were no records of a deposit or how the money got there.

Sandi paid off the credit card debt and has continued tithing ever since. She told me, "It's just something you do. You don't even think about it; you just tithe."

God knew Sandi's heart. Did God put that $17,000 in the account? I'd say yes! "With God all things are possible" (Matthew 19:26).

Offerings

Our tithe is 10 percent of our gross pay. Our offerings are what we give over and above the tithe. Offerings are what we give to various Christian ministries.

In 1988, God told me to join the Gideon Ministry. Through this ministry, I would "reach the world for Christ." My wife and I have been part of the Gideon organization for twenty-five years. We support this ministry financially as well as with our time.

Three years ago, I learned of a good ministry in Asia that was reaching the lost for Christ. I sent them a check. The next month, I sent another. Then, the next month, as I was about to send a third check, I heard the Lord's voice. He said, "I told you to reach the world for Christ through the Gideon ministry." I had blown it. I had looked into the Asian ministry myself and found it was a very good ministry. I did not pray about it. If I had, God would not have needed to correct me on my giving. For me, I'm to support the Gideons to reach the world for Christ. Pray and ask God where He would have you give your time and money. It may be a national organization, or it may be a local soup kitchen feeding the homeless and introducing them to Christ.

The Choice

Someone once said, "If you don't know where your priorities are, others will tell you." It's simply a matter of priorities. Choose to be a disciple. Don't turn back.

CHAPTER 6

PRAYER

Some of my Christian friends say they have never heard God's voice. I believe one reason is because we are sometimes so caught up in the world and in all the clutter of the world (job, family, church, hobbies, TV, entertainment...), that we simply don't hear God when he speaks to us.

Before God spoke to Elijah, there first came a great and powerful wind, then an earthquake, and then a fire. After this, Elijah heard God's voice in a "gentle whisper" (cf. 1 Kings 19:11–13). In order to hear God's whisper, we need to be close to Him.

For the first forty-four years of my life, I never heard God's voice. Of course, I never listened for it either. The night before I became a Christian, I talked with God. I confessed my sins and told God how sorry I was. Each time I told God how sorry I was, He would speak out loud and say, "I know." In those two words, He was telling me that He understood, He believed me, and I was going to be OK. How do I know this? God gives us the ability to know His voice and to *understand* what He's saying to us.

Jesus said, "My sheep listen to my voice; I know them, and they follow me" (John 10:27). Jesus also said, "But they will never follow a stranger; in fact, they will run away from him because they do not recognize a stranger's voice" (John 10:5). Once we become Christians, we continue hearing God's voice. God has spoken to me out loud on two different occasions while I was sitting in the sanctuary at our church. Even though I clearly heard God's audible voice, the people sitting next to me did not hear God speak. You may think, *How can that be? How can one man hear God's voice out loud and the people sitting beside him do not?* The answer is, "With man this is impossible, but not with God; all things are possible with God" (Mark 10:27). I absolutely believe God can do anything. We think in terms of what we can see, touch, taste, hear, and so on, and of what we have personally experienced. We often assume that if we have not personally experienced something, it can't be true. I call that belief *pride*. Who do we think we are, if we say that we must personally experience something of God before it can be real?

> *My good friend, Dave, who is a deacon and an elder in our church, heard God speak out loud. Dave started drinking when he was eighteen years old. As part of his recovery process, and to help save his marriage, Dave began a thirteen-week out-patient drug/alcohol treatment program. As a requirement for successful completion of that program, each participant was required to write an autobiographical history of their life, in an attempt to learn what had led to the addictive cycle. His first attempt was rejected by his group therapist. The very next morning, as Dave was picking out clothes for the day, and struggling with how to rewrite the bio, he heard the words, "You don't have to do that anymore." As Dave explains it, he felt physical weight being lifted from his shoulders, and a sense of absolute and total peace. Dave went on to say that he immediately fell to his knees in total and complete submission to what he could only interpret was God's intervention into his life just at that crucial time. He stated that he wept uncontrollably*

throughout the day, and never attempted a rewrite of his bio. After listening to his testimony, his therapist waived the bio rewrite.

I have heard God speak silently many times in healing-prayer sessions. We are sometimes going in a wrong direction as we pray for healing. God will silently speak and redirect us and our prayers. Many times at night, lying in bed, I hear God's voice. It's usually after all the clutter of the day leaves my head. I can then be still and focus entirely on listening to God. Once we've heard God's voice, we know it. When I was growing up, I could turn the radio on and flip through the channels until I heard the voice of Casey Kasem and his *American Top 40* radio program. I immediately recognized Casey's voice. We also immediately recognize God's voice.

I was once struggling in a spiritual battle with a man at church who was telling lies and hurting others. I was lying in bed, praying and asking God for guidance. I clearly heard God say, "I'll give you revelation. Pray for understanding." At the time, I didn't understand what God was telling me. A short time later, I did understand. The spiritual battle came to a head, and an early-morning meeting was scheduled. As I walked down the hallway to the meeting, I silently prayed. I asked God to "Help me call this man a liar to his face, but to do it in a Christian manner." As I prayed those words, God clearly spoke to me. He said, "I want you to be a doormat." I responded, "God, a doormat! You mean for me to let this man scrape his feet on me? I haven't done anything wrong! I need to take a stand and fight!" But God said no more.

When God speaks, He often uses words or terms that are not normally in our daily vocabulary. I know what a doormat is, but it has probably been ten years or longer since I used that word. I simply don't talk about doormats.

In the meeting, the man tried to attack me with words but could not. God put a spirit of confusion on him, and he couldn't even think logically. I just sat silently, as a doormat, and watched God clean his cage. The Lord fought and won this spiritual battle.

In meetings at work, I often silently prayed and asked God if I should speak up or remain silent. God answered in one of two ways. If I was not to speak, God would simply say two words: "Shut up." God never wastes words when He speaks. If I did not hear the "shut up," then I knew it was OK to speak what was on my mind. God also knows our thoughts. "Before a word is on my tongue you, Lord, know it completely" (Psalm 139:4).

God also uses others to speak to us. As described in the chapter "Go See Delores," God used Delores to share Scriptures of freedom in Christ with me. Four years later, God used me to deliver His confirming message of her husband's healing to Delores.

I often hear God's voice when reading the Bible. I may have been praying about something and then, out of the clear blue, the answer is staring me in the face. Often when I hear God's voice, He gives me a Bible verse that is an answer to my prayer.

After hurricane Hugo, we learned of a missionary who needed an electric generator. As Connie and I prayed for this missionary and his need and asked God, "What would you have us do to help?" I clearly heard God speak. He said, "You have no power, and you have a generator. Buy one for the missionary." I said, "Yes, Lord." We wrote a check, and the missionary had the generator he needed. Be careful what you pray for. A friend once told me, "If you can't handle the answer, don't ask the question."

The majority of times I have heard God speak audibly were during my first years as a Christian. As time passed, God's voice went from an audible voice to a silent one, but His voice was always as clear as a bell. His voice was so clear, I expect some of those times, God may have actually spoken out loud and I didn't know the difference. When God speaks, He does not mumble. In the twenty-five years that I've been a Christian, I've never asked God to repeat what He just said. Each time He speaks, He uses only a few words. Each time He speaks, I understand exactly what He is telling me.

Mr. Herman: How to Pray

Four months after being born again, I joined the Gideons. I was invited to a 6:30 a.m. prayer breakfast. Every Sunday morning, some of the Gideons would meet to pray for our churches, our pastors, and other needs. Then we'd eat a short stack of pancakes before going to church. I thought, *Sure, praying for the churches and the pastors in our area is important. I'll do that.* I assumed one of the older men would pray, we would eat our pancakes, and then we would go to church.

The first Sunday at the prayer breakfast, all the Gideons were glad to see me. We chatted a few minutes, and then one man said, "Let's pray." He prayed what I call one of those beautiful "stand-up" prayers that some older men pray in church. It was a "King James Version" prayer. It went something like, "Oh, mighty God, thou art our Creator. Here ye therefore..., we tarry not..., howbeit we seek the...," and so forth. While he was praying this beautiful prayer, I prayed silently, "Thank you, Lord that I don't have to pray one of those prayers." I didn't know how to pray like that. "I only know how to talk with you, God."

I thought the one stand-up prayer would do just fine, and then we'd eat. Wrong! After that man finished his prayer, the man sitting next to him prayed. He also prayed one of those "old-man, stand-up prayers." Then it hit me. They were going around the table, and each man would pray. Soon, real soon, it would be my turn. I listened to how they prayed and what they prayed. When it was my turn, I tried to pray one of those "King James Version" prayers, and it was a complete disaster. I'm not sure who was embarrassed most: me or the other men.

The next week, I went by a Christian bookstore and bought a small book on prayer that had examples. I tried to put together a prayer for the next Sunday prayer breakfast. I even tried to memorize the prayer. I guess I still have some dyslexia hanging around, because I couldn't memorize the prayer. It just wasn't me.

Sunday came, the prayers started, and then it was my time. I tried to pray the prayer I had tried to memorize and, again, it was a disaster. I was embarrassed, and I knew the other men were embarrassed for me.

As we were leaving the restaurant, Mr. Herman put his arm around me and said, "Ellison, I see you're struggling a little with prayer. Let me tell you how to pray. Don't pay any attention to how or what we pray. Don't try to be us. It's not about us. It's about you, and only you, talking with our God. When you pray, just pray what's on your heart, and it will come out right every time. Don't worry about what anybody else thinks. Just tell God what's on your heart. Your prayer is between you and God."

"Just pray what's on your heart, and it will come out right every time."

I took the book on prayers and put it on the bookshelf. It's still collecting dust today. From that point on, when I pray, I just talk with my God and say whatever is on my heart. As Mr. Herman said, it comes out right every time. When we are real with God, He will be real with us.

Fasting and Prayer

Yep, fasting is Biblical. Throughout the Bible, God's people fasted and prayed. I have a good Christian friend who fasts one or two days each week. He's been doing this for years.

I've had seasons of fasting and praying over the years. In my early years with the Lord, I tried fasting one day each week for a full year. I thought that if I fasted, God would reward me in return, which is incorrect. To me, fasting meant a little water is OK, but no food. So I assumed that each time my empty stomach growled at me, I was supposed to pray. But I don't think that's what fasting and praying is all about.

A few years back, I stepped into another spiritual battle. It really hurt me when I saw what a husband and wife were doing in one of the churches that we often visited. They were Christians, but Satan certainly had a hook in them. I won't go into any of the details, but I will talk about where the Lord took me.

As we were leaving church one Sunday, I confronted them in the parking lot about all the damage they were doing to the church. The wife struck back and said, "You're not a Christian! You have the spirit of the Antichrist in you!" That really threw me for a loop. Satan immediately took her statement and started messing with my head.

It was then that the Lord took me on a fast. He took the desire for food away from me. For the first few days, I did not realize what the Lord was doing. He did not tell me He wanted me to fast. I simply had no desire to eat anything. After several days with no food, Connie said she wanted to go to a restaurant for breakfast. Breakfast is usually my favorite meal. But I was not hungry. Connie said, "You have to eat something." So I ordered a waffle and a glass of water. I tried eating the waffle, but it was like eating a piece of cardboard. I couldn't eat the waffle or anything else. I simply had no desire for food.

I did not realize it at the time, but during the fast, I again drew close to the Lord. One night as I lay in bed, I questioned God about my faith and what this woman had said to me. This is the only time in twenty-five years that I have ever questioned my faith. I said, "Lord, your word says that we should test the spirit". I said, "Forgive me, Lord, but I need to know for sure. I need to know if I have been listening to your voice all these years or to the voice of the masquerading Antichrist. You allowed Gideon to question you with the fleece. I need to know for sure. Have I been listening to your voice, or the voice of the lying Antichrist?"

I then asked two questions. I asked, "Who is Lord?" I clearly heard God answer, "Jesus is Lord." (Satan will not acknowledge that Jesus is Lord. Satan hates the name Jesus.) I was then going to ask if He had risen from the dead. I asked, "Has He risen?" and before I could say "from the dead," God interrupted and said, "He is risen indeed." A huge peace came over me.

I then said, "Lord, I sure wish I was back on the mountain" (like in my mountaintop experience). The Lord answered, "You are." I laughed as I realized that I was, in fact, back on the mountain. I was again walking and talking with the Lord.

A few days later, Connie and I drove to Jacksonville to visit her aunt who was in a nursing home. Every time we had visited her in the past, she was alone in a semiprivate room (the other bed was empty). But on this visit, a woman was assigned to the other bed. As we entered the room, I felt a very strong presence of the Lord in it. I didn't understand what God was up to. Connie wanted to put her aunt in a wheelchair and take her outside for some fresh air. I helped Connie with her aunt and told her to go ahead; I would be out in a few minutes.

Then, for no reason, tears welled up in my eyes. I looked at the woman in the other bed and said to her, "Lady, God's telling me that you're supposed to pray for me."

She said, "Yes, I am. Sit on the edge of my bed." I could feel the overwhelming love of our Lord coming from this woman. She never said a word about my tears. She put her hands on my head and started praying—in tongues. Then she said, "Young man, you are slam-full of the Holy Spirit!"

Our God of love had just given me a second confirmation that I had been listening to His voice all these years and not the voice of the Antichrist. We talked and prayed about other concerns. I absolutely know our God put this lady in front of me, right when I needed her. A short time later, the fast was over.

What happened to the husband-and-wife team who were doing all the damage? The Lord Himself dealt with them, and they left that church.

Teach Us to Pray

During their three years with Jesus, the disciples asked Jesus to teach them only one thing—how to pray. In Luke 11, Jesus taught the disciples the Lord's Prayer. Jesus told the disciples to be bold when they prayed. Jesus said, "Ask and it will be given to you; seek and you will find; knock and the door will be opened to you. For everyone who asks receives; the one who seeks finds; and to the one who knocks, the door will be opened" (Matthew 7:7–8). Before Christ, only the High Priest could approach God on one day of the year. When Jesus died on the cross, the curtain in the temple separating the Holy Place from the Most Holy Place was torn open. You and I now have direct access to our God.

In Ephesians 6, we are told by God to put on our armor and stand firm against Satan and his enemy forces. One of the two offensive weapons we are to use in our battle with Satan is prayer. The other offensive weapon is the sword of the Spirit, which is the word of God.

When I am asked to pray aloud in a group, I usually first pray silently and ask the Holy Spirit what I should pray. Then I pray out loud what the Holy Spirit gives me. I pray all during the day and even in the middle of the night when I wake up. I just talk with God as though He were right beside me, because He is.

There are two times when I do most of my serious praying: before I go to bed at night and when I wake up during the night. If I go to bed with something bothering me and I need an answer, God will often wake me in the middle of the night. I sometimes say, "I'm here, Lord," and just lie there in bed, wait, and listen. In the quiet, with the clutter of the day gone, I soon hear His voice.

The other time I do my serious praying is when I'm by myself, sitting high in a tree in a deer stand. I usually take either a Bible or a Christian book with me and read while I'm sitting in the tree waiting on a deer. I talk with God about what I'm reading. If there are burdens on my heart, I talk with God about the burdens. Sometimes, I just sit silently and listen.

"Early morning in a deer stand looking over a bean field"

The Bible says, "Be still, and know that I am God" (Psalm 46:10). Sometimes, after all the clutter leaves my mind, I sit silently and just know what God is saying to me, without hearing Him say a single word.

Let me try to explain what I'm talking about: my wife and I have been married for twenty-five years. We have a growing relationship. I know her better as each day passes. I like being with her. We talk throughout the day. We're so close that sometimes she doesn't have to say anything; I just know what she's thinking. We're that close. I know my wife, and she, likewise, knows me.

I have known my God for twenty-five years. We have a growing relationship. I know Him better as each day passes. I like being with Him. We talk throughout the day. We're so close that sometimes He doesn't have to say anything; I just know what He's thinking. We're that close. I know my God, and He, likewise, knows me.

You may still be questioning how someone can just know what God is saying, without hearing Him speak. If you've been married twenty or thirty years, you probably understand. Your spouse will tell you,

"You read my mind." If you're that close to God, you also understand. He too wants to have that close personal relationship with each of us.

Sometimes, you just know. Sometimes you do not need to hear God speak. You just know what He's saying to you. I call this "having the mind of Christ." Jesus said, "I am in my Father, and you are in me, and I am in you" (John 14:20). We have the Spirit of Christ in us. We have the heart of Christ in us. We have the blood of Christ flowing through our veins. As we draw closer and closer to Christ, we also have the mind of Christ. "But we have the mind of Christ" (1 Corinthians 2:16).

I read a note in *Healing Line* magazine that explained how Mother Teresa of Calcutta responded in an interview. It's called "Prayer in Silence." The interview went as follows:

> Mother Teresa, when asked by an interviewer what she says to God when she prays, answered: "I don't say anything. I just listen." When the interviewer asked what she hears God say, Mother Teresa replied: "He doesn't say anything. He just listens. And if you can't understand that, I can't explain it to you." In Christian tradition this is called the "Prayer of Quiet"—a listening beyond words. In that silence we know and are known by God.[5]

I think Mother Teresa is saying the same thing. You just know. I really can't explain it either, but many of my Christian friends have also been there and understand.

Some of my prayers with God are not exactly what I would consider serious prayers. I became a Christian In June 1988. Deer season opened August 15, and for the first time in twenty years, I did not go deer hunting on opening day. As a matter of fact, I only went deer hunting one time during the entire 1988 deer season. I was too busy studying the Bible and telling people about Jesus.

In 1989, as deer season approached, I thought about trying deer hunting again. I thought I might run into a deer hunter who needed to know the Lord. I, like most deer hunters, have many deer-hunting stories. Here are two Christian deer-hunting stories.

A Prayer and Two Six-Pointers

When deer season opened in 1989, I went to one of my favorite hunting spots in the Francis Marion National Forest. As I sat in the tree that morning, I talked with my Lord. We talked about all of His creation. As we talked, four huge gobblers (male turkeys) flew down and landed right in front of me. I thought, *You turkeys better be thankful that I'm a Christian today and not the heathen I used to be.* It was a beautiful morning, but I saw no deer.

It was about time to climb down out of the tree and head for home. I thought about the empty freezer at the house. During the last year, we had eaten all the venison, fish, and shrimp in our freezer. I jokingly said to God, "Hey, Father, my freezer's empty. We need some meat. So why don't you just let a nice six-point buck walk out over there on that little hill. Oh, and while you're at it, why don't you just let two nice six-pointers walk out? I don't need a big, trophy deer. My ego is gone. I just need some meat in the freezer. Thanks, Father." Then I laughed.

I was only joking. When I first got saved, I was scared to death of God. Now, a year later, I had a growing relationship with my Heavenly Father. I would even occasionally joke around with Him.

I picked up my pack and my rifle. As I turned to climb down the ladder, I glanced over to the spot of high ground about a hundred yards away. There stood a nice buck. I couldn't believe it. He wasn't there fifteen seconds earlier when I prayed. Nothing had been there all morning. I sat down and looked through the scope on my rifle at a nice, six-point buck. I said, "Thank you, Lord," and squeezed the trigger. Bam!

I looked through my rifle scope, and there stood a six-point buck. I said to myself, "Man, I know I didn't miss that deer. My rifle is dead-on at a hundred yards." I couldn't believe that six-point buck was still standing there. As I looked through the rifle scope at that buck, I saw something on the ground. The deer I had just shot was on the ground beside the second buck. Then I remembered what I had jokingly said to God: "Why don't you just let two nice six-pointers walk out?" God had answered the prayer. He immediately sent two bucks, both nice six-pointers!

I told God I was just kidding. I really didn't need two bucks. One would do just fine. I told the Lord I'd be glad to shoot the second deer and give the meat to friends, but I really didn't need two deer right now. Then I said, "Lord, if there is another hunter in the woods today who needs this second buck more than I need it, please let the deer turn right now and walk back down into the swamp." The second buck turned and casually walked back down into the swamp and out of sight. Hopefully that second buck was going to be the answer to another hunter's prayer.

The Turn-the-Other-Cheek Buck

Several years ago, my cousin, Boyd, and his friend came to visit and hunt with me. We went to the hunt club, and I picked out three of the best deer stands for us to hunt that evening. We signed in the hunting log for the three stands. The procedure is, whoever arrives at the club first gets his pick of the deer stands, and we were the first to arrive.

Fifteen minutes later, Jim drove up. He looked at the log and saw the stands we had selected. He obviously wanted to hunt one of the stands we had reserved, and he really became upset. My goal at the hunting club is not to shoot deer. My goal is to be Christ to the other hunters and hopefully lead some of them to Christ. One new Christian brought into the Kingdom of God is far greater than a hundred trophy deer.

Jim started complaining and saying he wanted to hunt in one of our stands. I remembered what Jesus said: "Give to everyone who asks you, and if anyone takes what belongs to you, do not demand it back" (Luke 6:30). I told Jim to go ahead and take the stand he wanted, and we would hunt another area.

We signed in for three other stands that were not as good as our first choice. Shortly after we signed for these second-choice stands, Frank drove up with his guests. I asked Frank where he planned to hunt. Of course, he wanted the stands we had just reserved. Again, I told Frank to go ahead and use those three stands. I then picked three stands on the outer edge of the club. They were not exactly great deer stands. I did not expect to see any deer from the stand I was going to hunt; I just wanted to get the hunt over with.

After sitting in my third-choice stand for about two hours, a couple of does came by. Then a third came by and stopped, urinated, and casually walked off. When a doe comes into estrus (meaning she's ready to mate), the scent of her urine is what attracts bucks. I silently prayed, "Lord, I hope she's in estrus." Sure enough, she was. Buck deer started coming out of the woodwork. Eight different bucks came to the spot where she had been, all with their noses in the air, looking for the doe. At one point, there were two eight-pointers standing in front of me. They left, and a larger eight-pointer came out of a thicket and stood in front of me, looking for the doe. I was thinking about shooting this nice eight-pointer when a *huge* eight-pointer stepped out. I quickly prayed, "Thank you, Lord." Bam! I aimed over the head of the first eight-pointer and shot the "grown" eight-pointer.

This buck was a 220-pound eight-pointer, which is the largest deer I have ever shot in fifty years of deer hunting. Had I not obeyed God's command of, "Give to everyone who asks you" (Luke 6:30), I would not have had the opportunity to shoot this deer. I would have been sitting in the wrong stand. I truly believe God honored our obeying his command when we gave up our deer stands, not once, but twice. God sent the doe in estrus that attracted all the bucks, including the big one. No one else at the hunting club saw a buck that evening.

"The Turn-the-Other-Cheek Buck"

A Farmer's Prayer

A few years ago, I met Brian. He is a young Christian and an extremely hardworking young man. He owns and runs a great hunting club. He also farms thirty-two-hundred acres of cotton, corn, soybeans, and peanuts. Each year, Brian has to make it. He could easily lose everything in a season. At the beginning of the season, he takes out a bank loan to purchase seed, fertilizer, chemicals, equipment, and to pay labor and land-lease charges. After the harvest, his loan comes due.

The 2011 season was a good one for cotton. Brian, as well as neighboring farmers, had a bumper crop. This caused cotton prices to drop. It's simply a matter of supply and demand. Brian chose to "warehouse" about $900,000 worth of his cotton rather than sell it at a loss or just break even. He hoped cotton prices on the commodities market would rise after the flooded market cleared out.

About six months after storing his cotton, the bank called. They needed Brian to pay off the balance of his loan for the 2011 season, but he couldn't until he sold his cotton, and the market prices were still too low. The market continued to drop, day after day. The bank suggested Brian cut his losses and sell. Brian did what we all sometimes do: after everything else fails, we pray! Brian prayed for the market to rise—and rise a lot.

After a couple of days of prayer with no rise in the market prices, Brian put in a sell order at the price he needed. The market was far below it. He still prayed as he went to bed: "Lord, let it hit. Let it hit my price." He then put it in the Lord's hands.

Cotton is bought and sold on the world market twenty-four hours a day. During that night, something happened. The cotton market had a spike and hit Brian's sell order. After Brian's cotton sold, the bottom again fell out of the market. The next morning, when Brian checked the market, he couldn't believe what he saw. God had answered his prayer. The spike in the market was just high enough and long enough. All of his cotton sold.

Brian asked me how this miracle could happen. I told Brian it was because "God knows your heart." Brian has always had a humble heart before God and has honored God as best he could. Even though he is one of the youngest and largest farmers in the county, he remains humble and gives God the glory for his farming success. When we live our lives to honor God, we will be blessed in return. Brian will tell anyone who asks that "God did this for me. There is no other explanation." Would Brian still have trusted God if the market had not spiked and his cotton later sold at a loss? Absolutely yes!

Pray to the End

Shortly before my dad died, I received a telephone call from him. He made small talk for a few minutes and then he said, "Son, you really need to start going to church." At that time, I had not been to church in twenty-two years. I was a member of the church back home but not a Christian. Dad was a member of the church and a deacon there, but he was not a Christian either. At some point, Dad had also quit attending.

Mom later told me that as Dad lay in his hospital bed, a young pastor from our home church visited him each week. It was during these visits that Dad surrendered his life to Christ and was truly born again. He was sixty-four years old. He then recognized that I was not a Christian and, as best as he could, he tried to head me to church, hoping I too would find Christ.

I'm sure my dad prayed for me every day until he died. He died knowing that his son was a member of a church but not a Christian. Eight years after his death, his prayers were answered. I became a Christian. The point is, keep praying for your loved ones and friends. The Bible says, "Then Jesus told his disciples a parable to show them that they should always pray and not give up" (Luke 18:1).

CHAPTER 7

Why My $5,000?

I began deer hunting when I was a teenager. It was a trial-and-error experience, because my only training had come from *Field & Stream* magazine.

One sunny afternoon I drove to the Broad River Game Management Area to scout an area for hunting later in the fall. I drove my car to the end of the dirt road, where there was a flat, swampy river bottom between the river and the dirt road. I had learned from the Boy Scouts to check the location of the sun before I entered the woods. I checked, and the sun was over my left shoulder. Since it was in the afternoon and the sun sets in the west, I knew the sun would be over my right shoulder when I walked out of the swamp.

The only things I took in the woods with me were a pocket knife and an old, cheap compass that I had never used. I really didn't think I'd need either of them. I knew from the map that the dirt road ran east-west and the river was due north of where I parked. I entered the swamp and found many deer trails and possible spots to hunt.

It was a beautiful afternoon, and I let the time slip away. The weather had also changed, and the sky became heavily overcast. I could not find the sun, but I wasn't worried. I knew I could find my way out of the woods, even without using the sun to guide me. As I walked in the direction of where I thought the car was parked, I realized it would be dark soon. I didn't want to spend the night in the swamp. I thought I might just check my compass to confirm that I was walking in the correct direction. I knew I needed to walk due south to get back to the car.

When I checked the compass, it showed that I was walking north, not south. I looked around the swamp and thought, *This cheap compass must be wrong*, because I knew I was walking south. I put the compass in my pocket and continued walking. Through the woods, I could see an opening about fifty yards ahead of me, and I knew that opening was going to be the dirt road and my car. I felt relieved that I had made it. I would not be spending the night lost in the woods tonight.

As I approached the opening, my heart sank. It was not the dirt road—it was the river. I had been doing it my way rather than trusting the compass to guide me out of the woods. It was almost dark, and I was about to panic. I checked the compass again. Sure enough, it had shown me the correct direction, but I hadn't believed it. My way was the wrong way.

I kept the compass out and followed its south direction through the swamp. I tore through the briars and brush as fast as I could. It would be dark in a few minutes, and I had no flashlight. The compass would be useless in the dark. Just as dark was setting in, I could see an opening in the woods ahead of me. The opening was the dirt road and my car. When I stepped out onto the dirt road, it was dark, but I made it!

This was definitely a defining moment in my life. I learned that I must trust my compass in the woods. From that point on, I always carry a good-quality compass and flashlight when I am scouting or hunting. So what does a compass have to do with the chapter "Why

My $5,000?" It has nothing to do with the $5,000 but everything to do with trust.

I remembered my parents taking me to Wednesday night prayer meetings when I was a child, so now, thirty years later; I thought I'd give it a try. I went to church Wednesday evening to what I thought was going to be a time of prayer. As it turns out, the church had called a business meeting for that evening. Wow! I had never seen so much arguing and shouting in a church before. I did not know it at the time, but our church was in the middle of a huge, spiritual battle that was causing a split in the congregation.

That evening, the pastor talked about the financial situation in the church. It had just built a new Christian Life Center (CLC) building. Now some of the main donors were leaving the church because of the fighting, and others just simply quit tithing.

The pastor looked out over the congregation, and there was a full house that night. He said, "If a hundred of you would each write a check for five hundred dollars, we could put a huge dent in the debt we owe on the CLC." As I sat on the back pew, I looked around and thought, *Preacher, there aren't a hundred people here with that kind of money*. (I learned later that there were actually many wealthy people in the church.) I thought about the $5,000 I had in my "emergency" savings account.

Five years earlier, I had gone through a divorce and was broke. I became a single parent working two jobs. I managed to get out of debt and began saving an emergency fund just in case I lost my job or encountered a large expense. My goal was $5,000, and I had recently reached that goal. I now had my $5,000 emergency fund in a money-market savings account.

As the preacher spoke, I thought about my emergency savings. I could do my part and give $500. Then I thought, *Sure, preacher, I'll chip in five hundred dollars*. As soon as that thought ran through my mind, I heard God speak to me out loud. He said, "From you, Ellison, I'll have five thousand dollars." I had heard God speak out loud before, but never with other people around.

I immediately looked to my left at the two elderly ladies sitting there. I thought they would be staring at me, but they were not. I looked to my right at the men sitting next to me, and they were not staring at me either. For the first time, I realized that God could speak out loud to one person and others nearby would not hear His voice.

I thought, *But, God, that's all I have.* God repeated, "From you, Ellison, I'll have five thousand dollars." I thought, *OK, God, it's all yours anyhow. Easy come, easy go.* Then I thought, *No. It's not yours. That's my money. I had to work two jobs for five years to save that money. God, why do you want my money? You're God, and you can do anything. Why don't you just print your own money? Why do you want my life savings?* God did not answer. When God speaks to me, He never explains why; He just expects obedience.

James tells us, "Consider it pure joy, my brothers and sisters, whenever you face trials of many kinds, because you know that the testing of your faith produces perseverance" (James 1:2–3). There was no "pure joy" in me. I was really upset. I'm just grateful that our God had more patience with me than I had with Him.

The next day I went to the bank, closed out my emergency savings account, and put the $5,000 in my checking account. The following Sunday, June 26, I dropped my $5,000 check into the offering plate.

I kept the canceled check to remind me of the experience.

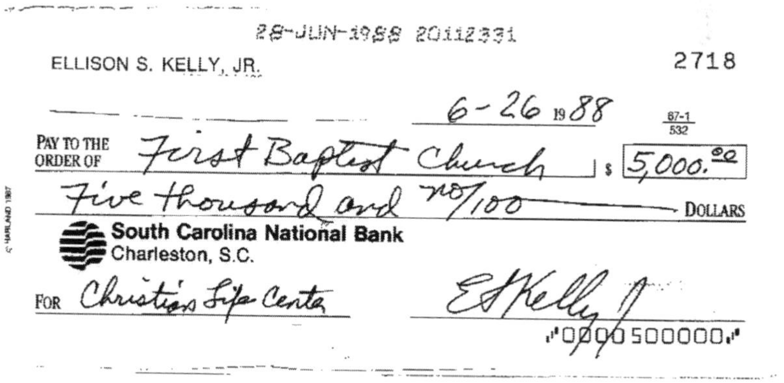

28-JUN-1988 20112331

ELLISON S. KELLY, JR. 2718

6-26 1988 87-1/532

PAY TO THE ORDER OF First Baptist Church $ 5,000.00

Five thousand and no/100 DOLLARS

South Carolina National Bank
Charleston, S.C.

FOR Christian Life Center E S Kelly Jr

0000500000

"The $5,000 check, which was my life's savings."

I was absolutely not a happy camper. If you've ever been a single parent and living hand-to mouth, you know what I'm talking about. I had an old car with a diesel engine that was nothing but trouble. I had already replaced two fuel-injection pumps and knew the next pump could go out at any time. I told God, "OK, God, when the next fuel injection pump on my car goes out, I want to see you leaning over the engine, replacing it. You took all my money, and I can't pay for it, so, now it's up to you. I still have to drive to work, and I still have to feed my family. Why did you take all my money?"

My daughter, Susan, was entering the ninth grade. She tried out for the soccer team and made it. It was also time for the parents to meet the new teachers and pay school fees. I came home after the meeting at school and sat down at my desk. I started going through the stack of papers and bills and started writing checks. I had to pay a ten-dollar lab fee, a fifteen-dollar book fee, and then another fee and another fee. I came to an accidental insurance policy bill, which was optional. The policy paid for medical bills if your child was injured doing school activities. As I remember, the insurance cost twenty dollars for the year.

I looked at the twenty-dollar bill and thought, "*No, I don't need it. I have a good insurance policy at work that covers my family.*" I threw that bill in the trash can, and then I heard God speak out loud. He said, "Take it out of the trash." I reached in the trash can and took the bill out and looked at it again. I said, "God, I don't need this insurance. I have good insurance at work. Besides, I don't have an extra twenty dollars lying around to pay for this. You took all my money." I threw the bill back into the trash can. God spoke again. "Take it out of the trash." I leaned over and took it out of the trash again and looked at the bill, thinking, *What's going on here?* I threw it in the trash again and again, and each time, God told me to take it out. This went on five or six times. All God would say was, "Take it out of the trash." I finally quit arguing with God and wrote a twenty-dollar check for the school accidental-injury policy.

A few months later, I got a call at work. Susan had been injured at soccer practice. She and another girl had kicked the ball at the same time, and her knee gave way. Susan had surgery on her knee. The doctor, Randy, was a friend, and he did the surgery and follow-up work for what my work insurance policy paid. I didn't have to pay anything out of pocket.

One day, I was sorting through copies of all the doctor and surgery bills. I thought about that twenty-dollar school accidental injury policy. I called the school and asked if that policy would pay anything on my daughter's injury. The lady said, "Yes. That's what the policy is for." I asked if she had a form to fill out, and she said, "No, just mail copies of your bills to the insurance company." So I gathered up copies of a few of the bills, totaling around $2,000, and wrote a short note to the insurance company explaining what had happened. I expected that I would never hear anything from the insurance company. What can you really expect from a twenty-dollar policy?

A few weeks later, I received a letter from the insurance company. In the envelope were a nice letter and a $2,000 check. They said to send any other bills regarding Susan's injury and that they would process them. I thought about it. My work insurance had already paid for all the bills regarding the injury, so I wondered if it was legal to collect from two insurance companies on the same injury. I was a Christian now, and I did not want to cheat anyone.

The next day, I called the insurance company and explained that my work insurance had already paid for the surgery. I asked if it was legal to collect from two insurance companies, and the lady said, "Sure. We don't care how many policies you have. You paid for a policy with us, and we're going to cover all the legitimate bills you send us."

I called the personnel department at work and asked them the same question. The lady said she didn't know. No one had ever asked that question before. She called my work insurance company and they told her the same thing I had been told by the school insurance company.

I gathered up copies of all the remaining bills for the injury and mailed them to the school's insurance company. A short time later, I received another check in the mail. Insurance companies don't work that way today, but twenty-five years ago, things were different.

You've probably guessed it by now: the total amount paid by the school policy was just over $5,000. God returned my money, with interest. I put the $5,000 back in the money-market savings account.

This was another defining moment in my life. I learned two things from those two God experiences. One, I need to totally trust God and depend on God to take care of my family. When I was lost in the swamp, I learned to trust my compass. I've learned to trust God as I walk through life. Money comes and goes, but God does not. He loves His children as much—even more—than I love my daughter. God says, "I will never leave you nor forsake you" (Joshua 1:5). Second, I learned about obedience. I could have refused to obey God and left that twenty-dollar insurance policy application in the trash. That mistake would have cost me $5,000.

There's a song we sing at church called "When We Walk with the Lord." The refrain goes, "Trust and obey, For there's no other way, To be happy in Jesus, But to trust and obey."

CHAPTER 8

THE GIDEONS

I was born again in June 1988. I was having a mountaintop experience, but I did not know it at the time. I had never heard of a mountaintop experience. All I knew was that I walked with God and talked with God every day—all day long. I realize today that many Christians have mountaintop experiences, but this was all new for me. I assumed that since I was a Christian, it would be like this the rest of my life.

One day after work, I stopped by the preacher's office. I asked the preacher, "Where do I sign up?"

He said, "Sign up for what?"

I said, "To be a missionary."

He asked what I was talking about, and I opened my Bible to Matthew 28. I told him, "See, God is telling me to go all over the world and tell people about Jesus. I need to be a missionary or a preacher to do that. Where do I sign up?"

He said, "No, no, Ellison. Sit down and let's talk. God's not telling you to be a missionary." He said that Matthew 28 is "the Great Commission" and that it applies to all Christians. He told me to look around at church on Sunday at all the people who worshiped there. They weren't missionaries.

I told the preacher, "That's their problem. God says right here in the Bible to go into all the world, and I'm going to obey God. If they want to just sit here on Sunday, that's their business."

He asked me, "Ellison, if you leave here and go into the world, who will take care of your daughter, and who will take care of your elderly mother?"

I said, "God will. He's the one telling me to go. He's the one who will care for my family."

The preacher again said, "No, no, that's not what the Bible is talking about." The discussion went on for almost an hour. He finally said, "Ellison, I'll tell you what I'll do. You go home, read the Bible every day, go to church every Sunday, and learn all you can. Six months from now, if you still feel strongly that you need to go into the world as a missionary, I'll help you."

I did not like his answer but agreed.

Coming Down off the Mountain

As I was about to leave, the preacher said, "Ellison, I need to prepare you for something. You're having what we call a 'mountaintop experience.' Right now, you're on the top of a mountain with God. That usually lasts a day or two for most, and even a week or two for some. I want to prepare you. When you come down here into the valley with the rest of us, it's really going to hurt you. I just want to prepare you for that hurt."

I told him, "Preacher, you're an old man, and you've been preaching that Bible for a long time. I may be, as you say, on a mountain. If I am, I'll tell you this: I like it up here. I'm not coming down. I walk with God and talk with God." I said, "Preacher, do you see God? He's standing right here beside me. Don't you see Him, preacher?"

The preacher looked beside me and said, "No Ellison, I don't see Him. There was a time when I did see Him as you now see Him, but I don't see Him standing beside you."

I really didn't like the preacher's answer, but I trusted him. I agreed to spend my time learning all I could about God in preparation for "going into the entire world." I certainly didn't like his comments about coming down off the mountain, but he was right on both accounts.

About two months later—I don't know the exact day or time—I realized God was no longer walking right beside me. Where had God gone? I fell on my knees and cried out to God, asking where He had gone. I asked what I had done wrong to cause Him to leave me. I was truly devastated. I prayed and apologized for whatever I did wrong, but He just was not there. I had been on the mountain with God for over four months, and now I was down in the valley, just like the preacher said. This was one of the most horrible experiences of my life. It was definitely a defining moment that I'll never forget.

Today, I understand that God did not leave me. God says, "I will never leave you or forsake you." (Joshua 1:5) And God doesn't lie. I was a brand-new Christian and had no support group to guide me and keep me on track. God used Dr. Charles Stanley and our pastor those first few months, and God, Himself, walked with me. Yes, God loves us that much. He allowed me to walk beside Him for just over four months. Now it was time to go down into the valley and get to work.

The Ham Radio

Shortly after talking with the pastor, I went by Connie's parents' house. Her dad, Mr. Wimbish, was sitting at the table with a telegraph machine, practicing Morse code. I asked what he was doing, and he told me he was brushing up on his Morse code so he could get his ham radio license. Its first phase included showing proficiency in Morse code. He showed me a picture of a small, $200 shortwave radio. He said that when he got his license, he planned to buy this radio. With it, he could talk to anyone in America. He showed me a picture of a $2,200 radio and said it would reach anyone in the entire world.

My head started spinning. If I had to wait six months to go into the world as a missionary, I could use a shortwave radio to reach the world now. I could tell people all over the world about Jesus using one of those $2,200 radios. I asked Mr. Wimbish if he had an extra telegraph machine. Early in his career, he had worked for the railroad as a telegraph operator. He loaned me his extra telegraph machine, and I took it home. I had learned the Morse code as a Boy Scout, so I knew I could learn it again. I started practicing: *A* (._), *B* (_...), *C* (_._.), *D* (_..), and so on.

By October 1988, I was on a roll with the Morse code. I decided to forget about the small radio and just go ahead and buy the $2,200 radio. I needed to start telling people all over the world about Jesus, even without the license. That Friday, I had almost $2,000 in my checking account, and I knew I could borrow the remaining $200 from Mom. I planned to get with Mom after church on Sunday and buy the $2,200 radio on Monday.

Connie and I were watching Dr. Charles Stanley on TV that Saturday evening, and his message was about stepping out and serving God. He cautioned us, saying that before we jump out and tell God what we're going to do for Him, we should pray and ask God if He really wants us to do that work. He said that sometimes we get the cart before the horse. He said that even though the work we want to do for God is a good work, God may not be ready for us. He said we may kick a door open and find there is nothing on the other side. Dr. Stanley said that God's timing is very important and that we should pray first and listen to God's voice.

This message, like all of Dr. Stanley's sermons, made sense to me. That night, I got on my knees and told God what I was going to do for Him. I told Him, "If you don't want me to buy that radio and tell the world about Jesus, you need to tell me right now. On Monday, I plan to buy the radio." I waited a few minutes, and there was no answer. I told God I guessed that meant it was OK to buy the radio.

Sunday at church, the preacher introduced a guest speaker. He said the man was a Gideon and that he wanted to share with us some of the work the Gideons were doing. I thought, *I don't want to listen to some Gideon, or whatever he is. I want to listen to the preacher. I want to learn about God.* I thought about just getting up, leaving, and going home where I could study my Bible. But Mom was sitting a few pews behind me and I didn't want to leave and embarrass her, so I just sat there. I opened my Bible and started reading. I did not pay one bit of attention to the man who was speaking, because I was starving for the word of God.

Toward the end of the Gideon's message, he said, "Last year, the Gideons distributed over twenty-seven million Scriptures all over the world." Even though I was paying absolutely no attention to the speaker, I could still hear his voice. When he said "twenty-seven million Scriptures all over the world," those words kept echoing over and over in my head. The man continued talking about other things, but all I could hear was "twenty-seven million Scriptures all over the world." Then the Gideon's echoing voice stopped, and I clearly heard God speak. God spoke out loud and said, "Ellison, this is the way I want you to reach the world for Christ."

About that time, the man thanked the pastor for letting him speak, and he sat down. I did not have a clue what he was talking about, but I clearly heard God's voice and understood what he told me to do. I now understood why God did not answer my prayer that Saturday night. He answered the prayer Sunday at church instead. I knew I was to join the Gideons and forget about the $2,200 radio.

Every Sunday after church, Mom came by the house. That afternoon when she came by, I asked what that man was talking about. She told me he was with the Gideons, and they were the people who put Bibles in motel rooms and give Bibles to school kids. She said they also send Bibles to other countries throughout the world. I did not tell Mom that God spoke to me. I only asked her where to sign up to join the Gideons. She told me several of the old men in the church were Gideons and that I should ask one of them.

Even though God had told me to join, I was a little embarrassed to just walk up to one of the old men in the church and ask about the Gideons, but God still had His plan for my life. The next Sunday, Shirley made an announcement in church. She said, "Tuesday evening, we are going to start our Tuesday Night Visitation Program." Shirley invited everyone to come and participate. I did not have a clue about the Tuesday visitation; so again, I waited for Mom to come over. She explained that people in the church would go out into the community, visit folks, tell them about Jesus, and invite them to come to church.

Mr. George

I showed up at church Tuesday evening, and there were about twenty-five to thirty people there, just hanging around, talking, and waiting to get started. I did not recognize anyone, so I just stood there in the corner like a wallflower. Then Shirley came into the room and told everyone, "Pair up with your partner, pick up a couple of visitation cards, and let's go!" In about sixty seconds, the room was completely empty, except for me. I just stood there and had no idea what to do. I looked at some of the visitation cards on the table, but had no idea what to do, so I decided to just go home.

As I was about to leave, I felt a hand tap me on my back. I looked behind me, and there was an old man standing there. He had just walked into the room. He said, "Sonny boy, it looks like you need someone to pair up with. Why don't we go together?" I told him I'd be glad to go with him, but I had no idea what we were supposed to do. He said, "You come on with me. I'll show you what to do." The old man was Mr. George, a man I learned to love and respect.

We made a couple of visits and then headed back to the church. As we were driving back, I remembered Mom telling me to ask one of the old men about the Gideons. But I couldn't remember the name "Gideons." So I asked Mr. George if he knew anything about the missionary who had spoken at church the previous Sunday. He didn't understand what I was talking about, because the man was not a missionary; he was a Gideon. I explained a little more, and then I said, "You know, the man who talked about 'twenty-seven million Bibles all over the world.'"

He then realized I was talking about the Gideons. He said, "Yes, I'm a Gideon. Are you interested in joining us in doing this work for God?" I didn't tell him God had told me to do it; I just told him I was interested in possibly joining.

Mr. George said, "Young man, you look like you might have gone to college. Did you?" I told him I had gone to Clemson. He asked, "Did you graduate?" I told him I had. He said, "You qualify." Then he whipped out an application for membership in the Gideons and handed it to me. He explained that to be a Gideon, we had to pay annual dues that were used to fund the organization's operating costs. He said that all the money the Gideons raised was used for buying Scriptures to distribute all over the world. The dues were $25 a year, or I could pay a lifetime membership fee of $600. I asked which he had chosen, and he said he was a lifetime member.

I took the application home and read it over. I discussed it with Connie and asked what she thought about the membership fee. She agreed that if God had told me to join, it would be a lifetime commitment. So I filled out the application, attached a $600 check, and gave it to Mr. George the following Sunday.

At this point, I knew God (the Father), I knew Jesus (the Son), but I still did not have a clue who or what the Holy Ghost was all about. God had told me to "Go tell Doug about Jesus," and I did. I had also started telling others about Jesus. Now God was telling me to join the Gideons to "reach the world for Christ." God had given me two mission fields: one was the world, and the other was here in the Lowcountry.

I have now been a Gideon for twenty-five years, and I love it. It's a great ministry. We get to put New Testaments in the hands of children and adults and place Bibles in motel and hospital rooms. We take Scriptures all over the world and tell people the good news of Jesus Christ. Since the beginning of the ministry, the Gideons have placed over 1.9 billion Bibles and New Testaments all over the world. We should hit the two-billion mark soon.

At the College

We were at the College of Charleston, handing New Testaments to the students as they walked by. Across from me, five employees came out of a building to take a break. I walked over to them and asked if they would like to have New Testaments. They all said they would. I returned to my station across the street. Four of the workers put the New Testaments in their pockets. One woman opened hers and started reading. The other four employees went back inside. As the woman read, her facial expression looked like she had the weight of the world on her shoulders. She would look at the New Testament, read a few words, and then rock back and forth, as though she were in pain. I walked across the street and sat down beside her.

She had the New Testament opened to Revelation. I said, "Ma'am, I see you're reading Revelation. Sometimes parts of Revelation are difficult to understand. I don't understand all of it myself, but I can help you with some of it if you would like my help."

She said, "Is this about the end of the world?"

I said, "Yes ma'am, part of it is about the end of the age we're living in." She looked even more worried now than before. So I said, "If you're a Christian and know Jesus, you don't have to worry about those terrible things that are to come."

She replied, "I've been baptized four times in four different churches. Does that make me a Christian?"

I told her, "No, ma'am. That only means you took four baths at four churches. Would you like for me to tell you what God says in the Bible about how to become a Christian?" She told me yes, and I explained to her why Jesus went to the cross—it was for her.

I asked her if she wanted me to help her pray and ask Jesus into her heart, and she said yes. I told her that when I pray, I usually get on my knees. Without hesitation, she dropped to her knees even before I could kneel down. I placed my hand on her shoulder, and we started praying.

At that time, there was a lot of controversy and friction in the news about praying in school. People complained about bringing the Bible into schools. There were two police officers on the street corner watching everything we did. I thought about the friction and thought, *I wonder if we'll be arrested for praying on the sidewalk in downtown Charleston.*

As we were praying, someone tapped me on the shoulder. I thought, *It's those two police officers. We're going to be arrested for praying on the sidewalk.*

I looked up, and it was not the police. There were two students standing beside us. One of them said, "Mister, could we have one of your Bibles?" I gave them both New Testaments from my pocket, and the woman and I continued praying.

As we got up off our knees, the lady looked as if God had just lifted a thousand pounds off of her shoulders. The Holy Spirit had been convicting her. She had been searching for answers and, with the good news, it all came together. She was born again. We talked a few more minutes, and she went back to work.

I watched her as she walked back into the building, and it was as if she was walking on air. Jesus said, "Then you will know the truth, and the truth will set you free" (John 8:32). Jesus broke her chains of bondage and set her free.

Quite often, students will take New Testaments and walk a short distance and stop. They start reading as if they have never seen God's word before. When we can, we talk with the students and share the gospel with them. Quite a few students have accepted Christ on the sidewalks of downtown Charleston.

The Middle School

Unfortunately, Gideons are not allowed to take New Testaments inside public schools anymore. A minority of Americans have been successful at having God's word removed from our schools. But we are able to stand on the public sidewalks and hand New Testaments to kids as they leave school.

One afternoon, we were handing out New Testaments at a middle school. A woman came over to me and I thought, *Oh, no, she's going to tell me she doesn't want me giving Bibles to the kids.* To my surprise, she said, "Sir, may I have five or six of those New Testaments?"

I told her, "Sure." As the students came out of school, it was obvious that some of the parents had told their children not to take anything from strangers. A few kids would not accept a New Testament from me. As they walked past me, the kids recognized this woman, and she asked them to come over to her. She gave the kids New Testaments and explained to them that the little Bible is about God.

God sometimes works in mysterious ways. He gets the job done. God says, "So is my word that goes out from my mouth: it will not return to me empty, but will accomplish what I desire and achieve the purpose for which I sent it" (Isaiah 55:11).

CHAPTER 9

The Vanishing Hitchhiker

This chapter is about another one of the "God things" that I don't tell my Christian friends about, because most of them will not believe me. In the past twenty-five years, I've only told two or three very close Christian friends about the experience. But now, God said, "Write it down."

When I was a student at Clemson University, I didn't have a car. So whenever I wanted to come home, I'd hitchhike. I did this for five years, and I could write a book about those experiences. So today, when I see people hitchhiking, and if they look clean (no knives, guns, drugs, or anything like that), I give them a ride.

A few years after becoming a Christian, I had been deer hunting in the Waterhorn section of the Francis Marion National Forest. It was a beautiful day in the woods, but there were no deer. Sometimes that's better than shooting a deer. I left the forest and started driving down Highway 17 toward home. There is a long stretch of road with woods on both sides and no access roads entering the highway.

I saw a hitchhiker on my side of the highway. I slowed down to check him out. Normally, when you're hitchhiking, a driver will drop you off at a highway intersection where the driver needs to make a turn or where the hitchhiker needs to make a turn. If you see a hitchhiker on a stretch of open road with no intersections, it may mean his previous driver had a problem with him and kicked him out.

There were no intersections or houses along this stretch of road, so I was hesitant to pick up this fellow. He was an old, gray-headed, African American man. He looked to be well over eighty years old. I thought, *This old man looks harmless*, so I stopped and picked him up. His name was John. I asked where he was headed. He answered, "Miami." I told him I'd drop him off at the Cooper River Bridge, where he could easily catch his next ride.

After driving a few miles, I noticed what appeared to be blood on John's head, which made me a little anxious. My mind started coming up with all these scenarios to explain where the blood had come from. Has he tried to rob someone, been cut in the attempt, and thrown out of their car? Is he now going to rob me? Does he have a knife?

I thought, *Make a plan, fast.* I had a pistol under the seat of the truck, but I knew that if I went for it, he would be on top of me before I could make my move. I decided that if he pulled a knife on me, I would speed up to eighty or ninety miles per hour and tell him to drop the knife or I'd wreck the truck. *If I'm going to die, I'll take him with me.*

As we drove farther down the road, I nervously chatted with the man. He did not seem like a robber. He actually seemed very nice. I finally got up some courage and asked him, "Are you aware that you have blood on your head? Are you OK?" He told me that he had hit his head on a tree limb. I thought, Likely story...but maybe true. He said, "I'll be OK, I just need to get home to Miami." I told him that I'd be dropping him off in Mount Pleasant near the Cooper River Bridge, where he could easily catch another ride.

As we got closer to my home in Mount Pleasant, the Lord spoke to me and reminded me of the parable of the Good Samaritan in Luke 10. In this parable, the Jews and Samaritans did not get along with each other at all, as is the case with some blacks and whites today. In the parable, there was a Jew lying on the ground. He had been beaten and robbed, and several Jews had passed him by and just left him lying there. A Samaritan came along, picked him up, put him on his donkey, and took him to an inn. The next day, the Samaritan paid the innkeeper for the overnight stay and gave him extra money to continue helping the Jewish man. He told the innkeeper that he'd pay anything else he owed when he returned.

I silently prayed, "Lord, I could take John to a motel, but I don't have any money to pay for his stay." Then the Lord said, "You'll be passing right by your house." This was not a command; the Lord gave me a choice. I thought, *Oh no, Lord, surely you don't want me to bring him into my house. He will probably rob me and may even kill me.* But the Lord did not answer. I knew I was to help the man, because that's what Christians are supposed to do.

I finally agreed with the Lord. I turned to John and asked, "Would you like for me to stop by my house? You can clean up the cut on your head and we'll eat a sandwich."

He said, "No, if you can just help me on my way, I'll be grateful." Whew! That was like lifting a hundred pounds off my shoulders. I thought, *OK, Lord, now what?*

As I drove through Mount Pleasant toward the Cooper River Bridge, I thought, *Well, I may as well take him to Charleston where it will be easier for him to catch a ride.* I told John what I would do, and he thanked me. As we drove through downtown Charleston, we came to what locals call "hamburger row," which is a stretch of fast-food restaurants.

I asked John, "When was the last time you had something to eat?" Since I had picked him up around 11:00 a.m., I figured he'd say either "breakfast this morning" or "supper last night."

But his answer was, "A few days ago."

Even though I didn't want to, I offered, "How about we stop, and I'll buy both of us some lunch?" He said, that would be OK, but that he could not pay me back because he only had a little change in his pocket. I told him, "No problem, it's on me."

After eating, I thought *Boy, you've got to do more than this.* I looked in my billfold. I had twenty-two dollars, and that was it. At first, I started to take out the whole amount and give it to him. Then my fleshly nature kicked in, and I only took out the twenty-dollar bill, keeping the two dollars for myself. I told John, "I don't have much money, but I'd like to give you this twenty dollars to help you buy some meals on the way home."

He said, "No, I can make it. I'll be OK." I insisted, and he took the twenty dollars.

Now, instead of feeling good about what I had just done, I felt terrible. Why didn't I just give him the other two dollars? I really didn't need it, and he certainly did. I thought, *Boy, that's exactly the condition of your heart.* I was too embarrassed to pull out my billfold a second time to give him the other two dollars, which I should have done in the first place.

I planned to drop John off on the other side of the Ashley River Bridge, and I had told him this. But as we were driving, the Lord spoke to me again and said, "Take him to Lands' End." This is at the far west side of Charleston, where Charleston ends and the country begins. After crossing a small bridge at Lands' End, there is wide-open country for a while.

As we approached the Lands' End area, I started looking for a spot to drop off John. There was a long stretch of highway with just flat marshland on both sides. There were no trees, bushes, or anything else, just open marsh. If he stood on the highway right here to catch his next ride, everyone passing by would easily see him. I stopped and wished him well on his way to Miami. I was still so nervous that I forgot to pray with him for a safe journey home.

I drove about forty yards farther down the highway and then looped around and headed back toward home. There were absolutely no cars on the highway going in either direction. I looked over to where I had just dropped off John ten seconds earlier. I was going to wave good-bye to him, but John was not there. He had completely vanished into thin air. I looked up and down the highway. There were no cars or trucks except mine, and there was nothing for John to hide behind—only open, flat marsh. In only ten seconds, John had vanished into thin air. He was gone.

I was a little shaken, to say the least, but I realized this was another "God thing." I really didn't worry about John vanishing, because I trust God. I thought, *Oh, well, this is another one of the "God things" that I won't tell anyone about because they won't believe me anyway.* I told my wife, and that was it. She believes because she too has seen God at work in both of our lives firsthand.

Our God is not bound by our logic. He tells us, "For my thoughts are not your thoughts, neither are your ways my ways, declares the Lord" (Isaiah 55:8).

I have a Christian friend who had a similar experience. Our local Baptist Association has a group of volunteers who do disaster-relief mass feeding for disaster victims. We were in Louisiana after Hurricane Katrina providing hot meals for the hurricane victims. One evening after work, we were sharing testimonies about Jesus. One of the men said, "Wayne has a good testimony."

Wayne said that he knew he needed the Lord in his life and gave his heart to God. He was reading the Bible when God spoke to him about acknowledging Jesus Christ. Jesus said, "Whoever acknowledges me before others, I will also acknowledge before my Father in heaven. But whoever disowns me before others, I will disown before my Father in heaven" (Matthew 10:32-33).

The next week, Wayne was on a ladder painting a house. A young man with auburn red hair stood at the base of the ladder and asked Wayne if he could speak with him. Wayne came down the ladder and the young man asked, "Are you a Christian?" Wayne told the young man that he had just last week given his life to the Lord. The young man then prayed for Wayne and turned to walk away.

As Wayne was climbing back up the ladder, he remembered what the Lord had told him about acknowledging Christ. He hurriedly climbed back down and looked for the young man, but he had disappeared. Wayne got in his truck and drove around the area looking for him, but he could not be found. He said, "It was like he vanished into thin air." Wayne said, "I believe to this day he was an angel sent by God to see if I would acknowledge Christ as my Lord and Savior." Wayne passed the test that day and continues acknowledging Christ today.

I also listened to John Paul Jackson's testimony when he appeared on *Joni Table Talk*. He was driving to a church in Floydada, Texas, to speak, when his pickup truck broke down. He was out in the middle of nowhere. He had not seen another car for an hour. Then a car came along, and the driver gave him a ride. The driver asked, "Son, where are you going?" He told the driver he was going to Floydada. The driver said, "Son, this is your lucky day. I'm also going to Floydada."

When the driver got to Floydada, he stopped his car in front of the church and said, "This is where you're going, isn't it?" John Paul got out of the car, looked at the church, and turned around to thank the driver. But in a period of two seconds, the driver and the car had vanished into thin air. He then realized he had never even told the driver where he was going in Floydada, but the driver had taken him directly to the church.

A short time later when I was reading the Bible, I came across the Scripture in Hebrews where God tells us, "Do not forget to show hospitality to strangers, for by so doing some people have shown hospitality to angels without knowing it" (Hebrews 13:2). Was my friend the hitchhiker an angel? Call him what you will; all I know is that God put him into my life to teach me a few lessons.

God put John on the highway out in the middle of nowhere, and I picked him up. Then I dropped John off on the highway out in the middle of nowhere, and God picked him up.

Yes, I believe John was an angel. People don't vanish into thin air, but angels do. I personally believe this was another one of God's tests. The Bible says, "What is mankind that you make so much of them, that you give them so much attention, that you examine them every morning and test them every moment?" (Job 7:17–18). Sometimes we pass the test, and sometimes we fail. But God never gives up on us. It's all part of that big church word, *sanctification.* It's all part of being a disciple of Jesus Christ.

CHAPTER 10

SNAKES AND DOGS

Snakes at the Savannah River Plant

My friend, Allen, and I drove down to the Savannah River Plant property in Barnwell County to deer hunt. We found a creek bottom that looked promising. We split up, and Allen walked south down the creek bottom, and I walked north.

It was late fall, and leaves had already fallen off of the trees. It was a beautiful, sunny morning, and the leaves crunched under my feet as I slowly walked and scanned the hillsides for deer. As I walked, I heard something rustling the leaves. It sounded like a deer slipping through the woods. I kept looking, but I did not see a deer. This happened several times.

I decided to stand in one spot and wait until the deer made the sound of rustling leaves again. I stood there two or three minutes. Then, on the ground right in front of me, I saw what appeared to be a black worm about four inches long, sticking up from under the leaves. This "black worm" was quivering and making the rustling sound in the leaves that I had been hearing.

All of a sudden, a huge, black snake reared up directly in front of me. He was about one foot in front of me and right between my feet. The small "black worm" sticking up from the leaves was the tip of his tail. My footsteps apparently had made him nervous, and his tail was quivering in the leaves. As he reared up, he opened his huge, white mouth. I knew I was looking eyeball to eyeball at a very large cottonmouth (water moccasin), a very poisonous and aggressive snake. His head moved from side to side like he was trying to decide which of my legs to bite. I learned in the Boy Scouts not to make any sudden moves, because snakes can sense sudden movements and that will often make them strike. We stood there eyeball to eyeball for what seemed like an eternity. I hoped the snake would chicken out and go away, but cottonmouths normally don't run; they attack.

One of us needed some relief, so I made my move. I hoped he would not beat me to the draw. I was carrying my 30-06 automatic rifle across the top of my shoulder with my right arm resting on top of the stock. In one swift motion, I pulled down hard on the butt of the rifle stock and caught the front end of the rifle with my left hand. I pointed it at the snake's mouth, and boom! I blew his head off. I thought, *I win. You lose!*

Then, directly in front of my left foot and directly in front of my right foot, two huge canebrake rattlesnakes reared up (canebrakes and timber rattlers are basically the same. Here in the Lowcountry, canebrake rattlers have a reddish streak down the middle of their backs. In the upper part of the state, these rattlers do not have this reddish streak and are referred to as timber rattlers). The snakes' coloration blended in perfectly with the leaves, and I had not even seen them. They were both also about one foot in front of me, and were coiled, with their tails high in the air. Their rattles were singing a duet. Their mouths were wide open, and I could see their long fangs. They moved their heads back, away from me, and then swiftly swung their heads toward my legs to strike. But for some reason, their heads stopped just inches away from my legs. They did not strike me, because for some reason, they could not. It was as if a sheet of glass had been stretched across in front of my legs, and when the snakes tried to strike, their heads hit the glass. They tried and tried, but they simply could not strike my legs.

I did not immediately shoot the two rattlers. I was so startled that I just stood there and watched as they tried to strike. They should have eaten me for lunch, but for some reason, they couldn't. Then I came to my senses and boom, boom! I still had not moved one inch from where all of this had started. Now there were three deadly snakes lying at my feet. Had I taken one more step with either foot, I would be dead. Had one of the three snakes struck my leg, I probably would have reacted by jumping up and down a few times, trying to stomp the snake, and all three snakes would have had at me.

The Bible says, "For he will command his angels concerning you to guard you in all your ways; they will lift you up in their hands, so that you will not strike your foot against a stone. You will tread on the lion and the cobra; you will trample the great lion and the serpent" (Psalm 91:11–13).

All over the bottom, I could hear leaves rustling with the sound of more snakes. I still did not move. There was no way out. Snakes were buried in the leaves all over the creek bottom. I thought about my hunting buddy. He was a mile or two away and couldn't help. Even if I was able to make it out of this place alive, he wouldn't believe me. He would say that I shot at a deer three times and missed all three times. To prove to Allen what had happened, I leaned down and cut the rattles off the two rattlesnakes and put them in my pocket. I then held up the first rattler to see how big he was. I was six feet tall, and the rattler was longer than that. The second rattler was about five feet long, and the cottonmouth was about four feet long. They were all full-grown snakes.

I knew I had to get out of there, but I couldn't casually stroll across this snake-infested bottom and just walk out. So I pulled up my pants legs and wrapped them tightly around my legs, because I didn't want them to get hung up on a briar bush, causing me to trip and fall. I held my rifle in the air and then ran as fast as I could to the hillside. I don't know how many snakes I crunched under my feet as I ran. I only hoped I would be off the snakes and several feet away before one of them could rear up to strike at me. It worked, and I made it to the hill and out of the snake-ridden creek bottom.

Allen was already at the car, waiting. He had heard me shoot and had come to help me drag my deer out of the woods. When I told him I had shot three snakes, he just laughed, as I knew he would. He, of course, said I had shot and missed a deer. Then I pulled the two sets of rattles out of my pocket, and he then believed me. When I told him how big they were, he encouraged me to go back and skin out the larger of the two rattlers. I told him, "No way. If you want the skin, you go get it."

The next morning was very cold, and frost was on the ground. Allen again encouraged me to skin out the larger snake. We both knew that with frost on the ground, there would be no snakes out. So I agreed, and the snakeskin still hangs on our den wall today.

"This is the snake skin off the six-foot long canebrake rattlesnake"

The Hunt Club

In 1987, Ron invited me to join his hunting club at Four Holes Swamp. We drove to the club near Dorchester, and he showed me around. It was a beautiful club, and I gladly joined and hunted with the men that year. In May 1988, I joined the club for a second year, but this time, I wasted my money.

In June 1988, I was born again. With the mountaintop experience, I had no desire to go deer hunting. All I wanted to do was to read the Bible, talk with God, and tell others about Jesus.

Shortly before deer season opened, the hunt club scheduled a work day. I felt obligated to help, since I had committed to be a member. Ron and I went to the club that Saturday to cut bushes, open shooting lanes, and work on tree stands. We stopped for lunch and sat under a shed roof on the edge of the Four Holes Swamp. While we were sitting there eating our lunch, a grown cottonmouth slithered right into the middle of our group of men. All the men except me jumped up and quickly retreated from the snake. I just sat there and continued eating my sandwich. At first, the men shouted at me to get away from the snake. Then Ron, who loves to joke around, said, "Hey, you're a Christian now. The Bible says you can pick up snakes. Go ahead and show us that you are a Christian." Ron and the others were laughing. (Before Ron said that, I had clearly heard the Lord's voice quote to me the Scripture in Mark where Jesus said believers would "pick up snakes with their hands" (Mark 16:18). The Lord had already told me it was OK to pick up the snake. He did not tell me "to pick up the snake;" He simply gave me the choice.)

I reached over, picked up the cottonmouth in the middle of his body, and casually tossed it over near my friend Ron. He immediately jumped back. He said, "You're crazy."

I said, "No, I'm a Christian."

He said, "Yes, you are."

> ***Stop right now! Don't pick up snakes! They'll bite you!*** *If you are absolutely certain you hear God's voice, then it's your decision. But remember, "For Satan himself masquerades as an angel of light" (2 Corinthians 11:14). If you hear Satan's lying voice (and I have heard Satan's lying voice before), and you pick up a snake, you'll probably have a painful, rude awakening. You may very well die from the snake bite.* ***I say again, don't pick up snakes! They'll bite you!***

The snake slithered back over in front of me and just lay there. The other men were talking about how crazy I was. Ron laughed and said, "Pick it up again, but this time, throw it down in the swamp."

I asked him, "Why don't you pick it up? You're a Christian."

He said, "I'm a Christian, but I'm not picking up that snake." And for Ron, that was the correct answer. God had not told him that he could pick up the snake. Had he done so without God's blessings, he most certainly would have been bitten.

I leaned over, picked up the snake by the end of his tail, whirled it around over my head a few times, and threw it down into the swamp. As we sat and talked, the other men asked, "Weren't you afraid of that snake?"

I told them, "No, I'm not afraid of snakes. However, I do have a certain respect for poisonous snakes. But this one time, God clearly told me it was OK to pick up that snake, and I take God at his word."

I have never again picked up a snake, unless it was already dead.

The Snake at the River House

One afternoon at the river house, as I walked past a patch of azaleas, I saw movement in the leaves. I looked closer and saw a copperhead. Copperhead snakes are somewhat shy when you leave them alone, unlike cottonmouths, which are aggressive and will sometimes come after you. As I walked closer to the copperhead, it slithered into a hole under a tree stump. I really do not dislike snakes, even poisonous ones. God created them all. But I don't want them in my yard. Sooner or later, they will bite me, my family, or my guests.

I went to my truck and took out my.38 special pistol, which was loaded with "snake shot." I went over to the snake hole and waited and waited and waited, but no snake came out. Impatiently, I told the snake, "I'll get you out of that hole." I shoved a garden hose as far as I could into the hole and let the water flow. After about five minutes, there was still no snake. I took a gas can and poured gasoline down the hole, but no snake. I took a can of wasp spray and sprayed it down the hole, but still no snake. I stood there and waited and waited.

Then the Holy Spirit reminded me of the Scripture in Genesis where God created everything—including all the critters that crawl on the ground. God gave man authority over them (cf. Genesis 1:28).

So I boldly said, "In the name of Jesus Christ, the Holy Son of God, I command you, copperhead snake, come out of that hole and show yourself. Come out right now. By the power of the Blood of Jesus Christ of Nazareth, I command you to come out now and show yourself." About three seconds passed, and the copperhead slithered out of his hole and just lay there motionless. Boom! We had one less poisonous snake in our yard. God gave us this authority, so why not use it?

The Mongrel Dog

I walk three miles a day, several days a week, in my neighborhood. We have leash laws in town, so folks are supposed to keep their dogs in a pen or on a leash. Dogs are not allowed to run loose. There is a house on a cul-de-sac road where I walk that has a four-foot-high fence around the front yard. The folks who live there have a huge, mongrel-looking dog that probably weighs over a hundred pounds. Every time I walk by the house, that mongrel dog runs along the fence growling, snarling, and in dog language saying, "I'm going to have you for my lunch one day." The fence always works, so I never really worry about the dog.

One day as I walked by the house, Old Mongrel—the name I gave the dog—was not in the yard. I walked to the end of the cul-de-sac and then turned and headed back up the street. As I walked by the fence again, there was still no Old Mongrel. I figured he must be in the house or in the garage. Then I noticed the garage door was open about a foot, and I thought, *Not good!* Just then, out crawled that huge, mongrel dog. He ran straight for me. I know he must have thought, *My day has finally come.* He ran wide open, growling, snarling, and slobbering; in seconds he was going to be on me. I quickly looked down for a rock or a stick or something to defend myself, but nothing was there. I knew I was dead meat, but then the Holy Spirit stepped in.

The Holy Spirit spoke through my mouth and said, "In the name of Jesus Christ, be still!" It was not me speaking. I had no such thought. The dog immediately slammed on the brakes, and his paws skidded on the asphalt. His eyes opened as wide as golf balls. Fear was written across his face. He lowered and turned his head away from me in a cowering motion. He tucked his tail between his legs and slowly walked back to his garage. On the way to the garage, still cowering, he occasionally looked back at me. He slithered back under the garage door and was gone.

From now on when I walk, I carry a five-foot-long walking stick. I believe: shame on the dog the first time, but shame on me if I go unprepared next time.

The Guatemala Mission Trip and Another Dog Encounter

In 2005, our church was planning a mission trip to Guatemala. I thought, as usual, *OK, y'all go right on ahead.* The deadline for signing up for the trip came and passed. A few weeks after the deadline, we were at our 6:00 a.m. Bible study. I was sitting next to Jim, and I asked, "Jim, the Lord has told me to go on this mission trip. Is it too late to sign up?"

He said, "No, but you'll need to go right now and apply for your passport."

We arrived in Guatemala without incident. Our mission was to go door to door, handing out tracts (the gospel of John) and sharing the gospel with anyone who would listen.

We split up into several small groups of five or six. The local missionary handed a broomstick to each of us, and I asked, "What are these for?"

He laughed and said, "You'll find out." There were not enough broomsticks for everyone, so I gave mine to one of the ladies in our group. As we started up the first hill, we visited several huts. Our translator, Vanecio, led the way for the five of us, and I brought up the rear. Then, as we walked up the hill, all Hell broke loose. Out of nowhere came a dog, growling, snarling, showing his teeth, and headed straight for me. I had no broomstick, but I remembered my previous dog experience. I looked straight at the dog and said, "In the name of Jesus Christ, be still!"

The dog did exactly the same thing as Old Mongrel. He slammed on the brakes, skidded on the dirt road, and his eyeballs opened as wide as golf balls. He lowered and turned his head in a cowering motion. He tucked his tail and walked away. The others in our group watched in disbelief. Vanecio came to me and in broken English said, "What did you say to that dog?"

I said, "In the name of Jesus Christ, be still." As he walked back up the hill to lead our group, he practiced saying "In the name of Jesus Christ, be still." He said it over and over again.

About two hours later, another dog appeared out of nowhere. His teeth were showing, and he was snarling and growling. This dog headed straight for Vanecio. He turned and in broken English said, "In the name of Jesus Christ, be still." The dog did the same as the others. Vanecio looked in disbelief at the cowering dog. He walked back down the hill to where I was standing and said, "It works! It works!" After that, even though there appeared to be stray dogs everywhere, none of them dared to bother us.

CHAPTER 11

Mom's Pure and Simple Faith

I've read several books about Mother Teresa of Calcutta. She was a most giving person who truly loved our Lord and gave her life serving others. Mom reminds me so much of Mother Teresa that when we get to Heaven, I expect to see the two of them walking and sharing together. If you had known my Mom and were asked to use one word to describe her, you would probably choose the word *love*. Mom loved everyone, but I would use the word *sacrifice* to describe her. She sacrificed her life for the good of others—first for our family, then for others around her.

Mom Comes to the Lord

When Mom was eight years old, Mordecai Ham, a famous revival preacher, came to her hometown of Laurens. Ham's group pitched a large tent in town, and they held church services each evening. Mom told me that Mama and Papa, her parents, took all the kids with them to the revival on Monday and Tuesday evenings but were unable to attend on Wednesday evening. Mom and one of her sisters received permission to walk to town and attend the tent meeting alone. Toward the end of the service, Mordecai Ham asked all those who wanted to ask Jesus into their hearts to come forward. Mom said her sister got up first. She asked her sister what she was doing, and she answered, "I'm going to ask Jesus to come into my heart."

To that, Mom said, "Wait for me. I want Jesus in my heart too."

When I talked with Mom about this, I asked her, "Did Jesus come into your heart?"

She said, "Yes, I had a child's faith, and that was good enough for God. He came in, He's there now, and, I know He'll never leave me." I was sixty-six years old when Mom died, and from my personal observations of her life and her witness for Christ, I agree that Jesus was definitely in her heart.

Mom's Angels

When Dad died in 1980, I talked with Mom about moving to Mount Pleasant where I could better look after her. She was sixty-seven at the time and really didn't want to move, so every few weeks I made the four-hour drive home to help her pay bills, work on broken items around the house, work on her car, and do whatever else needed to be done. This went on for almost two years. Mom often told me how she hated for me to make the four-hour drive to help her, because she knew it was a tremendous burden on me. I did not realize it at the time, but she apparently really struggled with the decision to move to the Lowcountry.

One afternoon it was raining, and Mom was praying about moving to Mount Pleasant. She knew she needed to move for my sake, but she really hated to leave her friends. She was asking God to help her with the decision. She told me that as she walked down the hallway toward the small utility room, two big men had stopped her in the doorway. They grabbed her arms, and she could not move. I asked her, "What did the men look like?"

She said she did not see anyone, but they both had real big hands, like Sam at church. She just stood there, because the men would not turn her loose. She said, "Then, I heard a loud 'boom' outside the house, and a huge ball of fire came through the back wall of the utility room. The ball of fire was larger than a basketball. It hit the floor, bounced and hit the wall to the right. It hit the ceiling, it hit the wall to the left, then the floor, then the wall again...around and around. The ball of fire kept bouncing off the walls, floor, and ceiling, and at the same time, it was coming toward me. Then, just before the ball of fire reached me, it went through the wall and left the house and the two men turned me loose." Mom told me she knew God had sent two angels to protect her. She also knew God was telling her it was time to move.

We found a condo in Mount Pleasant and sold her house. I had never told Mom that my first wife and I had been struggling with our marriage and that we were on the verge of a divorce. I felt Mom had enough problems of her own without worrying about me. Our divorce was final in 1983, and I was awarded custody of our eight-year-old daughter, Susan.

Mom always thought God sent her to Mount Pleasant so that I could better look after her, but I knew better. God sent Mom to Mount Pleasant to help me raise Susan. She was there to pick Susan up after school every day, feed her supper, and get her started on homework while I often worked two jobs. After work I would swing by Mom's condo and pick up Susan, and we'd go home.

Hurricane Hugo hit the Lowcountry in September 1989. Our house suffered very little damage compared to others. Mom's condo, however, did not fare so well. She had about two feet of surge-tide water in her condo, and the roof was badly damaged. There was no place for her to live, as all the livable houses and apartments in Mount Pleasant were already taken.

I asked my wife how she felt about having Mom move in with us. Her answer was, "No problem. I only ask one thing. Let me have the kitchen to myself when I get home from work. That's where I unwind."

It took a year for contractors to make all the repairs at Mom's condo. When they finished, we talked about Mom moving back there, but by then she had grown accustomed to living with us. Mom asked if she could just live with us and sell her condo. I talked with Connie, and again she again said, "No problem." Mom lived her last twenty years in our home.

I See Black

One evening, when we were sitting at the supper table, I put Mom's food before her, and I was about to say the blessing. She looked up at me and said, "What do you see when you pray?" I laughed and asked what she meant. She said, "When you close your eyes and pray, what do you see?"

I closed my eyes and said, "Mom, when I close my eyes to pray, I see black. I see nothing. What do you see?"

She very calmly said, "Oh, I see Jesus." When she said that, the Lord immediately spoke to me. I clearly heard Him say, "Blessed are the pure in heart, for they will see God" (Matthew 5:8).

I had been a Christian for probably ten years and had clearly heard God's voice many times. Often, when God speaks, He will quote a Scripture that pertains to what is going on at the time. Therefore, I was not shocked to hear God say this. I thought about what Mom had said and how God responded to what she said. I agreed that without a doubt, Mom had the purest heart of anyone I knew.

Mom's Visions

Mom was able to see things. I really don't understand how, unless she saw visions from God. When Janet, a friend of ours, died, I didn't want to upset Mom, so Connie and I went to the funeral home to pay our respects without telling her.

As soon as we got home, Mom looked at me and asked, "Is Janet dead?" I asked why she would ask that question. Mom answered, "Because I just saw you and Connie at the funeral home. I saw you look into a room, and there was Janet in a casket. Is she dead?" I told Mom that Janet was dead, and I asked her how she "saw" us at the funeral home, but she couldn't explain it. Oftentimes when God reveals things to us, it will be through a dream or a vision. I believe that Mom frequently had visions, but she was so close to God, it was just normal, everyday life to her.

Plan "B"

Mom and I would often sit on the side of her bed and talk about "God things." Mom had a tremendous faith, which was the same child's faith she had when she was eight. She had a very simple understanding of the Bible and was certainly no theologian. She always hungered to learn more, and I guess I take after her. I'm not a theologian either, and I always hunger to learn more about our God.

During the last ten years of Mom's life, she suffered from Alzheimer's disease. In 1988, I prayed, and God instantly healed her. So why wouldn't He heal her now? I absolutely believe that God is Sovereign, and He could have completely healed her Alzheimer's in a split second if He had chosen to do so. God is totally in control of everything, and He knows what He's doing. Sometimes we just suffer, and sometimes we just die. But we always trust God.

It's always good to have a "Plan B" just in case your "Plan A" doesn't work out. I completed all the paperwork to have Mom admitted to two nursing homes, just in case it became necessary. During the time she lived with us, I received several calls from both nursing homes telling me a bed was available for Mom if we wanted it. All costs would have been paid by Medicaid. Each time they called, I thanked them and told them we were still able to care for Mom at home. They kept her name on their lists, just in case. I still praise God that my wife and I were able to care for Mom in our home until she left to spend eternity with her Savior.

Jesus Takes Mom's Spirit

The last few years of her life, Mom was not able to get up or down. The little talking she did made no sense. If you really want to know what it's like to care for an elderly parent with Alzheimer's, go visit a nursing home. I could go into a lot of unpleasant details but won't. Then imagine doing all of those caregiver duties yourself. We were fortunate because we were able to hire Margaret, a caregiver, to stay with Mom five days a week. We took care of Mom at night and on weekends.

On Tuesday morning of Mom's last week here on earth, she had a major stroke. It just happened that a hospice nurse was at our house. The nurse worked with Mom for maybe fifteen minutes, and then we put her in her bed. She just lay there, not moving. Her eyes were glazed over. The oxygen was hooked up, but she was now basically a vegetable. She did not speak, eat, drink, or move. Her body just lay there, waiting to die. The nurse told us this was the beginning of the end. She said we should try to make Mom as comfortable as possible during this time. Mom usually complained when we changed her brief or rolled her around in bed to bathe her. Now she didn't even know we were there. It was as if she was already dead, but her body was still alive.

Here in the Lowcountry and possibly in other places, there is a name for this state of being. It's called "traveling." This is when the person isn't fully here, but they aren't fully there either. I don't think you'll find "traveling" in the Bible. I was with both Connie's mom and mine when they were in this state of traveling before death. From Tuesday through Thursday, I spent as much time as possible beside Mom's bed. I prayed with her. I sang her favorite song, "Jesus Loves Me," to her and just sat and held her hand.

I've been told that when people are on their death bed and are traveling, we need to tell them it is OK to leave. It has been said that the dying person is trying to hang on to this world for our sakes, rather than letting go and moving on to the new life. As I sat and talked with Mom, I told her it was OK to leave. I told her, "Jesus will be there to welcome you with His open arms. Dad, Mama, and Papa, and your brother and sisters will be there waiting on you." Telling Mom it was OK to leave was the hardest thing I've ever done in my entire life, but I had to tell her for her sake. She had suffered enough over the last ten years, and it was time to leave. It was time to be with her Savior and her family in Heaven. It was time to go home.

On Thursday afternoon, the hospice nurse came by to check on Mom. She still had not moved. She just lay there, staring at the ceiling. While the hospice nurse, Margaret, and I were standing beside her bed, Jesus entered the bedroom. I didn't see him, but Mom did.

Mom turned her head and looked over toward the corner of the room and cried out, "My Savior, my Savior, my Savior, my Savior..." After Mom said this five or six times, she slowly turned her head back and again stared at the ceiling.

We looked at each other and said, "She just saw Jesus. Jesus was here in this room."

During Mom's lifetime, whenever she talked about God, she would refer to God the Father as "God." She would refer to Jesus as either "Jesus" or "Lord." She knew Jesus was her Savior, but she never referred to Him by that name. The Jesus Mom saw enter her room that Thursday afternoon was her "Savior," and she knew Him well.

After calling out to Jesus, her Savior, Mom continued to just lie there. Saturday afternoon, I was sitting by her bed, holding her hand. I clearly heard God say, "She'll die tonight." I started to get up and go tell Connie what God had just said to me, but for some reason, I didn't. Maybe I just didn't want to believe what I heard.

I truly wanted Mom to go to be with Jesus, but at the same time, I didn't want her to leave. Love is a strong bond.

I checked on Mom at 11:00 p.m., tucked her in, and then I went to bed. I set the alarm clock for 3:00 a.m. so I could get up and check on her. About 2:00 a.m., I woke up and went to her bedroom. Her body was cold. She was gone. I believe that for her body to already be cold, she had probably died right after I tucked her into bed. It was as God said: "She'll die tonight."

My Dad had a similar experience. Mom told us how he died. The last three months of his life were spent in the hospital, dying of colon cancer. The doctors told him he would live only two weeks because his colon was completely obstructed with cancer. He could not eat or drink, so he just lay in bed waiting to die. Mom stayed beside his bed and even slept in a chair next to Dad those last three months.

When Dad entered the hospital, he was a deacon in the church and a very smart man. He knew all about Jesus and the Bible, but he did not "know" Jesus. A young preacher from our hometown church came to visit Dad in the hospital every week, and they talked about the Lord. It was on one of these visits that Dad "surrendered" his life to Christ, and the personal relationship with Jesus began.

Shortly after that, Mom said Dad had an encounter with the Lord. One day, Dad turned his head and looked over toward the door of his room. Dad later explained to Mom what had happened. He saw an extremely bright light enter the room and move across the room to the foot of his bed. He then felt the warmth and love in the light enter his body and move all the way up through it. Even though Dad had no strength left, both of his arms went straight up into the air, praising God. Dad told Mom he did not raise his arms; God raised them for him.

One afternoon, after three months in the hospital waiting on death, Dad told Mom, "Mary, come close. I have something to say to you. Tonight is the night I will die." And he did.

I always assumed the Spirit of God that lives in our hearts would not leave our bodies until the heart stopped pumping blood and the brain quit functioning. This may be true in many cases. But I truly believe that when Jesus came into my mother's room that Thursday afternoon, He took her spirit with Him when He left. I believe her heart continued pumping blood until shortly after 11:00 p.m. Saturday night, when her body died. But her spirit had left with Jesus two days earlier.

I wasn't in the room with Dad, but I think he had a similar encounter with the Lord. We'll let the great theologians sort it out. For me, I have a simple but strong faith, and I believe that "with God all things are possible" (Matthew 19:26).

CHAPTER 12

Susan, My Darlin' Daughter

Susan, my favorite daughter—and my only daughter—is both a beautiful and very smart young lady. She graduated from Clemson University with a civil engineering degree and a master's degree in hydrogeology. She made great grades in her undergraduate work and straight A's in her master's work. She has both her professional engineer and licensed geologist credentials, which is also somewhat rare, especially for a young woman.

Shortly before Susan graduated with her engineering degree, I put my affairs in order. I prepared for my death. In 1987, when I had the heart attack, I prayed and asked God to "let me live long enough to raise my daughter. Then, when she's old enough to take care of herself, if you still want me dead, kill me, I don't give a xxxx." God spared my life from the heart attack and let me raise my daughter. I truly expected God to answer the second half of that prayer now and take my life. But He allowed me to continue living. Then when she was about to graduate with her masters, I again put my affairs in order. This time I was sure God would answer the second half of that prayer and now take my life. But years later, I'm still here. Could be my Lord kept me around to write this book.

The Red Honda CRX

When Susan was in high school, she wanted to buy her first car. She wanted a red Honda CRX with manual transmission. My requirements were that it be a one-owner with low mileage and mechanically sound. She looked and looked but could not find the car she wanted.

At that time, when people around here sold used cars, they ran the three-day, weekend, special-rate ads in the newspaper. We checked the Friday and Saturday papers, with no luck. Saturday evening, we sat on the couch and talked about a car, because Susan was in a really down mood. I asked her if she had prayed about the car, and she said she had not. I suggested she pray and ask God for the car. That Saturday night, I prayed, and Susan prayed (at least, I did).

When we checked the Sunday paper, there was a red Honda CRX with a manual transmission. It was a one-owner with low mileage. It had never been wrecked and was in really good shape. Susan had her first car. Even though I truly believe God answered this prayer (no one lists a car for sale for just one day), I'm not sure that Susan gave God credit for finding the car. Susan reminds me a lot of myself. When I had the heart attack in 1987 and God spared my life, I did not bother to thank God either.

The 420 Mile Hike

After Susan graduated from college with her master's degree, she told me that before she started working, she and her friend, Maggie, wanted to fly to Southern California and hike about 420 miles on the Pacific Crest Trail. This trail is similar to the Appalachian Trail in the east. I thought, *Are you kidding me?* First of all, it would take six weeks to hike all those miles, and there are bears, panthers, and weird people out there, all of whom attack beautiful, young girls. I was totally against letting her go, but after much talking and persuading on Susan's part, and much prayer on my part, I agreed. I could tell how important this was to Susan, so I prayed and gave my daughter back to God and asked Him to take care of her. He did just that.

Susan and Maggie worked out all the details. They planned out all their food, clothes, tent, cooking equipment, water, and the most important item, a can of "bear spray." Susan also bought an expensive pair of hiking boots that would hold up to a 420-mile hike.

After several weeks of hiking, about three hundred miles down the trail, a problem developed: the stitches on the ankle support of her boot ripped apart. Susan and Maggie tied the shoe together the best they could. They still had over one hundred miles to hike. As they approached one of the trail stopping points, there, lying on the ground on the trail, was a pair of hiking boots. Not just a pair of boots, but a pair of size 7-1/2 women's hiking boots, like she wore. They were already broken in, and they fit perfectly.

Susan said that it's not uncommon for first-time hikers to pack too much gear and along the way to "toss" some of the surplus gear. The girl ahead of them had probably packed a spare pair of boots. Some people would call this a coincidence, but I don't. I call it another "God incidence." Things like that don't just happen. They saw no other boots on the trail during the 420-mile hike. But after three hundred miles, when Susan's boots were falling apart, these spare boots suddenly appeared. I had prayed and turned Susan over to the Lord for His safekeeping, and my God was answering my prayers.

Please Pray

Several times while at Clemson, Susan would call home and in a very sad and down tone of voice say, "Dad, I need for you and your friends to pray for me. I've got this big exam coming up, and I know I'm going to blow it." I would always call my good friend, Chris, and ask him to pray for Susan. Our prayers were always answered with high grades.

When Susan was preparing to take her licensed geologist exam, she called twice—before and after the exam. The before call was to ask us to pray for her when she took the exam. Her undergraduate degree was in civil engineering, not in geology. She had taken some geology courses in graduate school, but she hadn't taken all of the geology classes the other students had. We prayed for her to not only pass the exam, but to do well. After she took the exam, she called, very upset. She said she thought she had done well on most of the exam, but she didn't like the ways a couple of questions were presented. She wrote the exam officials a paragraph about how she felt the questions should have been asked and then gave her answers to the questions. She said it was legal to do this, but you had better be 100 percent right when you found issues with their questions. You had also better be 100 percent right in the way you presented your answer.

I can't imagine taking an exam in college and writing a note to my professor to say he doesn't know how to ask a question and then telling how the question should have been presented. We continued praying and turned the matter over to the Lord. When the test scores came back, she not only passed the exam, but she made a very good score.

All of Susan's prayers were answered with the outcome she requested. What is the probability of that happening? I don't think it would qualify for coincidence. It would certainly qualify as another "God incidence." Our God took care of my beautiful daughter.

For Dads and Moms

There are two things I talk about with anyone who will listen to me. The first, and most important, is Jesus Christ. The second is about being the man (or in some cases, the woman) of the house. Mom told me about my grandfather (my dad's dad), whom I never knew because he died when Dad was in college. He was a very smart and hardworking man, and he was very successful in the eyes of the world. Mom told me about how he raised my dad. My grandfather would wake the kids before daylight and give each of his children a list of chores to complete: some were to be done before school, and some were to be done after. When granddad came home, if the homework and chores were not completed successfully, Dad would usually get a whipping. I could tell you more, but the point is, my dad was "raised hard."

When it was time for my dad to raise his children, he did what he had learned growing up. He worked hard all day and let Mom raise the kids. Dad would come home from work and usually discipline me because my chores and my homework were not completed. There was usually very little family time. I remember Dad taking me squirrel hunting one time, and the hunt lasted about thirty minutes. Dad just didn't know how to spend time with us one-on-one, because he had never experienced that relationship with his dad. He knew only work.

It's a learning experience: children learn from their dads and moms, and these learning experiences are handed down from generation to generation.

Now it was time for me to raise my daughter. I learned from my dad to work hard, so spending "quality" time with my daughter was something I did not know about. I thought my job was to work hard, make money, and put groceries on the table. Even after I became a single parent, I worked two jobs, because I thought my number-one responsibility was to put the bread on the table.

I remember one summer in particular. Susan was twelve years old, and the school year had just ended. She came to me one Saturday morning and asked, "Dad, can we go out in the boat today?"

I told her, "No, darlin', I'm working two jobs. I have to work on this porch I'm building for some friends."

She said, "OK, Dad, maybe some other time."

The next Saturday morning, I was loading my tools in the truck for work on my side job. Susan again came to me and said, "Dad, can we go out in the boat today?"

This time I snapped at her and said, "No, Susan! I have to work two jobs so I can put food on the table and pay all our bills!"

She again said, "OK, Dad."

I worked my second job several evenings during the week and every Saturday and Sunday that summer. Then, the last weekend of the summer, Susan came to me again as I was loading my tools in my truck. She said, "Dad, I guess we're not going out in the boat this summer, are we?"

When she said that, I felt a knife go through my heart. The summer had come and gone, and I had spent very little time with my daughter because I worked two jobs all summer. I did not take Susan and her friends out in the boat one single time. The boat sat unused in our backyard. Once the time is gone, you don't get it back. That hurt was so painful that I never took another part-time job.

Parents, my purpose in telling you this story is this: so that you spend as much one-on-one time as you possibly can with your children. Spend as many hours as you can with them before it's too late. Once the time is gone, you don't get it back.

Dads, your sons and daughters also need to hear you tell them two things. First, hug them and tell them as often as you can that you love them. When they are old enough to understand, explain that you love them unconditionally and that you will always be there for them. Second, tell your son, "Boy, I'm real proud of you. You've turned into a fine young man, and I'm very, very proud of you." Your son needs to hear that from you, Dad. And tell your daughter, "Girl, I'm so proud of you. You've turned into an amazing, beautiful young lady, and I'm so grateful you're my daughter." You don't have to use those exact words, but whatever you tell them, make sure they know you truly mean it. In these early years, we guide and train our children. God says, "Start children off on the way they should go, and even when they are old they will not turn from it" (Proverbs 22:6). We only get one shot at raising our children.

Thirty Years' Worth of Hard Knocks

After Susan graduated from college, she would be heading to her first "real job." All her jobs up to that point had been summer and after-school jobs. Now she would be stepping into the real world as a professional.

I thought about what I could do to help her in this new environment. I had been a supervisor for over thirty years and had learned a lot, both good and bad. Most of what I had learned was by trial and error. I certainly had had my share of trials, and I made my share of errors. How could I help Susan avoid the mistakes I had made?

I decided to put together a list of brief pieces of advice to help her in her new job. Since I learned these things through "the school of hard knocks," I decided to call it "Thirty Years' Worth of Hard Knocks." I'm including the list here in the hope that it may help others.

Thirty Years' Worth of Hard Knocks for My Darlin' Daughter as She Steps Out into the Real World

1. You're a lady now...and a beautiful one at that. You'll be working in an engineering environment with mostly men. Don't try to be one of the boys just to be accepted, even though others might. You must earn the respect of others. Respect, trust, integrity, and honesty are the most important of all.

2. If you try to impress your boss, you will. It will be obvious. Just be yourself, and you will make a lasting good impression. Fakes are easy to spot.

3. Don't curse. You're a lady. Ladies don't curse. (Men shouldn't either.) If you curse, you'll be considered a trash mouth by others, and you will be talked about behind your back.

4. Don't be loud. Ladies aren't loud.

5. Choose your words carefully. Everything you say, even to your best friends, will be repeated...and probably to the person you're talking about. The employees who work for you one day will also repeat everything you say to them, even when you ask them to keep it confidential.

6. Look for the good in others. There's good and bad in all of us. It's just as easy to look for the good as it is the bad.

7. Don't live in the past. The past is gone. Learn from your mistakes and from the mistakes of others; then just carry on. Live for today, plan for tomorrow, and be thankful for your blessings.

8. Learn to listen. It's our human nature to want to butt in while others are speaking, but it's very rude. Rude people don't get ahead. I've observed company presidents and vice presidents in meetings...they do more listening than talking...and they don't interrupt others.

9. In a meeting, when you are talking and someone interrupts you, stop and let them talk. Then pick up where you were and continue with your statement. Don't try to talk over (louder than) them. Two wrongs don't make a right. You need to always be concerned about your reputation.

10. Never, never, never try to make yourself look good by making a coworker look bad. To the contrary. Try to help others, even if you are competing with them for a promotion. You'll win out in the long run.

11. Don't make end runs around your boss. Don't go over his or her head. If you don't like your boss, get another one: get another job. Work for your boss and support him or her—as well as your

boss's ideas. It's OK to disagree, but support your boss's final decision. Who knows? Your boss may actually be right.

12. Don't try to get even with someone who has wronged you. "What goes around will come around." They will get their just reward later...trust me, they will. If you try to retaliate, you will lower yourself to their level.

13. Don't take credit for work others have done. It's more important to give credit. When employees work for you, give them credit to their faces for their work. Give them credit for their work in meetings, even if they are not present. Word will get back to them, and they'll respect you even more. If you take credit for their work, they will dislike you, and the truth will eventually come out.

14. Pray for wisdom on when to speak and when to be silent and listen. A proverb says, "Even fools are thought wise if they keep silent, and discerning if they hold their tongues" (Proverbs 17:28).

15. When faced with a problem or when a customer comes to you with a request, don't give ten good reasons that something won't work. Look for at least one way to make it work. Those who continually give reasons that something won't work are considered negative roadblocks.

16. "I ain't got a dog in that fight": in meetings, when people are arguing about a matter that really does not affect you or your job, don't get in the middle of the argument or take sides. That's a no-win situation. If people ask why you haven't spoken, simply say, "I ain't got a dog in that fight!"

17. Choose your battles. If you know you're going to lose an argument or that your idea doesn't have a chance of being accepted,

then there's no point in arguing. It's better to lose a battle or two and win the war.

18. When people hurt you, your ideas are not accepted, or things just don't go the way you want, don't get hung up on it. Just forget it and keep moving ahead. Think back to thirty days ago. You can't even remember the things you were upset about. All things will pass, and time heals.

19. Most people just do the best they can. Sure, they are not perfect, but who is? Just accept and love people the way they are. Some people are smarter than others, but for their level of smarts, most people are probably doing just about the best they can. Concentrate on doing your best and don't be judgmental of others.

20. When friends are upset because of the loss of a job, a death in the family, or other hurts and disappointments, they are really not interested in your opinions or advice. You've probably never experienced what they're going through anyway. What they really need at a time like this is a friend who will listen. When they ask, "Why did God let my brother die?" you might answer, "I don't know. What do you think?" Or you might ask, "How do you feel about that?" Then sit and be silent. Just listen and let your friend pour out his or her hurt feelings. When people are hurting, they need someone who cares enough to listen, not to give advice. And never repeat to others what was said. Later on, your friend won't remember any advice you might have given but will never forget that you were there, you listened, and you cared.

21. When others cut down a coworker in a group or at a meeting, don't join in. If anything, say something good about the victim who is being stabbed in the back. Don't stoop to the level of the others.

It's better to have the respect of others than to be in the spotlight for a few minutes. True friends are hard to come by.

22. "Do not throw your pearls to pigs" (Matthew 7:6). Some people just will not listen to good advice. Even when you see them doing dumb things, they just won't listen to correction. So don't bother; they'll dislike you for pointing out their mistakes.

23. Always listen when others criticize you. If what they say upsets you a little, they may be right. You may deserve some of the criticism and might be able to change your actions to prevent future problems. If they are full of hot air, just stand there and let what they say go over your head, and then say something like, "I really appreciate you pointing that out to me, I never realized..."

24. WWJD: What Would Jesus Do? When you have a tough choice to make or you are uncertain about what to say, think: *What would Jesus do if he were here?* Because Jesus is here. God is always with us. Pray and ask Jesus what to do. Then listen, and you'll make the right choice.

25. Honesty is the best policy. It really is. Even if it means losing your job or a friend. If your boss asks you to lie, simply explain that because of your personal morals and values, you can't do that. If you lose your job because you would not lie or cheat, your good reputation will follow you. If you do lie, cheat, or even just "stretch the numbers a little," you will eventually be found out. The person who asked you to lie will no longer trust you either, because he or she knows you will lie. Be honest. You'll get a better job, and your reputation will be even stronger. No one has any use for liars and cheats, and no one trusts them. Your college degree won't get you jobs in the future, but your reputation will.

26. Dress like a lady. Your reputation depends on it. If you try to impress others with real short skirts and low-cut blouses, you will. If you dress like someone other than a lady, you'll be considered as

such by men as well as by other women (even if *they* dress like that). You're a professional now, so you need to dress like one.

27. Accept responsibility for your mistakes. Don't try to cover them up. We all make mistakes. The only people who don't make mistakes are the people who don't do any work. I've never fired anyone who made a mistake, even if it was costly to correct it. But I don't have any use for people who make mistakes and hide them. The hidden mistakes usually come out later and are often more costly to correct.

28. Give praise in public and criticism in private. When someone who works for you does something well, recognize him or her right away. Give a pat on the back and a genuine thank-you, or better yet, recognition in a meeting in front of others. But when your workers make mistakes, never discuss the problems with them in front of others. Go to your office or another place and talk in private with them. And don't put off talking with a worker about the problem. Deal with it and get it behind both of you.

29. Don't worry about the small stuff—and everything is small stuff. Worry doesn't help; it only clogs up your mind.

30. Where to get wisdom: There are thirty-one chapters in the book of Proverbs in the Bible. Read one chapter every day. On the first day of the month, read chapter one. On the second day of the month, read chapter two...then start over next month. By the end of the year, you will have read each verse twelve times. Then start over next year. You'll never understand all of the wisdom in Proverbs, but as you read and learn and apply the wisdom in Proverbs to your life, you'll grow in wisdom and stature.

31. Where to find love: Read 1 Corinthians 13. Love comes from giving, not taking. True giving is when you give and expect no recognition or anything in return.

32. Know your audience. I once told a man, "You lie a lot." I said it as a joke. He did not comment when I said it but obviously thought I was serious. A few days later, the president of his company wrote a letter to the president of my company and told him I had called his professional-level employee a liar. This was almost a JEM (job-ending mistake) on my part, but it all worked out. Be careful who you kid around with and what you say.

33. Don't always agree with others. A coworker may say something like, "Boy, did you see that dumb thing Jane did"? If you say, "Yes, I saw the dumb thing she did," it will get back to Jane that you said she did the dumb thing. Simply answer, "We all make mistakes. I've made a few myself, haven't you?"

34. Too much wine is a mocker. It's OK to have a glass of wine with your meal or a beer at an oyster roast. But if you have two, then it will become three, and then four...then there goes your reputation....and another JEM. You'll be talked about behind your back. Be the professional lady that you are.

35. When you are invited to eat lunch with the boss or an important client, don't pig out. You will be considered a glutton. Eat light. When invited to a meeting where sweet rolls and coffee are served, maybe drink a cup of coffee or a Coke, but pass on the sweet rolls. You can't talk if your mouth is full of sweet rolls. First impressions are important...very important. Pig out later.

36. Tell clean jokes, or don't tell jokes at all. Never tell racial jokes or use racial slurs, even to close friends. When others tell off-color jokes, don't slap your knee and laugh. If you do, you will condone them, and that's almost as bad. Remember...it's your reputation.

37. I want. I wish. It's our human nature to look at others who have better cars, better jobs, and bigger houses. But how often do we look at those who have less than we have? It's our human nature. Our eyes always see and want more. When you start wanting, stop for a moment. Look around and be grateful for what God has already given you. There is an old saying: "I once complained because I had no shoes until I saw the man who had no feet." Be grateful for what you have.

38. Eliminate "you" and "I" from your vocabulary. When correcting an employee, try not to say, "I noticed you were late three times this week." It's better to say, "We need to discuss this tardiness problem." Try to talk about the problem (tardiness) and not the person (you).

39. The Fool (taken from the book of Proverbs in the Bible):

"A chattering fool comes to ruin" (10:10).

"The way of fools seems right to them, but the wise listen to advice" (12:15).

"Fools show their annoyance at once, but the prudent overlook an insult" (12:16).

"A fool is hotheaded and yet feels secure" (14:16).

"A quick-tempered person does foolish things" (14:17).

"Even fools are thought wise if they keep silent, and discerning if they hold their tongues" (17:28).

"Fools find no pleasure in understanding but delight in airing their own opinions" (18:2).

"It is to one's honor to avoid strife, but every fool is quick to quarrel" (20:3).

"Do not speak to fools, for they will scorn your prudent words" (23:9).

"Wisdom is too high for fools" (24:7).

"Do not answer a fool according to his folly, or you yourself will be just like him" (26:4).

"As a dog returns to its vomit, so fools repeat their folly" (26:11).

"Do you see a person wise in their own eyes? There is more hope for a fool than for them" (26:12).

"Those who trust in themselves are fools, but those who walk in wisdom are kept safe" (28:26).

"Fools give full vent to their rage, but the wise bring calm in the end" (29:11).

"Do you see someone who speaks in haste? There is more hope for a fool than for them" (29:20).

And this is the greatest fool of them all: "The fool says in his heart, 'There is no God'" (Psalm 14:1).

40. Two things are absolutely certain in this life. Since you are now a brilliant engineer, you know all about absolutes. They are: (1) My love for you, and (2) God's love for you. Occasionally I may not like something you do, but that has nothing to do with my loving you. God will never turn his back on you, and neither will I. You're the best daughter I could ever have asked for. I would never even try to change anything about you. You are special. There is absolutely nothing you are capable of doing that can change my love for you. Never, never, never forget this. No matter what happens, no matter how well you do in the future, no matter how bad you might mess up in the future, no matter what...my door is always open. I will always love you. God's love for you is unconditional. My love for you is unconditional. One day when I leave this earth, please know for certain that I'll be with Jesus Christ in Heaven. Jesus Christ is real. He's alive and doing well. I am absolutely certain of this. And one day, when your life on this earth is finished and you come to join us in Heaven, Jesus and I will be there with open arms to welcome you home.

I love you, my darlin' daughter.
Dad

CHAPTER 13

"DOING THE BILLY"

I truly love working with the Billy Graham Telephone Ministry. I call it "doing the Billy." The Billy Graham Classics are on TV almost every week. These are replays of Billy Graham's and Franklin Graham's Crusades. While a classic is playing on TV, at the bottom of the TV screen, the words "To Begin a Relationship with Jesus Christ, call 1-877-772-4559" appear. When people call this number, the call goes to the Billy Graham telephone center. The call is then transferred to member churches throughout America for answering. In 2005, our church agreed to take part in this ministry and answer telephones for the Billy Graham Evangelic Association (BGEA).

At first, I was a little anxious that a caller might ask a question I could not answer. I quickly realized that the Holy Spirit of God was right in the center of this ministry. Probably 98 percent of the calls I have answered are relatively routine and to the point. People want to "get saved," and we guide them through receiving Jesus as their Lord and Savior. Other callers are hurting and ask for prayer, and it is truly an honor to pray with them.

There have also been a few calls that were not what I would consider routine. The Holy Spirit actually spoke to some callers;

there were calls where demons were cast out, and calls where curses were broken. Since our God has brought up these unusual calls, I'll share them with you. The names of the callers and certain details have been changed to protect identities, but the essence of each report remains factual.

The Brain Injury

Sam called the BGEA, and I asked if he wanted to receive Jesus Christ as his Savior. He said, "No, I'm already a Christian."

I asked, "Well, sir, how may I help you?"

He said, "Can you tell me why God is punishing me? I'm doing all I can, and I just can't take it anymore. Why is God punishing me?"

I told him, "Sir, I don't know. Tell me what's going on."

He said, "I have bleeding ulcers. I have problems with my knees. I have problems with an old back injury. I have financial problems, and I can't work because I have to stay home and take care of my wife. I can't take it anymore. I'm a Christian, so why is God doing all this to me?"

I don't think God punishes us right now. I know God tests us, but the day of punishment will come later for nonbelievers. I said, "God will not give us any more than we can handle, but it sure sounds like your plate is full."

He then started talking about his wife, Paula. He said, "Do you think God will make an exception for my wife, Paula? She has severe brain damage from an automobile accident nine years ago and is confined to a wheelchair. I have to spoon-feed her, bathe her, and do everything for her. I know I'm a Christian. I know that when I die, I'll go to Heaven. But my wife is not a Christian. I know she'll go to Hell, because she has severe brain damage from the automobile accident, and now she can't ask Jesus into her heart. Do you think God would make an exception for her and let her into Heaven to be with me?"

I asked if maybe she had accepted Christ as a child. He said she had not; they had talked about it in the past. He said they had discussed Jesus many times before her brain injury, and she just did not believe in God. His preacher talked with her, and she would not receive Christ. He said, "I know she's not a Christian, and I know she's going to Hell." He said, "I pray for her all the time—all day, every day."

I asked him when Paula was the most comfortable. He said it was when he spoon-fed her at the kitchen table. He said she could not talk, but he could tell when she was hungry, when she needed her brief changed, when she was ready for bed, and so forth. He said, "I know what she wants even without her being able to ask. We're that close." I asked him if I could speak with Paula. He said, "You don't understand. She can't speak. She sometimes makes noises, and I know what she wants because I love her, but no one else can understand her." He said, "And she hasn't spoken on the telephone in years."

I told him, "OK, here's what we'll do. I want to pray for you and Paula and about all that's going on in your lives. You truly have a tremendous load on your shoulders, and Jesus will share your load with you. After I pray, I'll hang up the telephone." I told Sam, "When I hang up, you roll Paula's wheelchair over to the kitchen table. She will feel comfortable with you. Then you tell her about Jesus and ask her if she wants to ask Jesus into her heart. Beg her if you have to. If she will come to Christ for anyone, it will be for you."

Sam said, "No, it won't work. I've begged her before, but she just doesn't understand what I'm talking about. The brain damage is too severe. It's just too late."

I told him, "Nothing is impossible for God. I want you to promise me that after we hang up, you will try. Give God a chance."

He said, "OK."

I prayed for Sam, and then I prayed for Paula. I prayed that Paula would be able to ask Jesus into her heart. As soon as I finished praying, I intended to say, "God bless you, Sam," and hang up. As I prayed, "In Jesus's name, amen" and was about to say, "God bless you, Sam," my mouth opened, and words came out. It was not me speaking. It was the Holy Spirit speaking through my mouth again. I was shocked when it happened, because I did not expect it.

Whenever God has done this in the past, He has never given me a "heads up" on what He's about to do—He just does it. Since this had happened before, I was not alarmed or afraid. I just rode it out and waited to see what would happen next. My mouth opened, and the Holy Spirit said, "Put Paula on the telephone."

Sam said, "I just told you, Paula hasn't spoken on the telephone in years. She can't even speak. She makes noises, and I can understand what she wants, but others can't understand the noises she makes."

My mouth opened again, and the Holy Spirit spoke those same words again. "Put Paula on the telephone."

This time, Sam said, "OK, but it won't do any good."

God says a lot in only a few words, and when He does repeat himself, it is usually with the same exact words. He does not explain what He's doing. He just tells us what to do and expects us to obey.

I could hear Sam say, "Paula, there's a man on the telephone who wants to talk to you." He repeated his statement. "Paula, there's a man on the telephone who wants to talk to you." Right then, I was thinking, *Is the Holy Spirit going to talk with Paula, or is the Holy Spirit going to give Paula to me?*

Then in a voice as clear as a bell, Paula said, "Hello." I paused to see if the Holy Spirit was going to again speak through my mouth. He did not.

I said, "Paula, my name is Kelly. I work with the Billy Graham Association. Have you been watching Billy Graham on TV with your husband?" And while I was speaking, I thought, *What do I do now? This lady has severe brain damage.*

Then Paula spoke. "Yes, I have."

I said, "Paula, at the end of the program, Billy Graham asked people if they wanted to ask Jesus to come into their hearts. Did you see that on TV?"

Paula answered, "Yes, I did."

I asked, "Paula, would you like to ask Jesus to come into your heart?"

Paula answered, "Yes, I would."

I then told Paula, "The Bible says, 'Everyone who calls on the name of the Lord will be saved'" (Romans 10:13). I told Paula that at the end of Billy Graham's program, many people come forward, and he prays with them to ask Jesus into their hearts. I asked, "Would you like for me to pray a prayer with you, and you pray it after me, asking Jesus into your heart?"

Paula again answered, "Yes, I would." I prayed the sinner's prayer with her, a few words at a time. She very clearly prayed each word of the prayer. As we were praying, it was like my brain began functioning again. I was thinking, *Can this be real? She's not supposed to be able to talk, but she's talking, and she knows what she's talking about. Does she really understand what's going on? Do I really understand what's going on?*

As soon as we finished praying the sinner's prayer, I wanted to make sure this was real. I asked, "Paula, do you understand that you and I are sinners, and we need a savior, and Jesus Christ is the only Savior that is acceptable to God?"

She answered, "Yes, I understand that."

I asked, "Paula, do you really believe that?"

Paula, in her clear voice, answered, "Yes, I believe that. *Do you really believe that?*"

I answered, "Yes I do, Paula. God bless you, my friend." And without thinking, I hung up the telephone. I often wish I had kept Paula on the telephone and talked with her further. I would like to know if God healed Paula completely or if God answered Sam's many prayers and gave Paula a five-minute open window to "get saved." I do know that when Sam and Paula die, they will both be together for eternity with our Savior in Heaven. God answered Sam's impossible prayer, and Paula is now a Christian.

The Lady with a Curse

A lady named Tracy called and asked, "Do you know how to break a curse that's been placed on a Christian?"

I replied, "Yes ma'am. Would you like for me to help you with that?" She explained she was a strong Christian and had been so for over sixty years. Her whole life had been OK until a few months prior, when everything began going wrong for her. She lost her job and had to move out of her house. She became sick, her car broke down, and she fell and broke her leg. Her list went on and on.

I asked if she knew who put the curse on her. She said she had prayed about it, and God had revealed that her sister had done this to her. They had had an argument a few months earlier, and that was when her troubles started. We prayed together and broke the curse. As soon as we finished praying, she said, "It's gone. I felt the curse lift off me. Jesus just set me free from the curse." When we pray to break a curse, we do not send the curse back to the originator. God says to "Bless those who curse you, pray for those who mistreat you" (Luke 6:28). Send the curse to Jesus and pray blessings on the originator of the curse.

The Lady from Hell

I answered the telephone and asked, "Did you call to ask Jesus to be your Savior and Lord?"

Janice said, "No, I want to know how to get to Heaven." It was obvious that Janice did not have a clue, because asking Jesus to be our Savior is the only way to Heaven. She said, "I've already been to Hell and returned. I know that if Hell is real, Heaven must also be real. Can you tell me what it takes to get into Heaven when I die? I don't want to go back to Hell."

I told Janice, "I'll be glad to tell you what God says we must do to get into Heaven. But first, would you tell me what Hell was like? I've never talked with anyone who has been to Hell." She explained that she had a bad heart problem. Her medication was not working, so she had called 911. While in the emergency room, on the table, something had happened.

She said, "I was in the air, looking down at my body lying on the table. I couldn't understand how that could happen." (She didn't know that she had a spirit in her body, and her spirit was leaving town. Her body was dead.) She continued, "The next thing I knew, I was in an awful place. Fires were burning everywhere. I was stretched out over this canyon, and fires burned under me. I felt the flames. The smell of burning flesh was everywhere. I heard others screaming. These ten-foot-tall 'beings' tortured me. They had ten-inch-long, razor-sharp fingernails that cut through my flesh. The pain was horrible, but I did not bleed, and I knew I would not die."

She said, "You know, I became aware of something very strange. Somehow, I knew time no longer existed. There was no longer night or day—just forever. I knew I was there forever." She continued, "Then, far off in the distance, I saw what looked like a hand coming toward me. As it got closer, I heard a voice say, 'It's not your time yet.' All of a sudden, I was back in my body on the table in the emergency room." She again said, "I know if Hell is real, Heaven must also be real. I want to know what I have to do to get into Heaven. Can you help me?" We talked, and she prayed and asked Jesus to be her Savior and Lord of her life.

Do I believe Janice visited Hell? Yes, absolutely. Books have been written by people who have been to Hell and come back. My friend Jack once talked with a woman who said she had been to Heaven and back, and she wanted others to know. God allowed these women to get a glimpse of Heaven and Hell and come back to tell us. I believe God loves us that much. The Bible says, "God our Savior, who wants all people to be saved and to come to a knowledge of the truth" (1 Timothy 2:3-4).

Janice told me, "Most of the people I tell about Hell don't believe me, so I don't talk much about the experience anymore."

I told her, "God allowed you to come back not only to give you a second chance, but for you to warn others. Share your experience and warn everyone who will listen to you."

The Man with Satan's Hook

I answered the phone and asked if the caller wanted to ask Jesus to be his Lord and Savior. Ron said, "No."

I replied, "Then sir, how may I help you?"

Ron was angry. He said, "You and Billy Graham say Jesus is the only way. I just don't believe that. I have good friends who are better people than some of you Christians. I have friends who are Muslims and Hindus, and they are real good people. Are you telling me they are going to Hell just because they don't believe in what you and Billy Graham believe?"

I told him, "Sir, it is about what you and I choose to believe. God loves all of us and gives each of us a choice. We can choose what God says in the Bible, or we can reject it. We can choose what Jesus did for us on the cross, or we can reject it. The Bible says that Jesus is the only way to eternal life in Heaven, and I personally choose to believe in Jesus." I had a three-page list of Scriptures pertaining to our sinful nature and God's plan for our repentance, forgiveness, and salvation. Each time I quoted a Scripture to Ron, he argued. I'd quote more Scripture, and he'd argue even more.

I told him whether or not he believes the Bible is God's word is immaterial. The Bible is still God's word. I told him he didn't have to believe in gravity either, but whether he believes gravity is real or not is also immaterial—gravity is still real. God's word is still real. His word is true and stands for us today. God's word never changes.

We try to limit our calls to fifteen minutes. If a person hasn't accepted Christ by then, or if we haven't prayed for their needs, we try to wrap up the call. There are often many other callers waiting for help. After fifteen minutes of listening to this man's arguments and slander of our Savior, I was ready to pray for him and hang up. But there were no other callers waiting, so I continued to quote Scripture and listen to his slanderous remarks.

When Jesus started His ministry, Satan tempted Him three times. All three times, Jesus responded by quoting Scripture, and then Satan left. I quoted Scripture for twenty-five minutes and was getting nowhere. Now other calls were coming in, and it was time to end Ron's call and take another.

As I opened my mouth to tell Ron I needed to go, the Holy Spirit spoke through my mouth using my voice. The words He spoke to Ron were, "Mister, I think Satan has a hook in you." When I heard the Holy Spirit say those words, I knew He was right on the money. For this man to have so much anger in his heart, Satan surely had a "hook" in him.

He burst into tears and said, "Yes, I've been listening to Satan's voice all afternoon. Can you help me?"

I said, "No, sir, I can't help you, but Jesus can. Do you want to ask Jesus to be your Lord and Savior?"

He answered, "Yes, please help me."

We prayed together the sinner's prayer, and Jesus set him free. We also prayed and renounced Satan's hold on him. When we wrapped up the call, he had the joy of the Lord in his heart. The Bible says, "Then you will know the truth, and the truth will set you free" (John 8:32). Jesus is that "Truth."

I've had the Holy Spirit speak through my mouth several times. I've witnessed the Holy Spirit speak through the mouths of others twice, both times while sharing the gospel over the telephone. I expect this is not very common, but God knows when we need help. We need only take that first step in faith and then trust God to work out the details.

The Preacher with a Demon

I asked the caller if he had called to ask Jesus to be his Lord and Savior. He said, "No. I'm already a Christian. I'm a preacher. I've been a preacher now for two years and I need your help."

I replied, "Well, then, sir, how may I help you?"

He asked, "Do you know how to cast out demons?"

I said, "Yes, sir, I do."

He asked, "Have you ever done it before?"

And I answered, "Yes, sir, many times over the last five years."

He said, "I have at least two demons in me, and I can't get them out. Can you help me with that?" I told him I could help and asked the preacher if he knew the names of the demons. He told me that Lust was the name of one, but he did not know the name of the other. Many times, if more than one demon is present, the demon spirit Confusion will also be present. No matter what their names, they are all subject to the authority of Jesus Christ (cf. Matthew 28:18).

I prayed with the preacher, and in the name of Jesus Christ bound the demons and cast them out. When we finished praying, I asked, "Preacher, what's going on now?"

He said, "They're gone! They're gone! I felt them leave me." He thanked me and went on his way. Jesus set the young preacher free.

Jane and Her Demons

Jane was full of demons and was hyperventilating when she called. She was really messed up, so I told her not to hang up the telephone. There was a powerful "strongman" present, and he did not want to budge. I think Jane was already a Christian, but we prayed the sinner's prayer anyway. I kept commanding the demons to leave in the name of Jesus Christ, but they wouldn't budge. Jane continued hyperventilating. She kept telling me, "They won't leave! Help me! Help me! Help me!" I asked if she knew the names of any of the demons. She said, "I know one is Pornography." Sure enough, Pornography was there, along with other strongmen.

> *When someone is oppressed by demons, it's as if a huge weight is sitting on their chests. The weight sometimes makes it difficult to function and even to breathe. When demons are cast out, breathing returns to normal.*

Finally, after fifteen or twenty minutes, the hyperventilating stopped. One by one, all the demons came out. Jane began breathing and talking normally. We prayed for the filling and protection of the Holy Spirit. I cautioned Jane about the demons returning (cf. Luke 11:24–26). I told her, "When they return, you rebuke them in the name of Jesus Christ. You're a Christian, and Jesus has given you the authority to do this." Jane said she would.

CHAPTER 14

Witnessing: Tell Them about Jesus

Saving Lives

Have you ever saved someone's life? I have. The first was my daughter's, when she was about two years old. Our friend, Teresa, and her two small children, my wife, my daughter, Susan, and I were at the beach. The ladies were in their beach chairs, working on their suntans and talking. The kids were playing in the sand, and I was waist-deep in the water, surf fishing. My wife called out to me to watch Susan, and I called back for *her* to watch Susan, because I was out standing in four-foot-deep water. As it turned out, neither of us did a very good job of watching our daughter.

As I fished, something inside me told me to check on Susan. I turned and looked behind me at the beach and saw everyone except Susan. I shouted, "Where's Susan?" She was not on the beach. She was gone. Then I clearly heard a voice tell me to "look to the deep water." I turned my head 180 degrees and looked out into the ocean. The heel of Susan's foot popped out of the water for less than half a second and then immediately went back under. She was caught up in a rip current that had already pulled her under the water, taken her past me, and was dragging her out into the ocean. I reached down into the water, grabbed her foot, and lifted her out of the water. She was gasping for air and crying, but she was OK. Thank you, Jesus!

One day as I was leaving work, I heard a man shout for help. I ran to him. His elderly father had just had a heart attack as he sat in his son's car. I told the young son to run to the first floor of the building across the street and tell the woman at the desk, "Code Blue, Parking Garage One." The son wanted to stay with his dad, who had no pulse and was not breathing. He was dead. I told the son again, "Go! Run! Now!"

I had taken Red Cross CPR training with our Southern Baptist Disaster Relief Group, but I had never done CPR on a dead man. Initially, I was so shocked that I did everything wrong. I tried to administer CPR while he was sitting in the car, which just doesn't work. I realized my mistake, pulled him out of the car, and laid him on the concrete. I began CPR again, but it still didn't work. Then I heard a voice say, "Check his airway." This is one of the first things I should have done. The man's false teeth were blocking his airway, so I removed them and started CPR a third time, and it worked. After I pumped his chest and breathed for him for about ten minutes, there was a pulse, and he started breathing on his own. About five minutes later, the Code Blue team from the hospital and the man's son arrived. One of the men said, "You did well. He's alive. We'll take over now."

A few years later, the same thing happened with another young man and his father. This time, I remembered my mistakes from the last heart-attack victim. The elderly man had no pulse and had stopped breathing. He was dead. His son and I laid his father on the concrete, and I started the CPR while the son went for help. By the time the Code Blue team arrived, the man had a pulse and was breathing. The Code Blue team took him to the hospital. His son thanked me, and I went on my way.

One summer, a group of families from church rented canoes, and we floated down the Edisto River. We would canoe for a while and then pull the boats up on a sandbar. The adults just relaxed while the kids swam in the river and played in the sand. At one stop, while the kids were playing and having a good time, Kim, who was sitting next to me under a shade tree, said, "Ellison, go help that little girl! She needs help!"

I looked at the little girl, who was maybe five years old. She was just standing there while the other kids near her were playing. I told Kim, "She's OK. The kids are just playing."

Kim again insisted, "No! Go help that little girl! Go now!"

I said, "Kim, that little girl is OK. If you think she needs help, you go help her."

Kim again said, "No! You go! Go right now!"

I casually got up and walked over to the little girl. I knelt down in front of her and said, "Darlin', are you OK?" She didn't say anything. I looked into her eyes and saw they were glazed over as she stared off into the distance. I asked again if she was OK, but she did not answer.

A little boy who was playing in another area of the beach casually walked over to us and said, "She can't breathe."

I said, "Little girl, can you breathe? Breathe for me, little girl!" I placed my hand on her chest, but it did not move. She was not breathing, but there was no indication she was choking. Normally, people grab their throats if they're choking, but she never did this or anything else. She just stood there.

Out of the corner of my eye, I saw the woman running toward us with her hand in the air, getting ready to slap the girl on the back. I shouted at her, "No!" She stopped dead in her tracks and didn't move. If you slap a choking person on the back, you will often drive the choking object further down into the windpipe. I moved around behind the little girl and placed my fist and hand at the bottom of her rib cage and did the Heimlich maneuver. I was afraid I'd hurt the little girl, so I didn't pull hard enough, and it didn't work.

She began to fold over, passing out from lack of oxygen. I grabbed her shoulder and straightened her up. The second time I pulled, I jerked the little girl three feet into the air, and a large piece of rock candy popped out of her windpipe. She gasped for air. She was OK. I went back and sat beside Kim, and we didn't even discuss what happened. It was just another day with the Lord.

> *If you don't know how to do CPR and the Heimlich maneuver, I encourage you to contact your local Red Cross office and take this training. Performing CPR and the Heimlich maneuver are not difficult at all. I've read that the sixth most common cause of accidental death in the United States is choking or strangling. You may one day have an opportunity to save someone's life and possibly the life of a member of your own family.*

Think about these four incidents. Think about the timing and all the things that had to fall into place at exactly the right time and sequence in order to have successful outcomes. My Christian friends and I don't call them coincidences; we call them "God incidences." Split-second timing was absolutely required when Susan's heel popped out of the water. Her foot had popped out for less than a half a second, and then she would have disappeared forever. I clearly heard the Holy Spirit's voice tell me to "look to the deep water." When the two men had heart attacks, I just happened to be working late both of those days, though everyone else in our department had gone home. If I had not been a Christian and part of the Southern Baptist Disaster Relief Unit, I would not have known how to perform CPR.

Why did Kim keep insisting that I go help that little girl? Why didn't she ask another nearby adult? Why didn't she, a mother of two, jump up and run to the aid of the child? Mothers do stuff like that, but men are too hardheaded. I asked Kim later why she kept insisting that I help the girl, but she didn't know. She said she just knew that I needed to help her. She did not know the girl was choking, but something prompted her to tell me rather than any of the other adults right beside us on the sandbar.

I know the Lord is always at work, and so are His angels. Out of the four above events, there was only one thing that I couldn't figure out at the time. How did the little boy, who was not playing with the girl, but playing on another area of the sandbar, know that she couldn't breathe? How did he know to come tell me? Today, I know the answer. It's called the "spiritual gift of knowledge." It is when the Holy Spirit gives you a word. The Holy Spirit speaks, either audibly, silently, or through someone else, and gives you a piece of information that you need for prayer, for healing, or for whatever is in your face at that point in time. I've received a word many times in healing prayer sessions and when casting out demons. I've seen the Holy Spirit give others a word when it's needed in battle. In the little girl's case, the Holy Spirit sent this boy with a word that was needed right then. I didn't have a clue that the girl was choking, and God knew I didn't know. I don't think the boy knew either, but God sent him with the message, "She can't breathe." The Bible says, "For he will command his angels concerning you to guard you in all your ways" (Psalm 91:11).

It's wonderful that four lives have been saved, but what does that have to do with witnessing and sharing the gospel? The answer is: both nothing and everything. It is nothing because these were lives that were saved, not souls; everything, because their souls will live on forever in Heaven or Hell. The answer is also everything because God's timing, as with these four lives, is also critical in witnessing for Christ.

If you look at all the "God incidences" that had to happen in just these four cases, surely you must realize that something is going on here. It's called "spiritual warfare," which is about the Kingdom of God and the kingdom of the evil one battling over lives and souls. When you choose to be a witness for Christ, you volunteer to step right into the middle of the battle.

In Ephesians 6:10–11, God tells us to "Finally, be strong in the Lord and in his mighty power. Put on the full armor of God, so that you can take your stand against the devil's schemes." If we choose to "get in the fight," our God has given us weapons for defending ourselves. But we don't have to just stand there and take what Satan and his demons dish out. Our God has also given us two offensive weapons to use in battle: prayer and the sword of the Spirit, which is the Word of God. He has given us the Holy Spirit to guide us and a crowd of His angels to fight alongside of us.

In church, we call this witnessing, sharing the gospel, leading someone to Christ, helping someone make a decision for Christ, going forward in church, an altar call, and many other names. I still call it "telling people about Jesus," because that's what God called it when He told me to "Go tell Doug about Jesus." The other names are OK to use, because it's not about what you call it, it's about doing it.

Over the last twenty-five years, I've told hundreds of people about Jesus. Most of them have come to Christ, but some have said, "No thanks." In this chapter, I'll share some of my learning experiences and some testimonies.

I totally agree with what the Apostle Paul said: "For I am not ashamed of the gospel, because it is the power of God that brings salvation to everyone who believes" (Romans 1:16). I'll tell anyone and everyone that I've been bought and paid for by the blood of my Savior, Jesus Christ. And if they'll listen, I'll share the good news with them. I'm not ashamed of being a Christian, and I'm not ashamed of Jesus Christ. Jesus died for me, so I live for Him. Telling people about Jesus is not bad news. The bad news is that they will spend eternity in Hell if they are not Christians. I'm telling them the good news of how to spend eternity in Heaven with our holy God of creation.

After telling Doug and Kathy about Jesus, I thought, "That was easy. Now, what about my neighbors? They, too, need to know Jesus."

My Neighbors

I went next door to Phillip's house. I knew his wife went to church but that he did not. He was a neighbor and a good friend, so right off the bat, I asked him if he realized that he was going to Hell. He didn't think so. He said that he was as good as anyone else, and he really was. I could not convince him that he was a sinner and needed to be saved. As I walked back to my house, tears were running down my face. I thought I had failed God and that Phillip would go to Hell because I couldn't convince him he needed to be saved. When I got to the house, I prayed and told God how sorry I was that I had failed Him. I thought it was my fault, but I told God I would not quit.

I regained my composure and drove to a friend's house. I rang the doorbell, and Linda invited me in and asked what she could do for me. I told her I needed to talk to her and Mike, her husband. We all sat down in the den, and I proceeded to tell them, "I just got saved, and now I'm a Christian. I'm going to Heaven when I die. I want to tell you all about Jesus Christ."

Mike got up and headed to the bedroom area of their house. Linda got up and walked into the kitchen and continued cooking supper. Without a word, they both just left me sitting there in the den by myself. After about five minutes, I finally realized they were not coming back into the den.

I walked into the kitchen and said to Linda, "I guess you're not interested in hearing about Jesus, are you?"

Linda answered, "Nope, but thanks anyway."

I said, "Well, I guess I'll be going," and I left. As I drove home, tears were again flowing down my face. I thought I had again failed God and that they were going to Hell because of me. Again, on my knees I apologized to God for failing him. I told God that if my neighbors didn't want to hear about Jesus, I'd tell my friends at work.

Witnessing at Work

It wasn't long before I had to counsel a mechanic who worked for me. As we talked, I learned that he had a lot of personal problems. I told him that I also had my share of problems, but that Jesus had turned my life around. I asked him if he would allow me to tell him about Jesus, and he told me to go ahead. I had a Gideon New Testament in my pocket and used the Scriptures printed on the inside back cover.

He listened and had only a few, simple questions. I was grateful for that, because at the time, I had a very simple understanding of the Bible. I asked him if he wanted to pray the sinner's prayer printed on the back cover and ask Jesus into his heart. He said he did, so we both got on our knees, and as we prayed together, something happened: tears started streaming down his face. As I watched his tears flow and listened to his prayer, I knew something bigger than me was going on. I knew it was not a matter of my doing a great job of sharing the gospel, but a "God thing" was happening. I still did not have any idea who the Holy Spirit was, but I knew God had done this right in front of my eyes.

Church Visitation

In October, we started our Tuesday Night Visitation program at church. Each Tuesday evening, we would pair up and go door-to-door, inviting people to come to church. I met a new friend, Pete, who became one of my lifelong friends. I memorized some Bible verses that pertained to salvation and marked other verses in my Bible. I had the "Roman Road" Bible verses, and I had the verses in the back of my Gideon New Testament. I now felt more comfortable talking with others about Jesus.

Pete and I made a good team. Pete was a very quiet man, but when it came to prayer, he was dead serious. He had a very close relationship with his Savior. Pete and I usually did three things before we went visiting and sharing the gospel. The first thing we always did was pray. On the way to the visit, we would pray. As we pulled into the driveway, we prayed again. Prayer is, in my opinion, one of the most important parts of sharing the gospel. I still had a child's understanding of the Scriptures, and I still did not have a clue who the Holy Spirit was, but I knew that if God did not go with us on our visits, we would definitely fail.

Once inside a house, we would both chat with the folks for a few minutes, and then I would start sharing the gospel. Pete did what he did best: he sat quietly and prayed the entire time I was sharing the gospel. He prayed for the people we were visiting, and he prayed that God would give me the right words to say. God heard Pete's prayers. On many of those Tuesday evenings, one or two people would pray and ask Jesus to be their Savior and Lord.

It did not matter to me if the folks we visited were members of a church and had not attended in a while or whether they were just plain heathen. At the time, I did not understand how, but I knew if the people we talked with were already Christians. Later, when we did a study on spiritual gifts, I found out how I knew. No matter who we visited, if I knew someone was not a Christian, I always asked this question: "If you died tonight and the next thing you knew, you were standing before God and He asked you, 'Why should I let you into my Heaven?' what would you tell God?" There is only one correct answer to this question.

If they had no answer or gave the wrong answer, I would tell them, "You know, I used to think something similar to that, but I've been wrong before. Since this is a matter of life and death, I thought I'd better find out what God says about getting into His Heaven. I read His book, the Bible, cover to cover, and found that God said there's only one way to get into His Heaven. Would you let me tell you what God said in His Bible?" People would almost always tell us to go ahead. Then I would share the gospel, using as many Bible verses as I could put together.

Names in the Bible

During this early walk with the Lord, I listened to Dr. Charles Stanley on TV every week. One week, Dr. Stanley said that after we have led people to Christ, we should continue praying for them as they begin their journeys with the Lord. He said we could even write their names in the front of our Bibles to help us remember to pray for them. I thought, *That's a good idea. I'll keep praying for those who accept Christ.* I thought about the people we had visited over the previous months and wrote the names of over twenty people in the front of my Bible.

One evening while I was studying the Bible, I read in the gospel of Mark where Jesus talked about how good seed sown would "produce a crop—some thirty, some sixty, some a hundred times what was sown" (Mark 4:20). At work, we were putting together our annual plan, which called for setting goals and objectives. I thought about those names in the front of my Bible, and the thought came to my mind: *Set some goals and objectives for witnessing too.* I set a first goal of thirty. I thought, *When I reach this goal of thirty souls saved for Christ, I'll set the next goal of sixty, and then a goal of one hundred.*

Pete and I continued sharing the gospel on Tuesday evenings, and I continued talking with people at work and with anyone who would listen. Quickly the number of saved souls in the front of my Bible went to thirty. I patted myself on the back and told myself out loud, "Boy, you done good!" I thought this was all my doing. I told God, "OK, God, now we'll go for sixty souls."

We continued sharing, and I wrote in my Bible a name beside the number thirty-one. Then something happened: "Wham!" It was as if God slammed the door. Pete and I visited five houses the next Tuesday evening. We could not even get people to talk with us. We knew something was wrong.

At home that evening, I told Connie what had happened and that I was going into the bedroom to pray. I told her to leave me alone and that if she got ready for bed and I was still on my knees praying to just go on to bed. I told her that on Wednesday morning when she got up, if I was still on my knees, to call in to my work and tell them I would not be in that day. I fully intended to stay on my knees until God told me what I had done wrong. I'm not the smartest kid on the block, but I knew the problem was me. I had offended God, and I needed to ask his forgiveness.

On my knees, I prayed, "Father, I know I've screwed up. I don't know what I've done wrong, but I'm going to stay right here on my knees until you tell me." I was on my knees about an hour. It took that long for all the clutter of the day to filter out of my head. Then I clearly heard God's voice. He said, "You quit witnessing from your heart and started witnessing for numbers." I knew exactly what He was talking about, so I apologized to God and asked for His forgiveness. I went into the kitchen and told Connie how I had blown it.

I've been a Christian for twenty-five years and truly understand that Satan is trying to destroy us and tear down the Kingdom of God. Satan is our enemy. The Bible says, "For Satan himself masquerades as an angel of light" (2 Corinthians 11:14). I don't know if I came up with the idea of setting a thirty-sixty-one hundred goal all by myself or if Satan put that thought in my head. I do know that God was not going to put up with it, and he quickly straightened me out. The next Tuesday evening, Pete and I went out visiting, and people were again saved. I never wrote another name in the front of my Bible.

Witnessing Training

My heart was totally sold out to Jesus Christ, but I still had a lot to learn about sharing the gospel. Let me share a couple of witnessing experiences where my heart was right with God, but I simply did not have any training in sharing the gospel.

I remember a visit that I made by myself. The visit did not go well at all. I visited a man and tried to convince him that he was a sinner and needed a Savior. The man told me he was not a sinner. I asked him if he had ever told a lie, and he said, "Yes, I have. Have you?" I told him I had, and he said, "See, that's not sin. Everybody tells lies." Then I asked if he had ever stolen anything, and he said, "Yes, I have. Have you?" And, again, I told him I had, and he repeated, "See, that's not sin. Everybody steals."

I tried for ten minutes to convince him that he was a sinner and that he needed a Savior, but I could not. Then I blew it. I lost my temper, which is a terrible thing to do when witnessing for Christ. I said, "One day you will stand before God, and you will try to say you didn't know about Jesus. Then God is going to flash a picture of my face in front of you and remind you that I came to your house to help you get saved. You'll remember me, but it will be too late for you. You will then be cast into Hell." With that, I walked out the door. I think that's the worst I've ever blown it when sharing Christ with others.

About two years after I became a Christian, we had a training program at church to teach us how to share the gospel. I think most Christians would like to "lead someone to Christ," but they simply don't know what to say.

The program we used was called Continuing Witness Training. It was a major learning experience for me. The first class was about the role of the Holy Spirit in witnessing. I often thought if someone was saved, it was because I had done a good job. I thought that if someone did not get saved, I had failed God, and that person may very well go to Hell because I failed to do my part. In the first class, I learned that my role in sharing the gospel was to be God's messenger. My job was to deliver the gospel message to the best of my ability. If someone is saved, praise God, and if someone doesn't get saved, it is not my fault. This was a huge relief!

I learned that it was God's job to draw people to Christ. Jesus said, "No one can come to me unless the Father who sent me draws them" (John 6:44). And it was not my responsibility to convince anyone that they were sinners and needed a Savior. That was the Holy Spirit's job. Jesus said, "When he comes, he will prove the world to be in the wrong about sin and righteousness and judgment" (John 16:8). I learned a lot in that witnessing training, but I still had a lot more to learn.

One evening, after the classwork was done, my friends Jane and Pete and I went out for a visit. We were going to visit some folks who were members of a church but had not attended in quite a while. The plan was simple: we would all chat with them for a while, and then Jane would share the gospel while Pete and I sat quietly and prayed.

We chatted for about fifteen minutes. I kept waiting on Jane to lead into sharing the gospel, but she never did. I tried to lead into the gospel and hand it over to Jane, but each time I tried, she cut me off and changed the subject. I tried again and again, but Jane kept cutting me off. I could not understand what was happening.

Finally, I became so frustrated; I just got up and walked out of the house. I blew it again. I did not even say good night to the people we were visiting. I got into my truck and waited for Jane and Pete. I was terribly upset. About fifteen minutes later, Pete and Jane came out of the house. Pete got in the back seat of the truck and was laughing at me for leaving. As Jane got in the front seat, she said, "Oh, Ellison, that was a great visit. Why did you leave?"

I said, "No, Jane! That was a terrible visit! Why wouldn't you share the gospel with those people? Why wouldn't you let me share the gospel? Couldn't you see they were totally lost?"

Jane said, "Oh, they are Christians; they just haven't attended church in years."

I said, "No, it was clearly obvious that they are not Christians. Couldn't you see that?"

Jane saw how upset I was and said, "No Ellison, I couldn't tell they were lost. I don't have the gift of discernment. You do have that gift." Since I didn't know what she meant by "discernment," I shut up, and we drove back to the church.

When I got home, I looked in my new Bible dictionary to see what *discernment* meant. It's a spiritual gift. I could talk with a stranger or with someone I knew, and I somehow knew if they were a Christian. I had assumed it was that way with all Christians. A year or so later, we did a spiritual gifts study at church. I learned that the Holy Spirit had given me the gifts of faith, evangelism, and discernment, which all work as one when sharing the gospel. Telling others about Jesus is the primary work our Lord has assigned to me.

I've also learned that gifts such as discernment, for example, may involve different avenues for others. I know several Christians who have the gift of discerning evil spirits. One friend told me she could talk with a person for two or three minutes and tell if there were demons in him or her. I know two other women who can talk with a person only for a few minutes and tell if he or she can be trusted or is full of hot air. So what I'm saying is, there are many facets to the spiritual gifts our Lord gives us. I realize today that our Lord equips us for whatever work He places in front of us. I still remember my good friend, Mr. Herman, telling me, "God has something else for you to do. I don't know what it is, but you will know it when you find it, because you'll love doing it for the Lord." We'll love doing it because the Holy Spirit has equipped us to do this work.

We later used another training program to train Christians to share the gospel. The training went well. I remember one man in our class said, "I love doing this so much, that I would pay good money just to be allowed to go out and share the gospel."

During one visit, I met Linda, who was already a Christian. Her husband, Jack, said he was also Christian, but I could tell he was not. We talked a few minutes, and he said that he had attended a Catholic church most of his life. I explained about sin, and the Bible said, "For all have sinned and fall short of the glory of God" (Romans 3:23). He acknowledged that he knew he was a sinner but suggested that we all sin. I asked him if he received a paycheck weekly or monthly, and he said monthly. I told him I knew his boss didn't just give him a paycheck. He was responsible for his work, and I was sure he earned his wages each month. He was fully responsible for what he did, and he therefore received his due payment.

Jack said, "Yes, I work hard, I and am responsible for my work. I earn my wages. They don't pay me just because they like me." I told him that the Bible says, "For the wages of sin is death" (Romans 6:23). I told Jack that he was totally responsible for his sin, and the due wages for his sin was death. I explained that death meant eternal separation from God in everlasting Hell. The Holy Spirit had already convicted Jack, and he knew he was guilty.

Jack threw up his hands and shouted, "Then we're all sunk! We're all sinners! We're all going to Hell! There's no hope for any of us!" The Holy Spirit was really working on Jack.

I told him, "No. God gives us one way out. It's Jesus. That Bible verse in Romans has two parts. Let me tell you the second half of the verse, which is the good news: 'But the gift of God is eternal life in Christ Jesus our Lord'" (Romans 6:23). Jack prayed and asked Jesus to be his Lord and Savior. Jack is now a deacon in his church.

Fear

There was still one big thing I needed to deal with: fear. Before going to visit someone, fear would engulf me. Negative thoughts would dart through my mind, and I would think, *What if they laugh at me? What if they spit on me? What if they throw me out?* What if? What if? What if? The fear was usually the greatest when I made a visit by myself. If someone went with me, the fear was minimal. Maybe that's why Jesus sent the disciples out in pairs.

On several occasions, I would have to stop the truck on the way, sit by myself, and pray for a while. Praying helped, but it did not completely eliminate the fear. I would still make the visit and share the gospel, even with the fear piled on me.

At the time, I did not understand Satan's tactics. Now, years later, I know his battlefield is in the mind. Satan attacks our thought process. Jesus said of Satan, "For there is no truth in him. When he lies, he speaks his native language, for he is a liar and the father of lies" (John 8:44).

> *Over the last twenty-five years, I've spoken with hundreds of people about Jesus, mostly one-on-one. I've never had anyone curse me out, throw me out, spit on me, or anything else. Not all the people accept Christ, but that's not my fault. It is my fault, however, if I don't tell them the good news about our Savior.*

When I go inside a house and start talking about Jesus, the fear leaves. I've learned that Satan hates the name of Jesus. When you mention the name "Jesus," Satan and his demons are out the door. I now know and understand much more Scripture than I did in the early years. I know that "the one who is in you is greater than the one who is in the world" (1 John 4:4).

Another thing I've learned is, we have to take that first step in faith. Peter knew he could walk on water, but he couldn't do it sitting in the boat. He had to get out of the boat and take that first step of faith. It's that way when we share the gospel. Our God-given faith and the name "Jesus Christ" send Satan and his demons of fear down the road. When we take that first step, the Holy Spirit takes over.

Fish the Deep Waters

I've learned how to be prepared. I pray a lot. I memorize Scripture that deals with the gospel. I carry a Gideon New Testament in my back pocket all the time, prepared to give it to someone who needs to know the Lord. I look for opportunities to share Christ with others. I don't just walk blindly through life, hoping I'll trip over someone who needs the Lord. I like going out into the deep water when I go fishing.

"Some went out on the sea in ships; they were merchants on the mighty waters. They saw the works of the Lord, his wonderful deeds in the deep" (Psalm 107:23–24). I've heard the saying that we can "sit on the dock and cut bait, or we can go fishing," and I choose to go fishing. Jesus told the disciples, "I will send you out to fish for people" (Matthew 4:19). The same applies to you and me today. Jesus said He will make us fishers of people, and I take God at His word.

I like fishing. I fish the creeks, the lakes, and the salt marshes. When I was younger, I went offshore to the Gulf Stream to fish. I still see the works of the Lord in the creeks and streams. But when fishing the deep waters offshore, where the water is several hundred feet deep, I get to see the clear, blue Gulf Stream water, the weed lines, flying fish, schools of beautiful dolphin under the boat, and the clear sky, horizon to horizon.

God gives each of us a choice. We can sit on the dock, cut bait, and talk and talk about fishing (sharing the gospel). Or we can go out fishing in the deep water and see His wonderful deeds. But to do that, we must take that first step. Over the years, I've made an important discovery:

The greater the challenge, the greater the fear, the greater the faith, and the greater the reward.

Today, instead of letting Satan and his demons harass me, I harass them. I take my prayers and the sword of the Spirit and go on the offensive. In Acts 19, Luke tells us about the seven sons of Sceva, a Jewish chief priest. They were not Christians, but they would go around casting out demons. They would say, "In the name of Jesus whom Paul preaches, I command you to come out" (Acts 19:13).

One day, an evil spirit spoke back to them and said, "Jesus I know, and Paul I know about, but who are you?" (Acts 19:15). Then the man with the evil spirit proceeded to whip all seven of their behinds.

I often pray and ask God to use me in such a powerful way, reaching the lost for Christ, that when I show up, the demons will say, "Oh, no, Ellison's here." I want those demons to say, "Jesus I know, and Paul I know about, and Ellison I know about..." I want to make such an impact for my Savior that Satan and his demons will know my name. Put another way, I once heard a preacher say, "Are there any wanted posters in Hell with your picture on them?"

Satan Pays a Visit

As described later in the chapter on near-death encounters, I had an accident on my ATV while deer hunting. I broke five of the seven cervical vertebrae in my neck. The doctors installed a halo brace on my head and placed me in a hospital bed. I asked the doctor, "How long will I be in the hospital?"

He replied, "A week," and he left the room.

I told my wife, who was standing beside my bed, "I'm not going to waste a week of my life just lying in this bed. Go home and get me a stack of Gideon New Testaments so I can give them out and share the gospel with people while I'm here in the hospital." She went home and brought back a stack of twenty Gideon New Testaments.

About fifteen minutes later, I went to work. I remember the first woman who came into the room to bring my first hospital meal. I remember saying, "Come over here, lady! I want to tell you about Jesus Christ!" And then everything in my head went blank. Things went blank for the next seven days. I had a concussion from the accident, and I did not know or remember anything or anybody for seven days. Connie said that people came by to visit and I talked with them, but I never knew it. My lights were out. To this day, I still have no memory of what happened in the hospital after the concussion set in.

One day after we came home from the hospital, I asked Connie what had happened to those twenty Gideon New Testaments. She said, "You gave out each one of them and shared the gospel twenty times." I never knew it.

I asked her, "How did I do?"
And she said, "You did a good job."

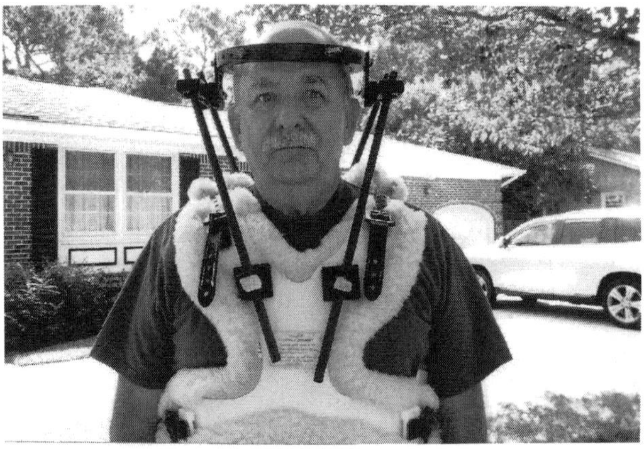

"This is the halo brace I wore for 3 ½ months"

When I was discharged from the hospital, I still could not even sit up in bed. The doctor had a hospital bed sent to the house, and Connie slept in a chair next to it. After a few days at home, it happened. I was lying awake in bed in the middle of the night, because the halo brace was painful. Connie was asleep in the chair at the left side of the bed. Then Satan came by for a visit.

I heard the voice of a man (out loud). He was standing on the right side of the bed, right beside my head. His voice was not overly loud, but firm, and he spoke very convincingly and with authority.

He said, "Ellison, you really messed up this time. You'll never be the same. You'll be paralyzed, and your wife will have to take care of you the rest of your life. Look at the burden you'll be on her. She'll have to take care of you, your mom, her parents, the kids, and she'll still have to work. You need to just go ahead and end it all right now. Get the pistol and end it now. You're a Christian. You'll go to Heaven. Just end it now. You have life insurance. Your family will be better off with the insurance money than with you paralyzed. Just end it now. Don't be a burden on your family."

He was so convincing that I was going to do exactly what he said. Even though suicide is a sin, I knew I would still go to Heaven, because Jesus died for all my sins. But the pistol was in the other bedroom, and I couldn't sit up in bed by myself. Connie would have to help me get up. I knew she would not help me get the pistol, so I put together a plan. I'd ask her to help me get up and walk me to the master bathroom. The pistol was only twenty feet away in the master bedroom, and I knew I could walk that far by myself. As I lay there putting together my plan to commit suicide, something snapped inside my head.

I realized who was standing beside my bed. I knew it was Satan. Without giving it any thought whatsoever, words flew out of my mouth. I shouted out loud at him, "Wait a minute! Who do you think you are, Satan? I'm a Christian! I belong to Jesus Christ! This house belongs to Jesus Christ! You have no business in my house! Satan, get out of my house and go to Hell right now!" I tried to turn my head to see what he looked like, but I could not turn over with the halo brace on my head and upper body.

The Bible says, "Submit yourselves, then, to God. Resist the Devil, and he will flee from you" (James 4:7). Satan left my house faster than a bolt of lightning. When I shouted, it woke Connie and she asked what happened. I told her, "Satan came by for a visit, but he just left." Connie just went back to sleep.

Satan never even raised his voice, but he spoke with power and authority. How do I know it was Satan? I know it was Satan's voice, just as I recognize God's voice. God has given us this knowledge. I have three very strong Christian friends who have also heard Satan's voice.

Up until that point in time, I often wondered how Eve could have so easily been talked into eating fruit from the tree of the knowledge of good and evil. Adam and Eve actually walked and talked with our God of creation while they were in the garden. So how could Eve, and then Adam, have been so easily convinced to disobey God?

I consider myself a strong Christian. I'm like Peter. I tell it like it is, and sometimes I put my foot in my mouth. I walk with God, as do many of my Christian friends. So how could Satan convince me, a strong witness for Christ, to commit suicide for the good of my family?

The only answer I can come up with is that Satan is a powerful adversary. He is the "ruler of the kingdom of the air" (Ephesians 2:2). He is the "prince of this world" (John 12:31). He has "blinded the minds of unbelievers" (2 Corinthians 4:4). Peter denied Christ three times when Satan "sifted" him. Solomon, the wisest man on earth, was tempted and married "outside the family" and then worshiped the false gods of his wives. Both of these great men blew it.

On our own, we will lose the battle every time. Without the Holy Spirit, we are "roadkill." Satan's words were powerful enough to convince Eve to blow it. He also convinced me to blow it. But the Holy Spirit revealed the truth to me, and Satan lost this battle. Today I have a greater respect for Eve, because I can easily see how she was deceived and ate the fruit. Satan put out the bait, and she took it. "'You will not certainly die,' the serpent said to the woman. For God knows that when you eat from it your eyes will be opened, and you will be like God, knowing good and evil" (Genesis 3:4-5).

Eve believed Satan's lie. Satan told me I'd be paralyzed, which was his lie. He told me my family would be better off with the insurance money, and I again believed his lie. Be careful out there; Satan is a formidable adversary.

A few years later, I took Connie to the hospital for a doctor's appointment. While we were sitting in the waiting room, a nurse walked by and stared at us and then walked on down the hall. A few minutes later, she came back and again stared at us and said, "Do I know you?" I told her my name and that I didn't recognize her, and she left again. Then she came back a third time and asked, "Have you ever been a patient here in the hospital?"

I told her, "Yes, a few years ago, when I broke my neck."

She then said, "You're the one! You're the one with the broken neck! You're the one who gave me the New Testament and told me about Jesus!" She smiled, turned, and walked away. If God can use a man lying in a hospital bed with a broken neck and a concussion, he can use anyone to share the gospel of Jesus Christ.

Ask Me

I ordered one of those personalized license plates from the State Highway Department. You could use up to seven letters on your plate, so I ordered a license plate for my truck that said, "ASK ME."

When I pumped gas or parked my truck, people would stop me and say, "Ask me what?"

I would answer, "Let me ask you a question. What two things in life are for certain?"

About 90 percent of the people would laugh and answer, "That's easy—death and taxes." I'd tell them they made a fifty on the test. I explained that my mother was old and had no money, so she didn't pay any taxes.

Then I'd tell them, "The Bible says the two things that are certain are death and facing God's judgment." I would quote the Bible: "Just as people are destined to die once, and after that to face judgment" (Hebrews 9:27). I would explain that we both agree that we're going to die, and the Bible tells us we will then stand before God in judgment. I would ask, "What will you tell God when He asks you, 'Why should I let you into my Heaven?'" If they answered correctly, we'd praise God together. If they answered incorrectly, as most did, then I'd share the gospel with them.

Wild Jim

Let me share the story of a visit with a man I call "Wild Jim." I call him that because he behaved like a wild man.

I made the visit by myself. Wild Jim's girlfriend invited me into the house. Wild Jim was sitting on the couch, eating supper and watching TV. His supper consisted of a huge piece of hamburger meat that completely covered his plate and a cold beer, nothing else. He wore blue jeans with no shirt. After a few minutes, I knew his girlfriend was a Christian, and Wild Jim was as lost as a blind bat. He also acted like one. When he talked, he used a lot of wild hand and arm motions. What he said didn't always make sense. He would argue over the smallest, most insignificant things. I shared Bible verse after Bible verse, and he argued about each one. He was quite loud and belligerent, and I wondered if he had been using drugs.

He was also quite threatening, telling me, "I could just kill you and dump your body, and no one would know." I told him that he probably could do that, but Jesus would know. And quite frankly, I had no fear of death, because I know my Redeemer lives. He argued about that too. By around 10:30 p.m., I told him I needed to get home. I asked if I could visit and talk more with him the next week, and he told me, "Come on back, but it won't do any good."

The next week, as I prepared to make the visit, I wrote Wild Jim's name and address on a piece of paper and gave it to my wife. I told her that if I was not home by 10:00 p.m. to drive by Wild Jim's house and see if my truck was parked out front. If I was not home by 10:00 p.m. and my truck was not at his house, she should call the police. I truly felt there was a good chance this would be the last visit I ever made.

Connie was not happy about me making the visit, but I told her it was something I had to do. I told her, "We all have to die in order to get to Heaven. And when I die, I'd like to be in the middle of doing the Lord's work."

At the time, I did not realize that Wild Jim was not angry with me. He was under the conviction of the Holy Spirit, and that's why he was so filled with anger. He knew he was a sinner and had a one-way ticket to Hell. His anger was meant for the Holy Spirit, not me.

I entered their house into the same hostile environment. I got nowhere with Wild Jim. All he wanted to do was to argue and threaten me. It was time to leave. I asked Wild Jim if I could come back a third time, and he agreed. When I left, it was after 10:00 p.m. Connie had already left our house to come check on me. My truck was not at Wild Jim's house, so she headed back home to call the police, but by then I was home.

I went back for a third visit, which was the worst visit of all. In addition to all his arguing and threatening, he said, "I'm coming to your church Sunday. I'm going to come in and tell you, your preacher, and everyone else they can just go to Hell." I really thought he was serious and tried to explain that this was not a good idea. I left his house again around 10:00 p.m. after another three-hour visit.

The next day, I went by the church and told the pastor what Wild Jim had said he was going to do on Sunday. The pastor told me not to worry about it, that he could handle it if Wild Jim showed up. The pastor went on the offensive and wrote Wild Jim a letter inviting him to worship with us Sunday.

As we sat in the sanctuary on Sunday, I looked around for Wild Jim, but he was not there. I felt a huge sense of relief. After the service started, however, l saw Wild Jim walk in and take a seat. I think I silently prayed during the entire service. I was so afraid that Wild Jim would make a scene, but nothing happened. At the end of the service, the pastor gave his altar call, and lo and behold, Wild Jim walked forward and surrendered his life to Christ.

The ten hours of listening to Wild Jim argue and threaten me were actually not meant for me. They were directed at the Holy Spirit, who had him under conviction to the point that he could hardly function normally. Sometime between that third visit and Sunday morning, Wild Jim finally broke under the Holy Spirit's conviction, and he surrendered his life to Christ. He made it official Sunday morning at church.

Hurricane Andrew

In 1992, the Charleston Baptist Association was in the process of putting together its first disaster relief mass-feeding unit. Then,

Hurricane Andrew hit Homestead, Florida and the people in Homestead needed immediate help. We put together what we could, and our feeding unit headed to Florida. In those days we did not have the fine commercial mass-feeding equipment that is used today. For example, our stoves consisted of old, metal milk crates with tobacco barn burners attached underneath and propane bottles attached to the burners. That's what rednecks here in the Lowcountry call a "cooker." These cookers are used mostly for cooking catfish, chicken bog, Frogmore stew, and other Lowcountry delicacies.

I was looking forward to providing hot meals for the hurricane victims, but more important, I looked forward to sharing the gospel with the locals. I took about thirty Gideon New Testaments with me to give out as I shared the gospel. While driving to Homestead, Angela sat beside me in our van and told me she was really looking forward to sharing the gospel with someone at Homestead. She said she had never led anyone to Christ and really felt God was calling her to share the gospel.

When we arrived, things did not work out the way we expected. We set up camp out in the middle of nowhere. We worked from before daylight until dark each day, preparing hot meals for the hurricane victims, but rarely saw any of the local people. We prepared thousands of hot meals and loaded them onto Red Cross trucks, which delivered the meals throughout the community.

We were there for almost two weeks, and there were no witnessing opportunities. The people we dealt with were mostly disaster-relief and Red Cross personnel who were already Christians.

The last morning, as we were packing and getting ready to head back to Charleston, an eighteen-wheeler truck pulled up. The driver, John, got out and came to our cook tent. He said, "I know you all do mass feeding here and you don't fix single meals for people, but is there any chance I could get something to eat? I haven't eaten in a while." We had already eaten breakfast and were now in the process of breaking camp. Since I was the cook and the man was hungry, I told him to come on over. I asked him if bacon and eggs would be OK. He gratefully said that would work for him. After preparing his breakfast, I placed it on a table for him. Angela was already sitting at the table with John. As she talked with him, I silently prayed for both of them. I knew she wanted to share the gospel.

As John finished his breakfast, another eighteen-wheeler pulled up, and the driver got out. He walked over and asked if he could get a bite to eat and said anything would be OK with him. We really didn't have time to feed anyone else, and I thought about telling him he was too late for breakfast. We had been working daylight to dark for almost two weeks, and we were tired and ready to head home. But the frying pan was still hot. I told him to come on over and I'd fix him some breakfast. These were the only two single meals we cooked during the two-week trip.

John had finished eating, and he and Angela walked out into the parking lot. I could tell Angela was struggling while talking with John, because she kept looking at me. I didn't want to interrupt, so I continued praying for both of them.

Then the Holy Spirit revealed to me that there was a problem. Angela wanted to share the gospel with John, but like many Christians, she didn't know what to say. I walked over to where they were standing, and Angela said, "Ellison, this is John. He's driving that eighteen-wheeler. I asked John if he was a Christian, and he said he didn't know." Then she didn't say anything else. I looked at John, and he had a worried look on his face. There was just silence.

I said, "John, let me ask you a question. If you were to drive your eighteen-wheeler down that highway and some drunken fool hit you broadside and killed you graveyard dead, would you go to Heaven or to Hell?"

John answered, "I guess I'd go to Hell, because I don't know how to get to Heaven."

I asked John, "Would you let me tell you what God says in the Bible about going to Heaven? It's not my opinion. My opinion and the opinions of others don't mean anything. Heaven belongs to God, and if we're going to get in, we must do it God's way." John agreed, and I shared the gospel. John bowed his head and prayed and surrendered his life to Jesus Christ.

As we stood there talking, John was all smiles because he had just been born again. Now the worried look was on *my* face. I was silently praying, "God, what are we going to do now? We can't just drive off and leave a brand-new Christian standing here in the parking lot by himself." We had not made contact with any churches in Florida. We had not even gone to church the two Sundays we were in Homestead, because we worked every day feeding the hurricane victims.

While I was silently praying, the second truck driver walked over to where we were standing. He said in a loud and bold voice, "It looks like you folks are standing out here praying!"

I said, "Yes, we are. We're praying with John. He's the world's newest Christian. John just asked Jesus to be his Savior and Lord of his life."

The truck driver said, "Praise God. My name is Phillip, and I drive this truck five days a week. But on Sunday, I'm the pastor at the AME church about three miles down the road." He said, "John, do you remember seeing that church when you drive the highway?"

John said, "Yes, I know where your church is located."

Then Phillip said, "John, I want you to come worship with us Sunday. If you will, I'll be standing out front waiting for you, and I will personally escort you into our church." John said that he would come and worship at the AME church on Sunday.

Phillip turned to us and said, "I know you're getting ready to leave and go home. You all go ahead and leave. I'll take care of John." We thanked Phillip, shook his hand, and were on the way to Charleston. For almost two weeks, we had been working at that site with the Red Cross personnel and had not seen a single truck driver or anyone else. Then, during the very last thirty minutes, two men drove up. One of them got saved, and the other was a preacher. Some people call things like this a coincidence, but I don't. I call it another "God incidence."

On the way home, Angela sat next to me in the van for part of the drive. I didn't say anything about her not knowing what to say to John, because it wasn't her fault. There are many who want to share the gospel, but like Angela, they don't know what to say.

After swapping small talk, Angela said, "I wanted so badly to share the gospel with John, but I just didn't know what to say. How did you know how to do that?" I explained to her that I spent many hours memorizing Bible verses and practicing what to say. I gave her a Gideon New Testament that has Bible verses and the plan of salvation on the back cover. I hope Angela won't get discouraged but will learn to share the good news with others.

Tracts

Years ago, a woman on TV explained how she used tracts to witness to the lost. She said that she found a particular tract she liked and bought it by the hundreds. When she paid a bill, she mailed one of her tracts in the envelope with her check. She said she also received a lot of junk mail that included self-addressed, postage-paid, return envelopes. She threw the junk mail away and put a tract in the return, postage-paid envelope, and mailed the tract back to the sender.

I thought that was a great idea. I looked through all my tracts and picked out the one I liked best. I ordered a thousand of them and began putting a tract in basically every envelope that left my house. Before long, those tracts were gone, so I ordered more. To date, I've mailed and given out over twenty thousand tracts and am still going strong.

We have our mail delivered to a post-office box. There are six tables in the lobby of the post office. Each day when I pick up our mail, I leave several tracts on each table. One day, I returned to the post office for some additional business. In a period of about thirty minutes, half of the tracts had already been taken.

When we're traveling, we often make stops at rest areas, and I'll leave a few tracts on the lavatory counters. Have you ever noticed that inside the toilet stall, the toilet-paper holder is sometimes busted loose? I stick several tracts into the opening between the holder and the wall. The next man to use the toilet has something to read while he's sitting there taking care of business.

Do I expect that all those who receive the tract will get saved? No, not really. But that's not my call. It's up to the Holy Spirit to convict them and draw them to Jesus. My job is to get the gospel message explained in the tract into their hands. My job is to deliver the good news any way I can.

Think about it. What if one out of ten reads the tract and gets saved? Or what if one out of fifty or even one out of a hundred gets saved? If, in fact, only one out of one hundred people gets saved—and I have given out twenty thousand tracts—then two hundred people will be saved. Is it worth the effort? It is to me if only one person gets saved. That one person might be your son or daughter, or it might be your mom or your dad. Is it worth the effort?

There are many, many good tracts available. I just happen to like the one that says on the cover, "God's Simple Plan of Salvation." This tract is published by Lifegate, Inc. (Post-Office Box 425, Beech Grove, Indiana, 46107).

Allen Said No

Someone gave me a note and asked me to go visit Allen, because he was not a Christian. When I went to his house, he was not home, but his mother was there. She was a very nice elderly woman, probably around eighty years old. She thanked me for coming to see Allen and suggested I try again the next week. Then she asked why I came by. I told her a friend of Allen's had asked me to come tell him about Jesus. I told her I understood her son was not a Christian.

I asked her where she worshiped. She began telling me the names of different churches she had attended over the years. Then she told me about mistakes she had made, and that she knew God was not pleased with her. She had been trying for many years to make up for all her mistakes. It was obvious that she was not a Christian, so I asked her, "If you were to die tonight, do you think you've done enough good things to make up for all the bad things? Do you think God will let you into Heaven one day?" She said no and started crying. I told her I had some good news and some bad news. The bad news was, she had not done enough good deeds to get into Heaven, because none of us can. The good news was, she didn't have to, because Jesus did the greatest good deed of all time for us. I asked if I could share with her what God says in His Bible about eternal life in Heaven, and she agreed. She bowed her head and trusted Jesus as her Lord and Savior. Jesus immediately took away her tears.

I went back the next week to see Allen. I shared the gospel with him, but he did not want to accept Christ. He said he had two friends at work that drank, cursed, lied, and did all kinds of other bad things. He said the two friends went to a revival and came back to work telling everyone they were now Christians. A few weeks later, they were back drinking, cursing, and telling lies again. He said, "I am a better man than they are," and he simply would not accept Christ. He was getting ready for work at a local restaurant, so I asked if I could come back the next week. When I returned, he had company, and it was obvious he did not want to talk about Jesus with his friends present. I asked if I could come back another time, and he said it would be OK.

I decided to wait a few weeks before returning to see Allen. One or two times during that waiting period, I felt the Lord was nudging me to return to see him. I did not hear God's voice, but I just had a feeling. Sunday at church, I was talking with Robert, a friend who had grown up in Mount Pleasant, and I asked if he knew Allen. He said, “Oh, yes, I know him well.”

I told Robert that I had shared the gospel with Allen, but he would not accept Christ. I asked, “What can I say to Allen to get him to trust what I say about Christ?”

He said, “Allen will never accept Christ.” I didn’t like that answer, because I fully intended to talk with him again. Then He continued, “Didn’t you read about it in the newspaper two weeks ago? Allen was killed in an automobile accident in Georgia.”

After Robert told me about the accident, I had many guilt feelings. For weeks, I heard those voices in my head telling me how I had failed and that I was a terrible witness for Christ. At that point in my walk with the Lord, I did not realize that it was Satan trying to discourage me from doing any further witnessing for the Lord. Satan slowed me down for a few weeks, but I prayed and talked with my Lord about Allen and his death. The Lord helped me understand that I had not failed. I delivered the gospel message to Allen as I was called to do. My hope is that in the days before his death, he pondered the gospel message and asked Jesus to be his Lord and Savior.

The Banker

One day I was in the bank, and I made small talk with Charles, the banker helping me. I had met him before, so we were not strangers. I asked him where he attended church, and he said he didn’t, but his wife sometimes attended a nearby church. We could not talk about Jesus while he worked, because other customers were waiting in line. I asked him if I could buy his lunch the next day, and he said that would be OK.

The next day as Charles ate his lunch, I asked if I could talk with him a few minutes about Jesus. He told me, “Sure, go ahead.” I shared the gospel with him and asked him if he wanted to pray and ask Jesus to be his Lord and Savior.

He said, "I listened to what you said. I evaluated what you said. I think you're telling the truth, and you're right. Yes, I want to be a Christian. I'll pray and ask Jesus to be my Savior." It was as if he was making a business decision. He listened to the facts, evaluated the facts, and then he made a decision based on those facts. I asked him if he wanted me to help him pray, and he said, "No, I can pray." He bowed his head and prayed a most humble prayer. He asked God to forgive his sins and asked Jesus to be his Lord and Savior. His prayer was very sincere, but it was also like a businessman talking with God about a business decision.

I kept up with Charles for a while. He joined his wife's church and became involved in various ministries. His conversion was the real deal. I've never had another person make a business decision for Christ the way Charles did that day.

His Parents

A hunting buddy asked me if I would visit his parents, because they were not Christians. When I entered their house, I told them I had spoken with their son and wanted them to know how much he truly loved them, and that's why he asked me to come by.

His father's two sisters, Jane and Lois, who were from Charlotte, North Carolina, were on vacation and at the house that evening. We sat in the den, and I asked if I could talk with them about God. They agreed. I asked, "If you die in your sleep tonight, and the next thing you know, you're standing before God and He asks you, 'Why should I let you into my Heaven?' What would you say to God?" The mother and father didn't really know what to say to God. I asked Lois, who had a huge smile on her face, what she was counting on getting her into Heaven.

Lois talked for five minutes about how each day, she did a good deed for someone. She said she might bake a cake for someone, she might go visit a shut-in, and she might take an elderly person to the grocery store. She was certain that doing one good deed a day and church membership would get her into Heaven.

I asked Lois, "What will happen if God tells you that the requirement for getting into Heaven is to do two good deeds each day? What will you tell God then?" Her smile went away. I then asked, "What if God were to tell you that all your 'good deeds' were like 'filthy rags' to Him?"

I told them I used to think that good people went to Heaven and bad people went to Hell. Then I read the Bible cover to cover and found out what God said about getting into His Heaven. I asked if I could tell them what God said in His Bible. The mom, dad, and Lois prayed and asked Jesus into their hearts. Jane was already a Christian. My friend's father and mother started attending church with their son. Lois continued worshiping at her church in Charlotte, but with a different understanding of grace and works.

The Strawberry Stand

There is a you-pick-it vegetable farm on John's Island. One morning, Connie and I went by to pick some fresh strawberries. As we picked up our strawberry buckets, I asked Lucy, the young lady managing the stand, if she was a Christian. She answered, "I'm a Catholic."

I said, "Well then, let me give you this little Gideon New Testament." She took it and thanked me. There were others in line behind us, so we couldn't stop to talk with her. We picked some strawberries and came back to the stand to pay Lucy. After the other customers left the stand, I asked her an opening question. I said, "I don't know a lot about Catholic doctrine. Tell me, what do you understand it takes for a person to have eternal life with God in Heaven?" Her whole answer dealt with being a good person and doing good deeds to please God.

I told her that at one time, I used to believe something similar. Then I read the Bible cover to cover to see what God said about getting into His Heaven. I asked if she would let me explain what God said in His Bible, and she told me to go ahead. I said, "In the Catholic Church and in other churches, there are statues and pictures of Jesus hanging on the cross. Do you know why Jesus died on that cross?" She said she didn't know, so I explained it was because of her sins, my sins, and the sins of all of us throughout the world. I shared the gospel with her. She had a few questions, and then she bowed her head and prayed and asked Jesus to be her Lord and Savior.

Jack Wanted to Believe

I met Jack, an elderly man, when we were building our house in Awendaw. I was going to use the name "Jack Ass" for him, because he was truly a rude, crude, and belligerent jackass of a man. Even with that, he was a friend of mine. I guess we were a lot alike at one time. I went by Jack's house several times and shared the gospel with him, but it did no good. He would not accept Christ, because he just didn't believe in God.

One Friday afternoon I went by to see Jack, and I again shared the gospel with him. Again, he would not accept Christ. He told me, "Ellison, I wish I could believe as you do, but I just don't believe in God." He said, "You've never met my son. He's a Methodist preacher. My son has talked with me many times about Jesus, but I just simply don't believe in God. I wish I could believe."

That evening at home, I got on my knees and prayed. I told God, "Jack is so stubborn and prideful that he will never get saved unless you humble him." I asked God to, "Humble the man so he can get saved and won't die and spend eternity in Hell. He's my friend." All weekend Jack was on my mind, and I prayed for him.

Monday, when I arrived at work, a mutual friend came up to me and said, "Did you hear about Jack?"

I said, "Hear what?"

He said, "Jack had a stroke. He's in the hospital." I immediately left work and went to the hospital to see Jack.

I arrived at his hospital room, and the door was cracked open. I could see Jack lying there with monitors hooked up to him. As I eased the door open, its hinges squeaked. Jack rolled his head over and looked at me standing in the doorway. Jack stretched out his arm and held his hand out to me. I said, "Jack, do you want Jesus?"

He answered, "Yes, help me." I went over and knelt beside his bed and briefly talked about Jesus and being saved. I asked him if he wanted to pray and ask Jesus to be his Lord and Savior. He said yes, and he surrendered his life to Christ.

After Jack was released from the hospital, I watched him. Sure enough, he was a new man. He had been born again, and he was no longer prideful, rude, crude, and so forth. He now had the love of Christ in his heart. He joined a nearby church. Jack was an old man and had been fighting medical problems most of his adult life. A few years later, he died. Today, he's with our Savior.

As the saying goes, "Be careful what you pray for. You may get it." I never again prayed for God to humble anyone, but if I felt it was the last option, I would pray that prayer again. Heaven and Hell are real places, and they are both places of eternity.

Scott Had Six Months to Live

Scott was a friend at work. He always seemed to be happy, no matter what. He was a friend to everyone who knew him. He just had that kind of personality.

There was a job opening in another department, and Scott got the job. It meant a promotion, and I was happy for him. He came by the office before leaving, and I wished him well.

After the promotion, I did not see Scott again for several years. One day I went to the Summerall building for a meeting. The lobby of the building was packed with people coming and going. Then I saw Scott get off an elevator, and I called out to him and asked how he was doing. He looked downcast. In all the years I had known Scott, I had never seen him look depressed. He said, "I'm not doing well. I just found out I have cancer, and it's too late. I have less than six months to live."

Without hesitation, I asked him, "Scott, do you know Jesus?" I did not whisper those words, and every head in the lobby turned and stared at us.

Scott didn't whisper when he answered. He said, "Ellison, there have been times in my life when I feel that I've walked with God."

I said, "Scott, I'm not talking about walking with God. Do you know Jesus?" He repeated himself, so I said, "Scott, have you ever had a drink of living water, the water that when you drink of it, you will never go thirsty again?"

He said, "No. Tell me about the living water."

We moved to the side of the lobby, and I began to share the gospel with him. I knew I only had one chance. I had not seen Scott in years, and now I was afraid I'd never see him again. As we talked, friends kept interrupting us. We left the lobby and sat in his car and talked. Then he said, "I live only a short distance from here. Why don't we go to my house and talk?" We drove to his house, and sitting on his front steps, Scott bowed his head and surrendered his life to Jesus. I saw the fear of death lift off his shoulders. Jesus took it. Scott again had that huge smile on his face, even though he had less than six months to live. He now knew the final outcome of his life. He knew that his Redeemer lives.

Over the next few months, Scott came by my office several times. Each time, he came to see how I was doing and to pray for me. He had a tremendous peace about him. The Bible says, "And the peace of God, which transcends all understanding, will guard your hearts and your minds in Christ Jesus" (Philippians 4:7). Scott was looking forward to spending eternity with Jesus.

Leroy Would Not Confess

One day at work, Don, a supervisor who worked for me, came by my office and asked if I remembered Leroy. He was a young man who had worked for us as a laborer until the police caught him with some stolen property and he went to jail. Don told me that if I wrote a letter to the police, they would let him out of jail on a work-release program. If I hired him, the police would bring him to work in the morning, let him work all day, pick him up in the afternoon, and take him back to jail. If he did well, he would be released in a few months.

I told Don that if Leroy was in jail, he probably needed to stay there. Don asked me, "Mr. Kelly, haven't you ever made a mistake and maybe just didn't get caught? I've made my share. Leroy made a mistake and got caught. Why don't we give him a second chance?"

I thought back over the years, and yes, I had made my share of mistakes. I told Don, "OK, I'll write the letter and get him out of jail. But it's up to you to keep track of him."

The first day at work, Leroy came by my office and introduced himself. He thanked me for giving him another chance. He said, "Mr. Kelly, I'm going to be the best employee you ever had. I don't ever want to go back to jail. When I first got to jail, they tried to make a girl out of me, and I don't ever want to go back to that place."

Leroy did, in fact, turn out to be one of our very best employees. He was willing to do anything asked of him. Leroy, like my friend Scott, always had a happy attitude. He was a friend to everyone. He always had a smile on his face, and nothing seemed to get him down.

One Friday afternoon, I was working late, and Leroy came by my office. He looked downcast, so I asked what was wrong. He told me, "The men in the shop told me to come see you."

I told him, "No, I don't need to see you. The men are just pulling your leg. Go on home, and have a good weekend."

He said, "No. They told me to come see you." I could tell something was wrong, so I asked what it was. He said, "My wife took my baby girl and moved out. I don't care if she leaves, but she won't let me see my baby. If I can't see my baby, I'm going to kill myself. I don't want to live anymore if I can't see my baby." I told him to come in and sit down. I could tell he was serious. We discussed his wife, the baby, and everything he had tried to do to make it work. He said, "I have tried everything."

I asked Leroy if he trusted me. He said, "Yes, Mr. Kelly, we all trust you. We all know you're a good man and an honest man."

I said, "Leroy, I know you've tried everything you can think of, but I know of one thing you have not tried. Will you trust me and try it for me?" He said he would, so I said, "Leroy, I want you to try Jesus Christ. He's the only one who can help you now. Will you let me tell you about Jesus, and you give him a try?" He told me he would try anything, and I shared the gospel with him. I used the Scriptures in the back of a Gideon New Testament when I shared with him, because I knew he wouldn't remember the Bible verses we discussed. I wanted him to be able to open the New Testament to the back cover and reread the Scriptures. I hoped he would take the New Testament and read more.

We got on our knees to pray the sinner's prayer printed on the back cover of this New Testament. I showed it to Leroy, and he started praying it: "I confess to God that I am a sinner..." Then he stopped and jumped to his feet. He said, "I'm not going to pray that! I'm not a sinner; no, not me! I'm not going to confess that I'm a sinner!" I tried to calm him down. I did not understand why he bowed up. I tried to explain to him that we were all sinners. He said, "You may be a sinner, but I'm not!" He really became very upset with me.

After he calmed down, I asked him if he would give me his word that he would not kill himself and let me talk with him again Monday. He agreed. I gave him the Gideon New Testament and told him to take it home and read it that weekend. I expected he might have trouble understanding the Scriptures, so I told him, "As you read this Bible, if you don't understand what you're reading, just look up and ask God to help you understand. If you really want to understand the Bible, God will explain it to you." He agreed and then left. I prayed for Leroy all weekend.

Monday morning, as I was entering our office building, there was Leroy with his Gideon New Testament. He was reading some of the parables out loud to some of the other mechanics. He was excited about those "stories." I asked him who had explained those "stories" to him. He said, "I didn't understand them at first. Then, I remembered what you told me. I just looked up and asked God to help me understand, and then everything became clear to me. Do you want me to explain the stories to you?"

I told him, "Don't stop. Keep on telling the men those stories. After you finish, come on up to my office."

When he came in, I could see "the joy of the Lord" all over his face. He explained how God had opened the Scriptures to him. He truly did understand. I knew Leroy had asked Jesus into his heart over the weekend, but I still did not understand why he had become so angry on Friday and wouldn't pray the sinner's prayer with me. I asked him, and he said, "Mr. Kelly, when you've been in jail like I have, the first thing you learn is—don't confess to anything. Even if you get caught red-handed, don't confess. Tell them you didn't do it." He continued, "When you asked me to pray this sinner's prayer and I started to pray, 'I confess that I'm a sinner,' I lost it. In jail, you don't ever confess. But yes, I'm a sinner, and you are too. We are all sinners. That's why we need Jesus."

Leroy did not get back with his wife, but he does get to see his baby girl. Jesus worked it out for him, and he was "born again" in the process.

I saw an advertisement that Billy Graham was going to be on TV in a few days. I called Leroy and gave him the date and time and asked him to watch the program. He assured me he would. That evening at home, when Billy Graham was about to come on TV, I got a telephone call from Leroy. He said, "Mr. Kelly, are you getting ready to watch Billy Graham?" I told him that I had forgotten about it and thanked him for calling and reminding me. Over the telephone, I could hear a lot of commotion in the background, and I asked him, "Where are you?"

Leroy said, "Mr. Kelly, you told me to watch Billy Graham, so I rented a TV, I bought a case of beer, and I invited all my friends over to my place to watch Billy Graham with me. Why don't you come on over and join us?" I thanked him and told him the program would be over before I could drive to his place. After I hung up, I immediately thought about how Jesus ate and drank with sinners. Leroy was already an evangelist, but he didn't know it.

A couple of years later, Leroy was in our office and I asked him, "How are you and Jesus doing?"

He said, "Just fine. We're doing great!" I asked if he still had that little Gideon New Testament I had given him, and he said, "I sure do. I don't go anywhere without my Bible." I hate to admit it, but I doubted what he was saying, so I asked him where it was. He reached in his back pocket and pulled out a bunch of pages of his Gideon New Testament with a rubber band around them holding them together. The front and back covers of the New Testament were worn off. He said, "It's torn up a little, but I can still read it. I don't go anywhere without my Bible."

I told him, "Give it to me. Let me give you a new Gideon New Testament, and when you wear this one out, I'll give you another one." I thought, *How many of us have our big, expensive, leather-bound Bibles and never read them? Here is Leroy, who has so little money he has to rent a TV to watch Billy Graham, and he has worn the covers off of his Bible.*

The Retreat

I attended a retreat in Myrtle Beach that was open to all Christian men. The speakers at the retreat would discuss various topics, and then we would break out into small discussion groups. There were six men in our small group. I had never met the other five. Our group leader had been given a list of questions regarding each topic the speaker was going to discuss.

As we discussed the first topic, I could that tell that four of the five men in our group were not Christians, even though they were all members in good standing at their churches. I started praying for God to give me an opening to share the gospel with them. The next day, the opening came. The speaker was supposed to speak on a certain topic, but he got sidetracked and spoke on an entirely different subject.

When we met in our small group, I waited for our group leader to speak. He said, "Well, these discussion questions are for a different topic. I think the speaker got sidetracked. Now I'm not sure what we're supposed to do for the next hour." There was the opening.

I spoke up and said, "It looks like we have some free time on our hands. Would you men allow me to ask you a question? I ask this question to almost everyone I meet. It's a very important question." They all agreed. I said, "Let's say we all go to sleep tonight at this beautiful retreat center, and we all die in our sleep. The next thing you know, we're all standing before God, and He asks, 'Why should I let you into my Heaven?' What would you say to God?"

Marvin, an older man, spoke up and said, "I know over the years that I haven't been very good at attending church, and I haven't been the husband I should have been. But the last few years, I have really been trying to do better. I attend church regularly, and I'm trying to be a much better husband. I think that's what I would tell God." I asked him if he thought that would be good enough to get him into Heaven, and he said he thought it would.

Jimmy, a young man, said, "I've been a member of the church for only a few years. I think I'd tell God that I love my friends. Doesn't the Bible say we are to love our friends? I think it's important that we love our friends. That's what I'd tell God."

Ralph said, "I agree with what both of you said, and I would also tell God I am a very compassionate man. I have a very compassionate heart. That's what I'd tell God."

I looked at Sammy, the group leader. I think he knew the other three men had incorrect answers, but he also did not know the correct answer, so he said nothing.

I told the men those were some good answers and that I used to think some of the same things myself. But since Heaven belonged to God, I knew that the only way to get into Heaven would be God's way, so I read the Bible cover to cover to find out what God says about eternal life in Heaven. I told the men I found the answer in the Bible and that God says there is only one way to get into His Heaven. I asked if I could share the answer with them. They all quickly agreed, and I shared the gospel. They all four bowed their heads and asked Jesus to be their Savior and the Lord of their lives.

The Hospital Visit

Janice told me her mother was in the hospital, and her condition was serious. I asked if her mother was a Christian, and she said she was not. I asked if she wanted me to go visit her mother, and she said, "It won't do any good. Mom has lived a very hard life just to survive. She's too hard to accept Christ." I asked if she would mind if I tried. She said, "Mom will probably be rude to you. She may even curse you, but you can go ahead and try. Who knows, she may even get saved."

The next day, I went to the hospital and found Janice's mother in a semiprivate room. The curtain was pulled between the two beds. I introduced myself and told her I was a friend of her daughter's. I asked if I could talk with her a few minutes. She said, "Sure, sit on the edge of my bed." We made small talk for a few minutes, and then I told her I understood her condition was serious. I told her we will all die one day, and with her serious condition, she would probably leave this world before I did. I asked if she thought she would go to Heaven or Hell. She said, "I hope I'll go to Heaven, but I expect I'll go to Hell." I told her that Heaven's gate was wide open to her if she would go through it. I asked if I could tell her what God says in the Bible about getting into Heaven. She said, "Please tell me." I shared the gospel with her, and she bowed her head and surrendered her life to Christ. She later joined her daughter's church.

While we were talking about Jesus, I could hear people talking on the other side of the curtain. As I was about to leave, a man stepped around the curtain and asked, "Sir, are you a preacher?"

I replied, "No, sir, but I am a Christian."

He said, "I heard you sharing the gospel with this lady. My daughter is here in this hospital bed. She has been in an automobile accident. I'm also a Christian and a deacon in my church, but I don't know how to share the gospel. Will you share the gospel with my daughter? My son is also here. Neither of them are Christians."

A young, seventeen-year-old girl was in the hospital bed. She was all bruised up from the accident. Her brother was sitting on the side of her bed. I said, "Young lady, if you had been killed in that accident, where would you be headed right now—to Heaven or Hell?"

She said, "I guess Hell." I asked if she'd like for me to tell her what the Bible says it takes to get into Heaven. She said, "Yes, sir, go ahead." As I shared the gospel with her, she steady looked me in the eyes. I noticed her brother had his head down the entire time we talked. He would not look at me.

After the young lady asked Jesus to be her Savior and Lord, I asked her brother if he also wanted to become a Christian. He still had not looked up, but he said, "Yes, sir." By now, tears were rolling down his face. The Holy Spirit was really working on both of them. We talked a few minutes, and he also prayed and asked Jesus to be his Lord and Savior. We then talked about joining a Christian church and baptism.

Needless to say, the Holy Spirit of God was in that hospital room doing His convicting works before I arrived. Putting all the right players in the room at the same time is not a coincidence. It's a "God incidence." It's another "God thing."

A Redneck and a Yankee

In 1993, computers were becoming friendlier. I was going to a conference in Madison, Wisconsin, to learn how computers could be used in our preventive maintenance programs at work. I knew my first airline flight would take me to Cincinnati, then another flight to Chicago, and then a third flight to Madison. I thought that if I sat in the middle seat on each flight and passengers sat on my left and right, I'd have an opportunity to share the gospel with six people before I even got to Madison. The same plan would work on my flights home. I told God, "Get ready. Here come some new Christians."

On the first flight, the woman sitting on my left immediately took a nap. The man on my right did not want to hear about Jesus. That's the way it was all the way to Madison; the other passengers were not interested in Jesus. Someone once said, "If you want to hear God laugh, just tell Him what you're going to do for him." Well, I guess God had a good laugh over my plan.

After the first day's meeting, I went out into the streets, but I didn't have any luck there either. Neither did I have any luck the next two days. Then, the last evening I was in Madison, I went into the streets again, just to relax before flying home the next morning. I had no intention of sharing the gospel with anyone, because I had repeatedly been shot down. I was going to take a break and just relax.

As I walked down one of the streets, I heard a man shouting. I walked in that direction to see what was happening. There was a park in the center of town with large buildings that looked like old government buildings. There was a statue in the park, and a man had climbed up on the statue. He wore what looked like a black church-choir robe, and he was shouting, "Repent, for the kingdom of God is at hand! You must repent now! Jesus is coming!" There were young men and women sitting on blankets, eating their picnic lunches. They were having their sunny afternoon in the park. Each time the man shouted for them to repent, they laughed and mocked him.

I silently prayed and asked God why he had brought me here. I told God those young folks certainly did not want to hear about Jesus. They were mocking the man who was calling out to them. Then I saw a young man sitting on the steps of a building on the other side of the park. I prayed and asked God if this young man is why He had brought me to the park, but God did not answer. He did not need to answer. I knew that God had brought me here for this young man.

I walked over and sat on the steps behind the young man and prayed silently for him. I did not say anything. I just prayed and asked God to give me an opening. The man standing on the statue had been silent, but now he started again with his, "Repent!" When he said, "Repent" again, I tapped the young man on his shoulder and asked him, "Do you believe all that repent stuff? Do you believe Jesus is coming?"

The young man, Bill, said he did not know. I told him, "I do know. Jesus is real, and he is coming. The old man is correct in what he's telling all these people." Then I asked him if he wanted me to explain to him what the old man was talking about. He said it would be OK, so I shared the gospel with him. He prayed and surrendered his life to Christ. We talked further about Jesus, church, baptism, being a Christian, and all that.

I asked Bill how he had wound up on these steps in the first place. He said he and his wife were driving through town and having an argument. He lost his temper and told her to stop the car and let him out. He had walked around town for a while. He said, "I felt like God was telling me to go sit on these steps and wait. I've been sitting here, waiting, even though I did not know why." He continued, "Now I know why God sent me to these steps. It was so I could meet you and I could ask Jesus to be my Savior and Lord." He asked me if I felt like this whole thing was a coincidence.

I told him, "No, this is the way God works. He sent a redneck from South Carolina to Madison, Wisconsin, to tell a Yankee about Jesus." That's no coincidence. It's a "God incidence."

I asked Bill what he and his wife were arguing about, and he said they always argued about money—they never had enough. I talked with him about my experience with saving money. I asked him if he would read a Christian book on managing money if I mailed one to him, and he said he would. When I returned home, I bought one of Larry Burkett's books on helping Christians manage money and mailed it to him.

We kept in touch by mail until he took a new job and moved to Oregon. During the time we kept in touch, he and his wife began attending church. He explained that they were using the book and putting their finances in order. He wrote me a letter saying,

> Thank you so much for the wonderful book by Larry Burkett. My wife Susan and I read it immediately and found it to be a good guide for living according to the principles of Christ. It has really helped us to see things as they should be. We've found a church here in Oregon where we feel the people are Christian in name and deed. Susan was hesitant at first about becoming Christ-oriented, but she is learning...I pray almost every day.

I had in mind leading fifteen or twenty people to Christ on that trip, but God had other plans. He wanted Bill and Susan in His kingdom.

The Agnostic

I was asked to go visit a young couple, Dave and Ann. After talking with them a few minutes, I could tell that Dave was a Christian and

Ann was not, so I focused my conversation on Ann. I asked what she believed, and she said, "I don't believe in anything." I asked again, and she said, "Well, my mom and dad are both atheists. They tell me there is no God." She said, "Our daughter, Lindajean, comes home from kindergarten at First Baptist Church and tells me Jesus is God. I simply don't know who or what to believe."

I said, "Deep down inside all of us, we have a belief. Dig down real deep and tell me what you believe."

Ann answered, "Well, sometimes I walk out into the yard and look at the trees and the birds. I look at all the beautiful flowers. At night I look up and see all the stars. I think about the birth of our daughter." Then she said, "I don't think all these things just happen. I think there must be a God somewhere."

I told her that what she had just said came right out of the Bible. Then I read "For since the creation of the world God's invisible qualities—his eternal power and divine nature—have been clearly seen, being understood from what has been made, so that people are without excuse" (Romans 1:20). I asked her if she would allow me to tell her about the God of the Bible. I shared the gospel with her, and she prayed and surrendered her life to Christ.

Dave and Ann both said they would come to church. I did not see them at church for the next couple of weeks, so I paid them another visit. They said they had friends who attended another Baptist church in our area and they were worshiping there on Sundays with their friends.

Imagine that. A kid in kindergarten is being used by God to tell her mom about Jesus.

The Fair

Our Gideon group set up a table at the Lowcountry Fair, and we handed out tracts and New Testaments to the folks who came by. One young man, Hal, took a New Testament and looked at it. I asked if he was a Christian, and he said no. I asked if he'd let me buy him a hot dog and we could talk about him becoming a Christian. We ate our hot dogs and discussed Christ and the cross. I told Hal there was only one thing in life that was free: God's gift of eternal life through Jesus Christ. He said, "No, that's not free either. It might be free to us, but it cost Jesus everything." He was right.

After he accepted Christ, I talked with him about reading the Bible and attending church. He said he had never attended church and didn't want to start now. I explained that in church, he could have help in studying the Bible and learning more about Christ. He said, "I'm not going to church. But if you want to, you can come to my place and teach me about the Bible." I agreed. For the next few months, every Wednesday after work, I drove to his home, and we studied the Bible together. I kept inviting him to worship with us at my church, but he would not attend.

Then, one Sunday, out of the clear blue, there stood Hal at the front door of our church. He was excited about being at our church. He worshiped with us a few Sundays and then joined a church near where he lived. He was now on the road of discipleship.

Harold and the Promise Land

Kevin, a good friend of mine, told me about a man who worked for him. Harold was a plumber and also an alcoholic. Kevin said he was on the verge of firing Harold because of his absences from work due to alcohol. I asked him to let me visit Harold and try to talk with him about the Lord. On each of the first two visits, Harold came to the door and said it did not suit him for me to visit at that time. The third time I visited, Harold gave up and invited me in. He said, "You may as well come in. If I don't let you in today, you'll just come back next week." As I shared the gospel with him, I saw tears well up in his eyes. I knew the Holy Spirit was working on him.

Harold understood the gospel message and prayed and surrendered his life to Christ, but he still could not shake the addiction to alcohol. He had been drinking since high school, and he simply couldn't quit. We prayed together and asked God to take the desire for alcohol away from him, but it did not happen.

A few weeks earlier, I had visited a man named Robbie to share the gospel with him. Robbie said that he had been an alcoholic on the streets of Conway. One night, he passed out on the street. A Christian man came along and picked him up and took him to the Promise Land, which is a Christian-based shelter near Conway. The folks there work closely with The Christian Church, which is located nearby. (Connie and I had visited The Christian Church, but we did not know about the Promise Land at that time.)

While visiting with Robbie, he told me about the Promise Land. He came to know Christ there. The people there worked with him and loved him to the point that he gave up alcohol. Robbie told me that if I ever ran into anyone who needed to dry out to let him know. He would be glad to help them get admitted to the Promise Land.

Kevin finally gave up on Harold and was going to fire him. Even though he was now a Christian, he still had the alcohol problem. I asked Kevin to hold off, because I had another plan. I told him about the Promise Land. He told me he would not fire Harold if he went to the Promise Land and dried out.

A few days later, I took Harold to Robbie's house and introduced them. They talked, and Harold agreed to give the Promise Land a try. Robbie drove Harold to Conway, and he was admitted to the Promise Land.

A short time later, I received a letter from Harold. I'll share part of it:

> I have met some real nice people who have all helped me understand and study the Lord's way. I have been praying a lot, just getting closer to God and letting Him control my future.
>
> I have totally surrendered myself to God and I never felt so relieved and relaxed in all my life. I want to thank you

again for everything you have done for me. At first I didn't understand, but now I understand the Christian way of life. I understand how good it must feel to turn someone into a Christian. I am looking forward to that reward myself someday. I know God has something real special for me too.

Several months later, Connie and I drove to Conway to worship at The Christian Church. When we saw the pastor, we asked how Harold was doing. He said, "I'll take you to him. You won't recognize him. Today is his first day at church as a Sunday-school teacher. He is so excited." When we saw Harold, he was a totally changed man. God had cleaned him up, and he was on that path of discipleship. He was learning and growing. He was also reaching out to others and helping them grow in Christ. Think about it: how can all these coincidences come together?

- Shortly after Connie and I became Christians, we looked for a small church near Myrtle Beach to visit, and we found The Christian Church.

- A year or so later, Kevin told me about Harold. Then, after three visits, I finally get in the door, and Harold surrenders his life to Christ.

- On another visit, I meet Robbie, who told me about the Promise Land near the same Christian Church that Connie and I had visited.

- We introduced Harold to Robbie, and Harold is admitted to the Promise Land.

- Several months later, we visit The Christian Church. Our visit just happens to be on the first Sunday that Harold is to teach Sunday school.

These are not coincidences—they are "God incidences." The Holy Spirit of God put all this together.

The Vagrant Witness for Christ

One day at work, I needed to attend a 9:00 a.m. meeting in the Summerall Building. I had to walk through the "hamburger row" area to get to the meeting. As I approached Hardee's, I saw a man sitting on the sidewalk curb. His clothes were dirty and he had not shaved in a while. I silently prayed, "Lord, let me get past this man. I need to get to my meeting. I don't have time to take this guy to breakfast." As I walked past the man, we looked at each other and said good morning. I kept walking and silently prayed, "Thank you, Lord."

Then, the man shouted, "Hey, mister, come back here!" I turned around and went back to the man. He said, "Give me fifty cents!" I reached in my pocket and gave him all the change I had, which was more than fifty cents, and he thanked me. As I walked away, he again shouted, "Hey, mister, come back here!" I turned and walked back. He was looking at the ID badge I had hanging on my pocket. At work, we were required to wear plastic ID badges with our picture, name, and department name. I had also attached a small gold cross as a symbol of being a Christian. The man said, "You have a cross on your ID badge. You're a Christian, aren't you?" I told him I was. He said, "Then why didn't you take me to Hardee's and buy my breakfast? That's what most Christians do."

I said, "Because you didn't ask for breakfast. You asked for fifty cents."

He said, "You know what I'm going to do with the money, don't you?" I told him I knew he would buy either beer or wine with it.

He said, "This morning, I had a dollar in my pocket, and all I needed was another quarter to have enough money to buy a beer. But my friend, Stanley, asked me if he could have some of my change so he could buy a beer, and I gave it to him. He needed a beer more than I did, so I gave him some of my money. Now I'm out asking for money again so I can buy a beer for myself. He said, "Mister, will you pray for me?"

I said, "Sure, I'd be glad to. What do you want me to pray for?"

He said, "My name is John-Claude Timberton, and I'm from Atlanta. Pray and ask God to take the desire for alcohol away from me. I came to Charleston to go to the VA Hospital. I need medicine, but the doctors won't give me the medicine I need because I'm an alcoholic. I can't take the medicine and drink alcohol at the same time. I know I don't look like it, but I'm also a Christian. I've prayed and prayed and asked God to take the desire for alcohol away from me, but He won't do it. Now I'm stuck here in Charleston without the medicine I need."

As I prayed for John-Claude, I was no longer in a hurry to get to my meeting. I thought, *Let them wait*, because I had something more important to do. We discussed the Bible together. He was indeed a Christian, and he knew the Bible better than I did. Then he said, "Did you read in the paper a couple of weeks ago where a vacant house burned down and a vagrant named Neal died in the fire?" I told him that I had heard about it on the TV news. John-Claude said, "Neal was a friend of mine. A few weeks before the fire, I led him to Christ. Now he is with our Lord in Heaven."

John-Claude could have returned home to Atlanta, but he said he knew God needed him here in the vagrant community, sharing the gospel with them. He had led many of them to Christ. He told me he had given his last Bible to a friend and asked if I had a spare. I told him I had a spare Bible in my truck and would bring it to him. I went to my truck and got the Bible for John-Claude, but I couldn't find him. I never saw John-Claude again.

That morning, God and John-Claude Timberton put me in my place. Here was a man, a vagrant, being used by God. He was my brother in Christ, and all I had wanted to do was to get away from him and go to my meeting. John-Claude was doing a much better job of witnessing for Christ than I was.

A few weeks later, Connie asked me, "What was that man's name you told me about?" I told her his name was John-Claude Timberton. Connie said, "He's dead. It was just on the news. A large truck was backing up and hit him."

I thought, "He's now with Jesus, walking those streets of gold." John-Claude Timberton was indeed a disciple of Jesus Christ.

CHAPTER 15

SHARING THE GOSPEL

R U a Christian?

Over the past twenty-five years, I've asked hundreds of people if they were Christians. I've heard just about every answer imaginable. Many give answers such as, "I think so, I hope so, I guess so. I'm a member of the church, Mom and Dad are Christians, I'm a Baptist (or some other denomination), I've been baptized, I'm counting on my priest, I believe there is a God," and many more. What would your answer be?

Now, if I were to ask you, "Are you married?" Your answer would be either yes or no.

John tells us, "I write these things to you who believe in the name of the Son of God so that you may know that you have eternal life" (1 John 5:13).

So can one *know* if one is a Christian? We are saved (from spending eternity in Hell) and become Christians by the grace of God when we surrender our lives to Jesus Christ. When we commit our lives to the lordship of Jesus Christ, we are "born again" (John 3:7). The Bible tells us, "For it is by grace you have been saved, through faith—and this is not from yourselves, it is the gift of God—not by works, so that no one can boast" (Ephesians 2:8–9). Jesus is the only way to eternal life. God tells us, "Salvation is found in no one else, for there is no other name under heaven given to mankind by which we must be saved" (Acts 4:12).

When a person surrenders his or her life to Christ, something supernatural happens. It's not something we do; it's something God does to us and for us. We are born again and start life all over with a clean slate. "Therefore, if anyone is in Christ, the new creation has come: The old has gone, the new is here!" (2 Corinthians 5:17). The change is often profound when someone gets born again later in life. But for a child, like my mom at age eight, the change may not be as profound. So how can someone know for sure that he or she has been born again?

Signs of the New Birth

Lives were changed at Pentecost. Has what happened at Pentecost happened to you? Is the fruit of the Spirit evident in your daily life (cf. Galatians 5:22)? I'll share a few of the changes that I experienced when I was born again and changes close friends have shared with me about their new births. I expect a Christian may not experience all of these, but we should each recognize in ourselves many of these signs.

1. Love of Jesus. We love the Lord because of what He's done for us. Sometimes we may not recognize this as love but as gratitude. We are truly grateful for the grace of God and Jesus's suffering in our place on the cross. "If God were your Father, you would love me, for I have come here from God" (John 8:42). Our lives are defined by Christ who lives in us, and the desire of our hearts is to follow Him. How many times during the last week did you mention the name of Jesus to someone? We recognize the guidance of the Holy

Spirit in our lives. "But when he, the Spirit of truth, comes, he will guide you into all the truth" (John 16:13).

2. Love of other Christians. We love everyone—unconditionally. We may not love what the person does, but we love the person. There is a special love in being around other Christians as compared to hanging out with the heathen. We like hanging out with Christians who are "like-minded." God tells us, "We know that we have passed from death to life, because we love each other. Anyone who does not love remains in death. Anyone who hates a brother or sister is a murderer, and you know that no murderer has eternal life residing in him" (1 John 3:14–15).

3. Sin. We know and recognize sin and hate it. Before becoming Christians, sin really did not bother us, because our mind-set was one of "everybody sins." The desire of our hearts is now to never sin again. Sin no longer pleases us. It is offensive to us. We forsake it. Then, when we do sin, the Holy Spirit convicts us, and we repent and ask forgiveness. If someone can sin and it doesn't bother him or her, there may be a problem. "No one who is born of God will continue to sin, because God's seed remains in them; they cannot go on sinning, because they have been born of God" (1 John 3:9).

4. Obedience. The desire of our hearts is to follow Jesus and to obey His commands and teachings. There is a "hunger" to read and learn the word of God so that we can live our lives in the likeness of Christ. We love to pray and talk with our God. We hear His voice and long to talk with Him.

5. Acknowledgment of Christ. We are not ashamed of being Christians. We will take a stand for Christ, even when it may not be the popular thing to do. Jesus said, "If anyone is ashamed

of me and my words in this adulterous and sinful generation, the Son of Man will be ashamed of them when he comes in his Father's glory with the holy angels" (Mark 8:38). We love to tell others about our Savior. When was the last time you invited someone to church or talked with them about Jesus?

6. No other way. We know that Jesus is the only way to eternal life. Without Christ, we know we're roadkill. We have absolute assurance in Christ's completed work at the cross. "Again, the kingdom of heaven is like a merchant looking for fine pearls. When he found one of great value, he went away and sold everything he had and bought it" (Matthew 13:45–46). We are "betting it all" on what Jesus did for us at the cross.

7. Living for Christ. Our desire for the finest car, house, boat, shotgun, purse, fashion clothes, etc., is gone. Our pride and the desire for the spotlight and the applause of man are gone. We no longer focus on spending our time and money on toys that we think will make us happy. We realize the world no longer revolves around us. We have committed our all to Christ and build our lives around Him. We now spend our time and money to glorify our Savior and to bring others to the cross of Christ. We have overcome the world. "Who is it that overcomes the world? Only the one who believes that Jesus is the Son of God" (1 John 5:5).

There is a difference between head knowledge and heart knowledge. That difference is the difference between eternal life and eternal death.

What to Say and What Not to Say

The Bible tells us, "For we are to God the pleasing aroma of Christ among those who are being saved and those who are perishing. To the one we are the aroma that brings death; to the other, an aroma that brings life" (2 Corinthians 2:15-16). To those who ask Jesus into their hearts, we are the aroma that brings life. To those who reject God's love and Jesus Christ, we are the smell of death.

Our response to God's offer of eternal life with Him in His Heaven will be a response of surrender and commitment. We will give up control of our lives and ask Jesus to be not only our Savior, but Lord of our lives. The desire of our hearts is to follow Him and to bring honor to Him through our love and obedience.

We are all born with a sinful nature. We don't have to teach a child to sin. We are all born with this inclination. We then choose to sin throughout our lives. But there is hope for even the vilest sinner. God tells us, "Whoever believes in him shall not perish but have eternal life" (John 3:16). The "whoever" means anyone.

For me, telling others about Jesus is a lifestyle. Every person I come in contact with is a potential person with whom to share the gospel. As I'm talking with someone, I'm usually silently praying at the same time. I'm asking God, "Should I proceed? Is the Holy Spirit already convicting the person?" Then I listen to God as He tells me what to do. If the Holy Spirit is not already convicting the person, I will hand them a Gideon New Testament and ask him or her to later read the Bible verses on the back cover, which is the plan of salvation. Most people who are working can't just stop work and talk about God, but this may be the time to plant a seed. Others are wide open for sharing the good news, and it's like delivering a winning lottery ticket to them.

Most people want to believe in something—a god. Many will choose the "broad road." Jesus tells us to "Enter through the narrow gate. For wide is the gate and broad is the road that leads to destruction, and many enter through it. But small is the gate and narrow the road that leads to life, and only a few find it" (Matthew 7:13–14). These verses in Matthew tell us that more people will choose death than will choose life. Many will choose the wide gate, and only a few will choose the narrow gate. That upsets me, but

God says that's just the way it is. "To whom can I speak and give warning? Who will listen to me? Their ears are closed so they cannot hear. The word of the Lord is offensive to them; they find no pleasure in it" (Jeremiah 6:10).

First, let me say that you and I are no better than those with whom we hope to share Christ. The only difference between us and the "heathen" is, we've been washed by the blood of our Savior and they have not yet. At one time I was a "heathen," and possibly you were too.

If I'm going to a house with an appointment, I begin praying ahead of time. I pray for those I plan to visit, and I pray for myself. I pray that God will give me the wisdom, knowledge, understanding, and a portion of common sense. I pray and ask God to help me know what to say, and especially what not to say. I ask the Holy Spirit to be there ahead of me to do His convicting work. I pray as I'm driving to the house, in the driveway, and I even pray silently while I'm talking with the residents. To me, prayer, the sword of the Spirit, and the convicting power of the Holy Spirit are the three most important parts of witnessing. Two out of three normally won't work. All three are needed.

One day, several Gideon men and their wives (the Auxiliary) went to a nursing home to place Bibles and hand out New Testaments. A good friend of mine began sharing the gospel with a man sitting in a wheelchair. After she finished, she asked him, "Don't you want to ask Jesus into your heart?" He said no. She came over to me and said, "Ellison, I shared the gospel with that man. He's not a Christian, and he doesn't want to accept Christ."

As we walked over to the man, I prayed a fast, silent prayer: "Lord, help him! Lord, help me!" Then I knelt down beside his wheelchair so I would be on eye level with him. I asked if he would accept Christ, and he again said no.

My friend got a little upset, because here was an old man who didn't have long to live, and he would not accept Christ. She said, "Well, then, let me pray for you." She prayed that the Holy Spirit would convict him and that he would later accept Christ. She then rejoined the other women who were placing Bibles in the nursing home.

I talked with the gentleman for a few minutes and explained the two choices that were before him: Heaven or Hell. After talking with him about the choices, I asked him again if he would choose Christ and life, and he said yes. We prayed the sinner's prayer together.

As we were leaving the nursing home, my friend said to me, "You prayed with him to ask Jesus into his heart. What did I do wrong?"

I told her, "We both forgot to pray first. Before leaving the man, you prayed and asked the Holy Spirit to convict him. The Holy Spirit then answered your prayer and did His convicting work."

Always pray first and ask the Holy Spirit to convict the person of guilt and need of our Savior. If a person believes he or she is not a sinner, then why should he or she need a Savior? It is the Holy Spirit's job to convict people of their guilt, and it's our job to deliver the good news of God's grace and faith in Jesus Christ.

If I'm going to a house to visit people and share the gospel, I try to learn about them before I make the visit. Do they attend church? Have they ever been involved in cult religions? Do they have children? Where do they work? What are their hobbies? I want to connect with them when I arrive. I want to find some common ground so that I can put them at ease with my being there. I don't want them to think I feel superior to them, because I'm not. I don't want to be the enemy. I want to be a friend.

> *I also look for this same common ground when someone shows up unexpectedly at my house and there is an opportunity to share Christ. For example, the week after Mom died, the rental company sent a young man to the house to pick up her hospital bed and oxygen equipment. While we were disassembling the bed, I explained that Mom had left us the week before and that she was now with Jesus.*

I asked the young man what he was counting on to get into Heaven when he died. His answer was all about good works. I asked him if I could tell him what God says in the Bible about getting into Heaven, and he asked me to tell him. He prayed and surrendered his life to Christ. The young man lived in Summerville, which is about thirty miles away. We discussed baptism and several good churches in his area, and he said that he and his wife would be baptized and worship at one of the churches we had discussed.

Sometimes we don't have time to plan ahead; we just take the cards that are dealt to us and play them. If the desire of our hearts is to share Christ with an unsaved person, God will give us the opening we're looking for. In this case, the common ground was the death of Mom.

When making a home visit, I normally talk about "the small stuff" for five or ten minutes. If the people don't already know why I'm there, I'll explain that I came to share some good news with them. I'll tell them I want to talk with them about the most important subject in the world: life and death. I'll then ask an opening question.

Sometimes, I come right out and ask, "Are you a Christian?" If the answer is yes, I'll ask to hear more about it. I'll ask where the person attends church, and I'll work the conversation around to: "Tell me what you understand it takes for a person to get into Heaven."

Sometimes I'll ask, "If you were to die in your sleep tonight and the next thing you know, you're standing before God and He says to you, 'My Heaven is over here, and I know you don't want to go to Hell, so tell me, why should I let you into my Heaven?' what would you say to God?" Or I might say, "Since we're all going to die one day, let me ask you a question. After you die, what do you understand happens next?" I sometimes ask, "In your church, what do you understand it takes for a person to have eternal life with God in Heaven?"

If people say they believe in God and that Jesus died and shed His blood for the payment of our sins and they're betting it all on Jesus, then I'm out the door. If I have any doubts about their answer, I'll try to confirm it with explanations of faith, grace, repentance, surrender, commitment, and receiving God's gift of love. These words may seem awkward at first, but they all easily come together when we discuss the atoning work of Jesus.

If the people are not Christians, they will probably say things like "being a good person, doing good things for others (good deeds or good works), trusting in their priest, attending church" and so forth that get them into Heaven. We're raised to believe that we are supposed to work for everything we get out of life and that nothing is handed to us on a platter. That's our mind-set. We think that for anyone, especially God, to die on the cross in our place just isn't American.

No matter what the answer, if people do not include "Jesus as Savior and Lord" in their answer somewhere, they don't have their Heaven tickets, because Jesus is the only way. Jesus said, "I am the way and the truth and the life. No one comes to the Father except through me" (John 14:6).

I don't ever say, "You idiot, how could you believe that," or, "Man, you're way off the track." That immediately puts people on the defensive, and you might as well go home. God did not call us to win arguments but to win souls. I usually say, "You know, I used to believe something similar. Then one day, I figured since Heaven belongs to God, if I'm to get in, I need to do it God's way. I read the Bible cover to cover looking for the answer to that question, and I found it. God says there's only one way into His Heaven. Would you let me share with you what I discovered in the Bible?"

Once I start talking about the gospel, I use as many Bible verses as possible. God says, "So is my word that goes out from my mouth: It will not return to me empty, but will accomplish what I desire and achieve the purpose for which I sent it" (Isaiah 55:11). I never change the intent of the verse, and I never water down the gospel. Occasionally, I've had people say to me, "Show me where the Bible says that," so I have lists of verses that I frequently use in sharing the gospel. I can go quickly to my list, find the verse, and open my Bible to show it to the person.

Below are seven topics I try to discuss when sharing the gospel:

God Loves You

The first thing I tell a person is that God created us and He loves all of us. He doesn't love some of the things we do. It's like that with our kids: we love them, but we don't love some of the things they do. I tell them, "I have a daughter, and I love her very, very much. I tell her and try to show her how much I love her. I tell her that no matter how much or how badly she screws up, I'll never stop loving her. I may not like what she's done, and we'll have to deal with that, but there is nothing she can ever do to make me stop loving her. That's the way God feels about us. My love for her is unconditional. Even if we reject God and His love for us, He still loves us unconditionally." The one greatest sin we can commit is to reject God and His love for us through his Son, Jesus Christ. Without Christ, we're dead.

Reference verses: (1 John 4:16, John 3:16)

Our Sin Separates Us from God

The second thing I talk with people about is sin. I'll explain to them that the Bible tells us we're all sinners and our sin separates us from a relationship with God. The Bible says, "Your eyes are too pure to look on evil; you cannot tolerate wrongdoing" (Habakkuk 1:13). Sin is the problem, and its penalty is death. I tell them, "I know I'm a sinner. How about you? Are you a sinner?" Most will look down and say yes. A few people will say no, but they don't look us in the eye when they say it. They know they are sinners. I don't argue with them, because it's the Holy Spirit's job to deal with them and their sin. We have the pleasure of sharing and explaining the "good news."

No matter whether people say yes or no, I quote a few Bible verses pertaining to our sin, because they need to hear God's word, not my opinion. Use the sword of the Spirit. "If we claim to be without sin, we deceive ourselves and the truth is not in us" (1 John 1:8).

Reference verses: (Isaiah 59:2, Romans 3:23, Psalm 53:3, Ecclesiastes 7:20, Isaiah 64:6)

The Penalty for Our Sin

The third thing I'll discuss is the penalty for our sins. I explain that if we get a traffic ticket, we must pay the penalty, and God says that the penalty for our sin is death. There is already a death sentence on each of us because of our sin, and God's justice calls for an execution. Death not only means we stop breathing and die, but more important, it means the spirit we're born with will be cast into Hell for eternity. The Bible describes Hell as a place where the worm never dies; there is torment and punishment, and it's eternal. We don't burn up and then our ashes just blow away. The torment and punishment go on and on for eternity. I've heard preachers say that Jesus talked more about Hell than he talked about Heaven. The Bible describes "God our Savior, who wants all people to be saved and to come to knowledge of the truth" (1 Timothy 2:3-4). Jesus is that "Truth."

I often quote John 3:16 because many people are familiar with this verse. The verse explains that whosoever believes in Jesus will not die, but have eternal life. All people have an opportunity to be saved.

Reference verses: (Ezekiel 18:4, Romans 6:23, Galatians 6:7, Hebrews 9:27, Revelation 20:15)

We Can't Save Ourselves

The fourth thing I explain is that we cannot save ourselves. Many people try to do good works or good deeds to make up for the sin in their lives. Some give money to the church, hoping it will cause God to erase their sin debt or the sin debt of a loved one. Some count on Mom or Dad, their preacher or priest, their wives, Mary, Peter, or another person to help them erase their sin debt and get them into Heaven. The Bible says, "Cursed is the one who trusts in man" (Jeremiah 17:5). We can't erase our guilt for sinning, and others can't pay our sin debt for us. God tells us, "No one can redeem the life of another or give to God a ransom for them—the ransom for a life is costly, no payment is ever enough" (Psalm 49:7–8). Our way simply will not work. The Bible says all of our efforts (good works) are like "filthy rags" (Isaiah 64:6). We're just not good enough to meet God's standard of perfect holiness. Jesus met that standard for us.

Reference verses: (Titus 3:5, Ephesians 2:8–9, Romans 11:6)

God's Remedy for My Sin Problem

Fifth, I explain how God provides a way for us to be saved. The Bible tells us, "Without the shedding of blood, there is no forgiveness" (Hebrews 9:22). We're not talking about just any blood. God the Father, Jesus, and the Holy Spirit are pure, holy, sinless, and perfect. For us to enter Heaven, we too must be pure, holy, sinless, and perfect. That is why Jesus had to shed His blood on the cross for us: to cleanse us, so we would have an opportunity to get into His Heaven. Sending Jesus to the cross is God's way of punishing our sin without lowering His standard. When we repent of our sins, surrender our lives to Christ, and put our total trust and faith in Jesus, we are then "washed in the blood of Christ." When the Father looks at us, He no longer sees all of our sin and filth; He sees the righteousness of His holy Son, Jesus.

People sometimes say they need to quit drinking, smoking, cursing, or something else before they can be saved. The Bible says, "But God demonstrates his own love for us in this: While we were still sinners, Christ died for us" (Romans 5:8). God takes us as we are, and His love is unconditional. Jesus said, "For I have not come to call the righteous, but sinners" (Matthew 9:13). When we repent, the cleaning up process begins. "Repent, then, and turn to God, so that your sins may be wiped out" (Acts 3:19). The Father's love is expressed in "Christ and Him crucified." We don't deserve to have God die for us. With our simple minds, we cannot even comprehend God's unconditional love.

Reference verses: (John 3:17, Acts 4:12, Galatians 1:3-4, 1 John 1:9, John 3:36, 2 Corinthians 5:19–21, 1 John 5:12, 1 Corinthians 15:3)

My Requirement for Being Saved

Sixth, after sharing the gospel, I often tell people they are at a fork in the road: one road leads to death and destruction in Hell, and the other road leads to life with God in Heaven. I tell them, "Now it's your choice." Sometimes they say they do not want to make a choice, and I explain that they have just in fact made a choice. They have chosen to reject God's love and eternal life through Jesus Christ. No choice is a decision for death and destruction.

So what must we do to be saved? We must do three things: repent, believe, and receive. We must recognize that we are sinners and need a Savior, and Jesus is the only Savior acceptable to God. We must ask God for the forgiveness of our sins, and we must repent (admit we're sinners and turn away from our sin), acknowledging, "Yes, I'm a sinner. I'm guilty, and I need help."

We must believe Jesus is God and that He died on the cross to pay our sin debt for us. That word "believe" means we're betting 100 percent on Jesus for eternal life. We surrender and commit our lives to Jesus Christ to be not only our Savior, but the Lord of our lives.

"Surrendering" is very important, because when we surrender to God, we become "slaves" to Him. Paul tells us, "But now that you have been set free from sin and have become slaves of God, the benefit you reap leads to holiness, and the result is eternal life" (Romans 6:22).

Billy Graham says, "Until you have surrendered to Christ by a definite act of your will, you are not a Christian."[6]

How do we "receive"? God tells us that "Everyone who calls upon the name of the Lord will be saved" (Romans 10:13). To me, this means we should pray a simple prayer and talk with God about our situations. We need to ask God to forgive us of our sins, surrender our lives to Jesus, and ask Him to be our Savior and our Lord. There are no "magic" words. If a person is truly sorry for his or her sin, repents and believes in what Jesus has done for him or her, that's what receiving is all about. The thief on the cross did not have a long, eloquent prayer. He believed in Jesus and said, "Jesus, remember me when you come into your kingdom" (Luke 23:42). Jesus knew the man's heart. "Jesus answered him, 'Truly I tell you, today you will be with me in paradise'" (Luke 23:43).

There is a huge difference between our head knowledge and our heart knowledge. It is the difference between eternal life and eternal death. The Bible says, "If you declare with your mouth, 'Jesus is Lord,' and believe in your heart that God raised him from the dead, you will be saved. For it is with your heart that you believe and are justified, and it is with your mouth that you profess your faith and are saved" (Romans 10:9–10).

After dying on the cross, God raised Jesus to life on the third day. This was God's way of telling us our sin debt had been paid in full. Just as Jesus was raised from death to eternal life, so we too will be raised to eternal life when the time comes. If a person chooses to reject Jesus as their Savior and Lord, he or she will need to pack a fire extinguisher in the coffin. It's that simple. If people die without Jesus, they will stand before God at the Great White Throne of judgment and will be cast into the "lake of fire," which is what we refer to as "Hell" (cf. Revelation 20:11–15). It's going to be a horrible sight, the most horrible sight that has ever been seen since the beginning of time.

I usually ask people if they would like for me to help them pray, because many who have never attended church have no idea of what or how to pray. So I tell them, "I'll slowly pray a prayer, and if you believe it and mean it, you pray it after me."

I pray something like, "Dear Lord Jesus, I know that I'm a sinner, and I'm asking you to forgive me for my sins. I believe you died on that cross to pay for my sins. I want to turn away from my sins and place my faith in you. I'm surrendering my life to you, and I'm asking you to come into my heart and be my Savior and the Lord of my life. Thank you, God, for saving me. In Jesus's name, amen."

If I feel we need to discuss it, I talk with people about being "sealed" by the Holy Spirit. Some of my friends believe they can lose their salvation, but I don't believe that. If we have to do works or deeds to earn and keep our salvation, then Jesus died for nothing. God also says our salvation is a "gift" (Romans 6:23) and confirms the gift is forever: "God's gifts and his call are irrevocable" (Romans 11:29). God won't take back the gift. The "gift of eternal life" is "irrevocable." God also says, "When I act, who can reverse it" (Isaiah 43:13). When a person gets saved, it's a done deal. Once you've been born again, you can't be unborn. Someone once said, "You can never be good enough to earn your salvation or bad enough to lose it."

Reference verses: (Luke 13:3, Acts 17:30, Ezekiel 18:30, Acts 20:21, Isaiah 43:25, John 1:12, Romans 8:1, John 3:18, Jeremiah 31:34, John 5:24, John 10:28–30).

Church and Baptism

The seventh thing we'll discuss is church membership and baptism. After someone has trusted Jesus as Lord and Savior, I explain the purpose of baptism and how Jesus was baptized by John. Through baptism, we publically identify with Jesus. We belong to

Him. Baptism is a symbol of death to our old sinful life, and we are now raised to new life in Christ. We talk about the importance of church attendance, Bible study groups, Sunday school, and other groups where we share together and learn together. I usually ask if they know of a good church in their area where they might worship. If they don't, and I know of one, I recommend one. It's important that they don't walk into a "cult" church. I'll also recommend some churches to avoid. Find a church where the Bible, and only the Bible, is taught as God's word and Jesus is the only way to eternal life.

When I'm out of town and someone accepts Christ, I ask if there is a church nearby where he or she can worship. If people don't know of one, I suggest they go to a Christian bookstore and explain to the salesperson that they are a new Christian and looking for a good church to attend. The bookstore personnel will often know about good churches in the area and can recommend one. I'll tell the person to pray and ask the Holy Spirit to guide them.

Since there are many cult churches, I may suggest that people go to the 4Truth.net website. This website identifies many of the cult religions in the United States. These are religions and cults that disagree with the traditional Christian understanding of God the Father, Jesus Christ, and the Holy Spirit. It would be very easy for a new Christian to walk into a cult church and be immediately misled. Jesus said, "If you hold to my teachings, you are really my disciples. Then you will know the truth, and the truth will set you free" (John 8:31–32). Cult churches bind people with trying to work their way to eternal life. Jesus paid our sin debt and gives eternal life to us as a free gift. Our only "work" is to "believe." Jesus said, "The work of God is this: to believe in the one he has sent" (John 6:29).

Theology

If a great theologian heard me sharing the gospel, he or she would probably say that some things I say are incorrect. For example, I know that eternal life for believers doesn't start when we get to

Heaven—it starts now. When talking about Judgment Day, I don't try to explain the Great White Throne, the judgment of nations, and the judgment seat of Christ. I simply say that Judgment Day is coming. I talk about Heaven and Hell.

I always remember something I learned in the army. We were taught to "K-I-S-S," which means "keep it simple, stupid." I've been told that many of God's evangelists try to present the gospel on a third-grade level so everyone can understand.

Have a Plan

I've heard it said that "if you fail to plan, you plan to fail." You and your partner need to have a plan before going out. Pray, pray, pray first, and then plan how you will share the gospel. Plan who will lead and who will pray, because it's extremely difficult for two people to share the gospel at once—each will head in a different direction.

My partner and I always agree ahead of time on who will share the gospel and who will pray. If I'm to share the gospel and I come to a point where I don't know what to say or how to answer a question, I'll turn to my partner and say something like, "Hey, Janice, you've been awfully quiet. What do you think about that?" From that point on, Janice is to share the gospel, and I'll do the praying. If she hits a bump in the road, she will turn to me and say something like, "Ellison, that's a good question he has. How would you answer it?" Then it's my turn to share again, and my partner starts praying again. Also, we plan how to interrupt and act on a word from the Lord if one of us gets one.

If one of us feels we're beating a dead horse and it's time to leave before we do any damage, we have a preplanned way to end the meeting. We'll plant a seed and then leave. There's a saying: "Don't bruise the fruit." If the person doesn't want to accept Christ at that time, we want to be able to come back on a follow-up visit. I've had several people accept Christ on a third visit. If we offend the person (bruise the fruit), we may not get a second chance.

Dos and Don'ts

Do pray for yourself. Ask God to cleanse you of any sin and reveal unknown sin. Ask God to help you empty yourself of all your self-sufficiency. Pray for the filling of the Holy Spirit.

Do pray that you will be sensitive to the leading of the Holy Spirit.

Do listen to what people have to say. Even comment on their opinions, but stick to the gospel.

Do provide them with accurate information (Bible verses) so they can make their decisions.

Do deal with facts, not opinions.

Do let them know you care about them and their futures; otherwise, you would not be there.

Do, after sharing the gospel, invite people to pray and ask Jesus to be their Savior and Lord.

Do discuss baptism, church membership, and Bible study with them.

Do invite them to your church and give them a bulletin with the service times. Offer to give them a ride.

Don't get emotional and try to influence their decisions.

Don't attack their beliefs. Discuss eternal life and eternal death using God's requirements.

Don't try to talk people into getting saved. If they pray a Jesus prayer only because of us, then they probably are not saved. They just want to get us out the door. It's the Holy Spirit's job to convict them, draw them, and encourage them to make a decision.

Don't attack their opinions. Simply ask, "How did you arrive at that conclusion?"

Don't try to tell them what's wrong with them. Focus on the good news.

Don't chase rabbits (get sidetracked). If they ask questions that require lengthy answers, just say, "That's a good question.

Can we come back to that one in a few minutes?" Then continue on with sharing the gospel.

Don't try to manipulate Bible verses to make them say what you want, because that's totally wrong and unnecessary. Let the Holy Spirit and the sword of the Spirit do their work.

Don't depend on yourself. Depend on the Holy Spirit to guide you.

Don't be surprised if you encounter Satan or some of his demons, because they don't want you there. Remember that greater is He that is in you (God) than he that is in the world (Satan). If Satan shows up, run him off. Jesus has given us authority to put Satan and his demons in the wind.

Just Do It

Some say, "I will start sharing the gospel tomorrow." Remember, today is yesterday's tomorrow. Just do it. Do it now. Put together your plan and your Bible verses and choose to be a disciple. Get out of the boat and take that first step in faith. Watch the Holy Spirit do His work. Remember, "There is no wisdom, no insight, no plan that can succeed against the Lord" (Proverbs 21:30).

CHAPTER 16

Demons: Our First Encounter

In late 1990, my wife and I had our "baptism of fire" into spiritual warfare and demons. This encounter is not something we went looking for; it came to us.

Like many Christians, when we read the Bible, we just skimmed over the parts that dealt with demons. Many of our Christian friends at church told us that demons do not exist today. They were something Jesus dealt with two thousand years ago. I had been a Christian for only a couple of years, so I really did not know what to believe. I had never heard a preacher give a sermon on demons or how to cast them out, although preachers occasionally talked about putting on the armor of God as in Ephesians 6.

Around 1:30 a.m. on a Saturday morning in December 1990, our telephone rang. Connie answered and started saying things like, "Who is this? What did you say? What do you want? I can't understand you. Speak clearer. I can't understand you. What are you trying to say?" This went on for several minutes.

I told Connie several times to hang up, because I figured it was a drunk or someone on drugs. I just wanted to go back to sleep, because I planned to get up early to go deer hunting. Connie finally hung up the phone. We didn't even discuss the call. We just tried to go back to sleep.

The telephone rang again. Connie again answered and started with the questions. "Who is this? What are you trying to say? What do you want?" I asked Connie for the telephone. I listened for a few seconds and then handed the receiver back to her and told her to hang up.

The telephone rang a third time. Connie picked up, and without answering, handed it to me and said, "It's for you." There was a man on the phone. He was screaming, hollering, making awful growling sounds, and trying to talk at the same time. It was easy to assume this man had overdosed on drugs or gone completely out of his mind, and unfortunately for us, he had our telephone number.

I could only make out a few words from each outburst. After listening to him scream and growl and try to talk, I was able to make out some bits and pieces. He was saying, "Ellison, do you have the Light? Please, help me find the Light! I'm in the darkness! You are the only one who can help me! Please, I'm begging you! Help me find the Light!"

I kept saying, "What Light?" He was begging for help. The voices on the telephone sounded like several different people making all of these sounds at the same time.

I asked his name several times, and he tried to tell me, but I could not understand him. I asked him to just tell me his first name, and he made several attempts. I finally asked if he was telling me his name was John, and he screamed yes! Then, after several attempts, I could understand his last name was Jones. I asked, "Are you telling me your name is John Jones?"

He said, "Yes, yes, you know me!"

Let me tell you about my friend, John. He is what I would call a Christian's Christian. He truly loves the Lord and daily looks for opportunities to serve God. At his church he has been chairman of the deacons, a Sunday school teacher, a singer in the choir, and active in many Christian organizations. He has always been one of the Christian men I respect and look up to.

The man said, "We've been friends for years! Why are you and Connie talking to me like this? You know me! Help me!"

I argued with him, saying, "No! This is not John Jones! Who are you? What do you want?"

He screamed, "You've got to help me find the Light! Do you have the Light? Please! You are the only one who can help me! I'm begging you! Do you have the Light?"

I handed the telephone to Connie and said, "Hang up!"

A few minutes later, the telephone rang a again, and Connie handed the receiver to me. John was screaming, and in what seemed to be a state of panic, shouted, "Why did you hang up on me? You're my friend! You've got to help me!"

I said, "I don't know who you are, but I know you are not John Jones!" I asked him, "What do you want me to do?"

He said, "Come to me and help me find the Light!" The man was totally out of his mind. I asked John if he was talking about a flashlight. He said, "No! You know, the Light!" I asked John if he was talking about a car headlight and again, he said, "No, no, the Light! You know the Light I'm talking about!" I did not hear God speak out loud, but I clearly heard God's voice. He said, "Jesus is the Light."

I said, "Are you talking about Jesus?"

He said, "Yes! Yes! Help me find the Light!" He could not say the name "Jesus." He could only refer to Jesus as "the Light." I told John he had been a Christian since childhood, and he already had the Light. Every Christian has the Light. He said, "No, no, I've lost the Light. You've got to help me find the Light!"

I said, "John, I have the Light! Jesus is the Light!" I told him again, "You also have the Light! You have been a Christian forever, and you have the Light in you!"

He said, "No! I've lost the Light! I'm filled with darkness, and I can't get out! Help me find the Light!" He continued begging. I had never heard a man this desperate before. I did not understand why he would not call Jesus by name. He kept calling Jesus "the Light."

I still felt that this was someone strung out on drugs or a completely crazy person. I did not want to get near the man. I knew that if I hung up, he would just call again. I knew he wanted me to come to him and help him. So, I said, "OK, where are you?" He started giving me directions to somewhere in the North Charleston area. The names of the streets were so jumbled and made so little sense that no one could have followed the directions.

He said, "Will you come to me right now?"

I said, "If you are my friend, John Jones, I'll come!"

He said, "I am. Please hurry!" And I hung up.

Connie asked, "You're not going to meet that man, are you?" I told her no. She said, "You told him you would come. You lied to him."

I said, "No, I didn't lie. I told him if he was John Jones, I would come, but I know he is not John. John is a stronger Christian than I am. It really doesn't matter how strong a Christian you are; once you receive Christ, you have the Light in you. John already has the Light. I don't know who that crazy man is, but I'm not about to go to him in the middle of the night."

Connie said, "That man is crazy enough to kill you." I told Connie to get some sleep.

About twenty minutes later, the telephone rang again. The man was screaming, "You said you would come! Why did you lie to me? You're my friend! Why won't you help me?"

I said, "I told you if you were John Jones, I'd come, but you are not my friend. I don't know who you are, but leave us alone!"

He screamed, "You've got to help me! You're the only one who can help me! Please!"

I said, "Look, if you're John, you know where I live! You come to me!"

He said, "I'm coming!"

Connie sat up in bed, turned on a lamp, and said, "Now what are you going to do? That crazy man is coming to our house! He's crazy enough to kill all of us!"

I said, "It's not John, and whoever it is probably doesn't know where we live!"

Connie said, "But what if the man does know where we live? He'll be here in twenty minutes! What are we going to do?" She was scared and jumped out of bed and started dressing. The fear I saw in her eyes made me a little uneasy.

I said, "What are you doing?

Connie said, "Some crazy man is on the way to our house, and he might break in. He's not going to catch me running around the house half naked. I'm getting dressed." Then she said, "I'm going to call the police right now!"

I said, "They won't do anything. No crime has been committed."

We both got dressed and went into the den. By now it was almost 2:30 a.m. We talked about what we would do if this crazy man came to our house. Connie said, "Maybe we should call John's house and just see if it really was John calling us."

I said, "No, I don't want to wake John and his wife at 2:30 a.m." Connie and I both felt certain it was not John, but after thinking about it a few minutes, I agreed to make the call. If John was home, I would just apologize and tell him we had a prank caller using his name.

I called John's house, and his wife answered. I said, "This is Ellison Kelly, and I'm sorry to bother you so late, but may I speak with John?"

She said, "He's not here. Why are you calling? Have you heard from John?" My heart sank. I knew it must have been John, and he desperately needed my help.

I said, "A man called the house and said his name was John Jones, but it did not sound like John's voice. I just wanted to see if it really was John who called."

She said, "It was John. He has not been home in over a week. John has gone totally out of his mind. He's completely crazy! We've tried to help him, and so have our friends, but no one can help him.

I said, "We'll do what we can." I thanked her and hung up. Connie and I looked at each other and said, "Now what?" We both knew John was on the way to our house, and his wife had confirmed he had gone crazy. I went to the bedroom and took a .38 special pistol out of the drawer. We sat on the den couch and discussed our options.

I told Connie that when John drove up, I would go out in the front yard to talk with him. I would lock the front door behind me. I did not want him in the house under any circumstances. I told her that if we started fighting, she should call 911, but under no circumstances was she to open the door. I told her I really was not ready to die, but I knew for a fact that if John killed me, I'd be with Jesus in Heaven. She knew this but still wasn't happy with that answer.

I told her that if he tried to get into the house not to shoot through the front door. If he broke down the front door, as soon as he set one foot inside the house, she was to point the pistol at his belly and pull the trigger five times. Connie wasn't completely happy with the plan. She didn't like the idea of me being killed and her not being able to help me. I told her that if he killed me, he'll kill her and our family, and she had to protect our family. She said, "If he tries to get in the house, I'll blow his ass away!" And I knew she would do just that.

We waited in the foyer. Our front door has a small window that opens. We opened it so Connie could watch us and listen. A few minutes later, John drove up. He drove his truck through the driveway and stopped his truck on the grass in our front yard.

I walked out of the house and closed and locked the front door behind me. John jumped out of the truck, leaving the door open, the headlights on, and the engine running. He ran across the front yard toward me with his arms swinging like a wild man's. He had an extremely wild look in his eyes. He grabbed my shoulders and started shaking me, saying, "Why won't you help me? Why won't you help me?" Then, in a hateful, laughing voice he said, "Aren't you going to invite me into your house?"

I said, "No, we both need some fresh air. Let's sit on the steps and talk."

He said, "But I want to go into your house!"

I said, "No, we need the fresh air. Sit on the steps, and let's talk." I did not realize until later that it was the demons speaking through John's mouth.

I asked John what had happened to him, and he said he didn't know. Something had "taken over him." He grabbed me again and said, "Ellison, do you have the Light? Please help me find the Light!" Then, in another voice (the demon's), with their hateful laugh, the demons said, "You can't help him! No one can help him!" The demons made similar statements throughout the conversation, broken with hateful laughs and hideous growls. This voice was not John's voice, and I do not think John could make these sounds even if he tried.

John and I talked a few minutes, and then I asked, "John, may I pray for you?"

In something close to his normal voice, he said, "Yes! Please!" Then the demons laughed and said, "It won't do any good! Your prayers won't do any good. Your prayers mean nothing." I prayed and asked God to help John, but I really didn't know specifically what to pray for. Even I felt like they were just "dry" prayers. There was no change in John. The laughs and growls continued, even as we prayed.

I asked John, "What has caused this?" He said that he did not know, but this darkness had taken over him.

I said, "John, let me pray again." And again the demon's voices kept mocking me and laughing at me as I prayed for John. I just sat there and had no idea what do next. John and I were both silent for a few minutes. Then I clearly heard God's voice say one word: "Demons." I asked John, "Did you hear that?"

John said, "Hear what?" I knew it was God who had spoken to me out loud, and I knew John did not hear God speak.

I said, "John, I think you have demons in you. Would you let me try to cast them out?"

He said, "Try anything." The demons in their hateful voices laughed and said, "It won't do any good. You can try anything you want, but it won't do any good! You can't cast us out."

The only thing I knew about demons was what I had read in the Bible. I remembered about Legion (cf. Mark 5:9). I also remembered that when the seventy-two disciples came back, they said, "Lord, even the demons submitted to us in your name" (Luke 10:17). I knew if I was going to cast out the demons, it had to be done in the name of Jesus Christ.

So, without really knowing how to cast out demons, I just started saying things like, "In the name of Jesus Christ, I command you demons to come out of John! By the power and the blood of the Holy Son of God, I command you to come out!" I told the demons, "It is not me, but Jesus speaking through me, commanding you to come out!" I continued, "I have been washed by the blood of Jesus Christ! Greater is He that is in me than he that is in the world!" I told the demons that in the name of Jesus, I had power over them. I told Satan, "You bruised the heel of Jesus, but He has cut your ass! I've read the book! I know how it ends—you lose! You may win a battle or two along the way, but you lose the war! You know it, and I know it! In the name of Jesus Christ, I command you to come out of John right now! Come out this minute! You no longer have power over him! Get out of him!" I kept making these and other commands, all in the name of Jesus Christ, who has given all Christians the authority to cast out demons.

A demon's voice said, "Don't you want to know our names?"

I first said, "No, I don't care what your names are. All of you demons, come out now."

Then the demon again said, "Ask us our names." John spoke up and said, "Go ahead; ask their names."

So I said, "Tell me your names!" They started telling me names like Lust, Money, Pride, and more. I really didn't pay much attention to the names. I commanded some of the names to come out, and then I just commanded all of them to come out.

John started shaking from side to side. I put my arm around his shoulders and held him. The deep, growling demon voice mumbled something I could not understand. I said, "Say that again!" The demon mumbled again, and I could not understand him. So I said, "I command you, in the name of Jesus Christ, to say that again so I can understand you!"

The demon voice then clearly said, "Where would you have us go?" I had no idea. Where do you tell demons to go? I sat there silently, still holding John. The demons started laughing at me and mocking me. The demons said, "I know where we'll go! We'll go into your house! Your family is in your house! We'll go into your family!" I think they even named the members of my family who were in the house, something John could not have known.

I said, "No! In the name of Jesus Christ, I command you to stay away from my family! I command you to leave them alone! Stay out of my house!" The demons laughed at me and argued with me. The demons continued saying they were going to leave John and go into my family! They said I couldn't stop them (demons are liars, and so is Satan). This really scared me, but I continued commanding them to stay out of my house and away from my family. We again sat silent for a few seconds, and I still had no idea of where to tell the demons to go.

My first thought was "the pigs" (cf. Mark 5:11-13). The demons either knew what I was thinking or made a good guess on their first shot, because they laughed and said, "The pigs."

I said, "No! I don't want to kill two thousand pigs!" I looked at the grass in my front yard and I thought, *No, I don't want them in my yard, because they'll kill the grass.* I looked at a large pecan tree in the median in front of my house and thought, *No, I don't want to kill the pecan tree either.* I looked at my neighbor's house, but they didn't need these demons either.

While I was thinking, the demons' voices continued mocking me because I did not know where to tell them to go. Then I heard God's voice again. He very clearly said, "Hell!"

I said, "In the name of Jesus Christ, I command you demons to come out of John and go to Hell! You belong to Satan, and Satan belongs in Hell! I command you to come out now! All of you come out right now! Go to Hell! Never harm John or anyone else again! I demand you come out of John now, this very instant, and go to Hell!" I repeated these and other commands.

I had my arm around John and held him tightly, and I said, "I claim John for Jesus Christ. He belongs to God, and you demons have no place in him! This man is a child of the Living God, and I command you to come out right now!"

John started shaking his head violently from side to side. He started gagging and spitting. Each time I commanded the demons to come out, John gagged and spat on the sidewalk. The spit looked green, like mucus. Then, in his natural voice, he started laughing and saying, "Do it again! Do it again!"

I said, "Do what again?"

He said, "You tell them to get out. You tell them to get out of me." (When demons are coming out of a person, the person often can feel them leave.) After several more times, John went limp. His shoulders slumped, and his head hung down. We were both silent, and I knew the demons were gone.

Exhausted, John looked at me and in a normal voice said, "Ellison, do you have the Light? Can you help me find the Light?"

I wanted to tell John he already had the Light, but I didn't. I said, "Yes, John, I have the Light. Jesus Christ is the Light. And when I got saved, Jesus and His Light came into me and will always be in me. It's a gift, John. God loves you. Do you want the gift? Do you want Jesus?"

John said, "Yes, help me find the Light!" I told John that Jesus said, "Ask and it will be given to you; seek and you will find; knock and the door will be opened to you" (Matthew 7:7). I told John all he needed to do was to ask for the Light, to ask Jesus into his heart. I asked John if he wanted me to pray with him and to ask Jesus into his heart. He said, "Yes! Let's move out to the front of the yard, away from all the green mess!" We knelt under the dogwood trees. I placed my hand on his shoulder, and we prayed the sinner's prayer. John hugged me and thanked me. He was laughing and happy. The demons were gone. John was normal again—he was the man I had known for the past twenty years.

After a minute or so, John's facial expression changed from happy to sad. I thought, *Oh no, here we go again.* I asked John what was wrong. He said, "I'm afraid they will get me again and take me back into the darkness." I couldn't believe what John was saying, but considering all that had happened to him, I guess he had a right to be afraid.

I held out a finger in front of John. I told John to grab my finger as tightly as he could and not to turn it loose. He grabbed my finger, laughed, and said, "I've got you, and I'm not going to turn it loose."

I said, "It is impossible for me to pull my finger out of your hand, isn't it?"

He said, "Yes! I've got you, and I'm not turning you loose!"

I said, "John, you know the Bible better than I do. Do you remember when Jesus said, 'no one will snatch them out of my hand'

(John 10:28)? Jesus has you in the palm of His hand, and no one, including the demons, can snatch you away from Jesus. Do you believe that?"

John said, "Yes. Jesus said it, so I believe it!"

John had been under the control of the demons for over a week. After the last demon left John, he changed from being a man totally out of his mind, struggling under the control of demons, back to being a perfectly normal man; a normal, Christian man.

I asked John to come into the house with me, and we'd have some coffee and talk. We got up and walked toward the house. As we approached the front steps, I remembered that Connie was standing at the front door with a .38 special pistol in her hand. I slowly walked up the steps, because I did not know what her state of mind would be. The experience in the front yard might have seemed exciting to some, but it was not. At first, I was almost certain I was going to die on my front steps. Then, when I saw the reaction of the demons to the name of Jesus Christ, the fear left me and I became bold in dealing with the demons. John was OK now, but I was afraid that Connie might be so upset, she would shoot through the door and kill both of us.

I tried to open the front door, but it was still locked. Connie was standing in the foyer, looking at us. I asked Connie to unlock the door and let us in, but she said nothing. John laughed and said, "What's the matter, are you afraid of me? You locked the door so I couldn't get in."

I shrugged off his question and again asked Connie again to open the door.

She finally answered, "Are you sure?" I told her again to unlock the door, and she did, standing aside in the foyer. As we walked in, Connie was holding the pistol behind her back. She looked very leery about letting John in the house. I carefully took the pistol out of her hand and hid it behind a picture that was on the foyer table, just in case it was still needed.

By now it was around 4:30 a.m. We had been in the front yard about two hours. We sat in the den, drank coffee, and discussed what had happened. John talked about how he had been taken captive and was in the darkness. It was black and very cold and very damp. He did not want to be there, but he could not get out. I asked him if he was in Hell, and he said that he knew it was not Hell. He did not know where it was, but he could not find the Light. He felt helpless. He did not know how he had lost the Light or how he had been taken captive by the demons. But somehow, he knew he needed to get to me for help.

Our children and Mom were home, and we did not have an empty bedroom. Connie put sheets, a blanket, and a pillow on the couch and asked John to stay the night with us. He at first agreed to stay. Then he said, "No, I need to go make right some of things I have done." I offered to go with him, but he said he'd go by himself. I told him he needed to go home and check on his wife and his family. He said he would as soon as he straightened out some things he had done.

We called John's house later that morning. His wife said John had not yet come home, but he had called her and said he was OK. She said he had told her how we had cast out the demons. She did not understand all that was going on but was grateful for our help. John came home later that day.

The next day, Sunday, John told his preacher that he needed to talk to the congregation. He stood before the congregation at his church and gave his testimony of how demons had taken control of him and kept him captive for over a week. He told how he had gone to a friend's house in the middle of the night and in the name of Jesus Christ, his friend had cast out the demons.

I asked John why he had told the folks in his church, because I thought it might embarrass his wife and his family. He said, "Yes, it embarrassed them. My wife is still mad at me, but I don't care." He said, "The people in my church are my friends, and they need to know; I had to warn them. If it can happen to me, it can happen to them."

I love John. He's my brother in Christ. He has been there for me when I needed help. I thank God I was there when he needed help. Today, John is just as normal as you or me.

Connie and I did not discuss this experience with each other or anyone else for several years. Quite frankly, we knew our Christian friends would not believe us. Some of our friends today still don't believe us, and they still don't believe in spiritual warfare, Satan, or his demons. We knew this was a "God thing," and we both just trust God without question and keep moving ahead, serving our Savior.

Listen to what Billy Graham says about Satan and his demons.

> There is no adequate explanation for what is happening throughout the world except that there is a moving of gigantic spiritual forces of evil that are gaining momentum and strength, and that behind these activities are the person and power of Satan.
>
> The Bible teaches that those outside of Christ can be organized and directed by Satan in a great evil federation. Because the world system has rejected Christ, it furnishes an ideal sphere for the operation of Satan and his demons.
>
> The world battle is being fought on a spiritual level. I am convinced that on the spiritual battlefield, Christ has taken up His position and is summoning His followers to stand with Him.[7]

CHAPTER 17

Healing Prayer and Spiritual Warfare

If you knew someone was coming to your house to steal, to kill and destroy you and your family, what would you do? I know what I'd do. I'd grab a gun and defend my family. I have good news and bad news for you. If you and your family are Christians, someone is trying to steal, to kill and destroy you. But the good news is that Jesus has given us the knowledge, the weapons, and the authority to defeat the enemy.

Healing prayer and spiritual warfare go hand in hand. We are told, "For our struggle is not against flesh and blood, but against the rulers, against the authorities, against the powers of this dark world and against the spiritual forces of evil in the heavenly realms" (Ephesians 6:12).

There is a war going on around us, and many Christian are not even aware of it. The battle lines have already been drawn. The two sides are the Father, Son, Holy Spirit, their angels, and their Christians versus Satan with his demonic forces. The battle is good against evil, the Kingdom of God against the kingdom of Satan. It's not a make-believe war; it's real. People's lives are destroyed, and people actually die. If you do not believe there is a war going on right now but believe our Bible is the word of our God, then listen to what God's word says about Satan and the war:

> "The whole world is under the control of the evil one" (1 John 5:19).
>
> Satan is the "ruler of the kingdom of the air" (Ephesians 2:2).
>
> Satan is the "prince of this world" (John 12:31).
>
> "For Satan himself masquerades as an angel of light" (2 Corinthians 11:14).
>
> "The god of this age has blinded the minds of unbelievers, so that they cannot see the light of the gospel that displays the glory of Christ, who is the image of God" (2 Corinthians 4:4).

There are more Scriptures that deal with the war, but we know the outcome: we win! Our victory came at the cross when Jesus defeated Satan. Now we who are in Jesus share in His victory. Satan is real, and his demons are real. I've actually seen demons. Some of my friends have also. I've prayed with many people and cast out many demons, and I've actually had demons cast out of me. I mentioned the night when I lay in bed with a broken neck, I actually heard Satan's voice telling me to commit suicide. Satan's goal is to "steal and kill and destroy" (John 10:10) you and me.

Ten years ago when I became involved in healing prayer, I also became involved in spiritual warfare. Up until that time, I thought I understood most of what I needed to know from the Bible. I had studied the Bible hard for fifteen years. Now, it was as if God had opened a new door to me. On the other side of this door was a huge, new work that I had never realized even existed.

The Holy Spirit gives us various spiritual gifts to be used in building up Christ's church. I personally believe that the work of healing prayer and spiritual warfare is a spiritual gift, and our Lord has equipped some of His Christians to do this work. I do not believe that all Christians are called to be active in this ministry, just as we are not all called to be pastors, teachers, leaders, or evangelists. But everyone should be aware of the war and the enemy.

I have taken many training classes and read many books on healing prayer and spiritual warfare. They are huge topics. I still don't understand much of what is said and done in these ministries, but I do know that God is in the center of this work. The majority of my training came from Francis and Judith MacNutt and their Christian Healing Ministries organization, located in Jacksonville, Florida.

If God has called you to get involved with this work, I encourage you to read some books on healing prayer and spiritual warfare. There are many good books available. These are only a few of the many I have read:

Healing by Francis MacNutt
Christ the Healer by F. F. Bosworth
The Power to Heal by Francis MacNutt
Power Healing by John Wimber
Deliverance from Evil Spirits: A Practical Manual by Francis MacNutt
The Bondage Breaker by Neil T. Anderson
They Shall Expel Demons by Derek Prince
Pigs in the Parlor: A Practical Guide to Deliverance by Frank and Ida Mae Hammond
Demolishing Strongholds: God's Way to Spiritual Freedom by Mike and Sue Dowgiewicz
The Handbook for Spiritual Warfare by Dr. Ed Murphy

God says, "My people are destroyed from lack of knowledge" (Hosea 4:6). Warren Wiersbe writes, "If you are going to win the battle, you must know the enemy, possess power and equipment to attack him, and also have protection against him."[8]

We really have no excuse for not knowing about healing prayer and spiritual warfare. The knowledge is right here before us. We need only to reach out and take it. To get started, Google the word "healing prayer," "spiritual warfare," or "demons." There is a wealth of information and help on the Internet. But be careful, because there are false prophets who would love to bind you in their chains.

When I was in the army, I spent my first ten months in training: boot camp, advanced training, and Officer Candidate School. Of those ten months, I'd say we focused 90 percent of our time on training to be American soldiers. We spent the remaining 10 percent of our time learning the tactics of the enemy and his weapons. My personal opinion is that we should spend at least 90 percent of our time studying the Bible and focusing on Jesus, and 10 percent of our time learning about our enemy and his tactics. We need to keep our focus on Christ, but at the same time, remember that Satan, our enemy, "prowls around like a roaring lion looking for someone to devour" (1 Peter 5:8).

Deer season opens in the Lowcountry of South Carolina in August. It's hot, and rattlesnakes are out and on the prowl. When I'm deer hunting, I focus 90 percent of my attention on hunting deer and 10 percent of my attention on watching out for the enemy: the rattlesnakes. In Ephesians 6, we learn to put on the armor of God to protect us from our enemy, Satan. When I'm deer hunting, I also put on armor. I put on a pair of snake boots so that as I walk through the woods deer hunting, I'm not worried about rattlesnakes. But I'm not careless either.

Satan's greatest lie is, "Trust me, there is no war going on around you." If you don't believe there is a war going on, then you're already defeated. Satan is going to try to steal, kill, and destroy you, your family, your joy, your health, your friends, and anything else he can get his hooks into. He's going to try to destroy and discredit your walk with our Savior. If you're not a Christian, you already belong to Satan.

Satan cannot own (possess) a Christian, because we are already owned and possessed by Jesus Christ. We have been purchased (redeemed) with the blood of Christ. We are in Jesus Christ, and we are sealed by the Holy Spirit. But if Satan can find an opening in our spiritual armor, he will try to get his "hook" into us and pull us down. A Christian can get a cold, the flu, and cancer. A Christian can also "get a demon." Satan's demons can wreak havoc on a Christian. In mild cases, this is usually referred to as being oppressed. In stronger cases, demons can actually control a person.

When Christians are oppressed with Satan's demons, they often feel like they have hundred-pound weights on top of them. One definition of *oppressed* is "weighted down." When the demons are cast out, the weight is gone, and a person often feels lighter. One man we prayed with not only felt the demons come out, he actually saw them as they left.

I gave an example of a strong Christian who was under the control of demons in the previous chapter. The demons controlled this Christian man's actions for over a week.

When we encounter spiritual warfare, there is good news in the Bible:

> Jesus said, "I have given you authority to trample on snakes and scorpions and to overcome all the power of the enemy; nothing will harm you" (Luke 10:19).
>
> Jesus said, "All authority in heaven and on earth has been given to me" (Matthew 28:18).
>
> Jesus is the "Lord of lords and King of kings" (Revelation 17:14).

> "Jesus knew that the Father had put all things under his power" (John 13:3).
>
> "The reason the Son of God appeared was to destroy the devil's work" (1 John 3:8).
>
> "For though we live in the world, we do not wage war as the world does. The weapons we fight with are not the weapons of the world. On the contrary, they have divine power to demolish strongholds." (2 Corinthians 10:3–4).
>
> Jesus said, "And these signs will accompany those who believe: In my name they will drive out demons" (Mark 16:17).
>
> "The God of peace will soon crush Satan under your feet" (Romans 16:20).

Listen to what Billy Graham says about the spiritual war:

> On the spiritual battlefield today, the Lord is calling for volunteers who will pay the price to throw back the enemy. It is in prayer and obedience that we fight the battle. Because of the authority that belongs to the crucified and risen Son of God, situations on the earth can be controlled, forces in the unseen realms moved, changes effected, powers of evil dislodged and routed, and the purposes of God pressed forward to final triumph.
>
> I am convinced that hell's legions can be stopped and turned back. I am convinced that the invading heathen darkness can be hurled back. It is not too much to believe that the Lord can endure people with the baptism of the Holy Spirit for this end-time ministry as He did at Pentecost.[9]

Jesus tells us that He does only what He sees His Father doing. He said, "the Son can do nothing by himself; he can do only what he sees his Father doing, because whatever the Father does the Son also does" (John 5:19). All through the gospels, Jesus healed the sick and cast out demons. As disciples of Jesus Christ, we follow His example. We rely on Jesus as we do this work today. Jesus said, "apart from me you can do nothing" (John 15:5).

Jesus has equipped us for the fight. Jesus expects us to get in the fight. He said, "Very truly I tell you, whoever believes in me will do the works I have been doing, and they will do even greater things than these, because I am going to the Father. And I will do whatever you ask in my name, so that the Father may be glorified in the Son. You may ask me for anything in my name, and I will do it" (John 14:12–14). When we fight, we fight in the name and in the power of Jesus Christ. Jesus and the Holy Spirit do their work through us. Without them, we would be dead meat. Satan is a powerful adversary.

How Does Satan's Hook Work?

How does Satan get a hook into a Christian? How does he oppress, influence, and gain control of our thoughts and actions? From all I've learned so far, it's by a habitual sin, a major hurt, or repeated disobedience to God. I've been told that we must give Satan a legal right to attack us. Satan will hook a child who has been abused, even though the abuse is never a child's fault. He will hook someone who has been exposed to trauma (for instance, a friend killed in a car accident). Examples of sins, hurts, and testimonies are given in many of the books on the subject.

Some people innocently join organizations that are not Christian based but don't realize it. The organizations do works that look good on the outside, but on the inside, the organizations are secretive, oaths and vows are sworn, curses are called out, and their leaders are exalted. Even non-Christian religions are accepted as equal to our Father, Son, and Holy Spirit.

Jesus tells us, "But I tell you, do not swear an oath at all: either by heaven, for it is God's throne; or by the earth, for it is his footstool; or by Jerusalem, for it is the city of the Great King. And do not swear by your head, for you cannot make even one hair white or black. All you need to say is simply 'Yes' or 'No'; anything beyond this comes from the evil one" (Matthew 5:34–37). Jesus says that when you swear an oath, your oath is from Satan, the evil one. James also tells us not to swear; "Otherwise you will be condemned" (James 5:12). Jesus tells us, "If you love me, keep my commands" (John 14:15). Jesus also says, "Anyone who does not love me will not obey my teaching" (John 14:24).

One good Internet site that compares the beliefs of cult religions and organizations to the beliefs of Christianity is www.4Truth.net. Click on its links for "New Religions and Cults" and also "World Religions."

The Elephant and the Chain

Elephants have great memories. When a captive elephant is a baby, a small chain is attached to its leg to keep it from wandering off. No matter how hard the baby elephant jerks on that chain, it can't break it and go free. After a while, the elephant quits trying to break the chain, because it knows it can't. As the elephant grows older, the keepers use the same small chain because the grown elephant doesn't realize that as a huge, seven-ton animal, it could easily snap the chain. The elephant is bound by the memory from its youth that it can't break the chain. People are like that too. We can easily be bound by hurting memories.

Many people are bound by hurting remarks that were thrown at them in youth. For example, "You'll never amount to anything, you're good for nothing, you're ugly, no one will ever love you, I don't want you," and other hurtful remarks. Children are abused and told it is their fault. They carry this guilt and are told never to tell anyone what happened to them, because it's their fault. Many people go through life in bondage to inner wounds, experiences, and memories. These remarks and memories can and will bind people throughout their lifetimes. I know a woman who was abused as a child and carried fear from the abuse all her adult life. Satan had her bound in his chains of fear for over seventy years, her entire adult life.

Don't allow the past to dictate and control your future. Jesus came to set the captives free. Live in the unconditional love and freedom of our Risen Christ.

Praying with People

Over the last ten years, I have come across several good prayer ministries, such as Christian Healing Ministries, Sozo, and the Order of St. Luke. These and others provide excellent training in healing prayer and spiritual warfare. We sometimes pray in a room at a church, at conference centers, in homes, and basically, wherever the Lord leads. The following testimonies have taken place here in South Carolina as well as in other states.

I'll share some of my personal experiences and a few things I have learned. Most of the names of the people involved and some circumstances have been changed. The number-one rule when praying with someone is to keep confidential the identity of the person being prayed for. However, in some of the testimonies that follow, the person healed said, "Go ahead and use my name. Others need to know that Jesus will also set them free." One man told me, "Absolutely! Go ahead and use my name. Use my wife's name and the names of my children. People need to know that Jesus is still healing people today." In those cases, the actual names are used.

In our prayer sessions, we deal with salvation, physical healing, inner healing, memories, experiences, forgiveness, birth, deliverance, and more. We rely on the Holy Spirit to guide us as we pray.

Jesus Heals Mom

The first time I ever prayed for healing was twenty-five years ago, long before I ever heard of healing prayer. I had just become a Christian. At that time, my mother, age seventy-four, had been sick for well over a year. Once or twice a month, I took her to three doctors at the Medical University in Charleston. They ran test after test, but they could not help her. Her skin would bleed through its pores for no apparent reason, and she was always in a great deal of pain. One Sunday morning, Mom was in church, and the woman sitting on the pew behind her tapped her on the shoulder and said, "Mary, your back is bleeding through your white blouse." Mom had to leave church in front of everyone, and it really embarrassed her. She would not return to church for fear the bleeding would start again.

Then, in June 1988, I became a Christian. During the prior year, Mom's condition had progressively worsened. I stopped by her condo on a Thursday after work, and she looked like death warmed over. I really felt like she would soon die. I told Mom that the next day, I was going to do three things: I would go to the hospital and reserve a patient bed for her. I would come to her condo and pick her up at 8:00 a.m. and take her to the hospital to be admitted. I would then bring her three doctors to her hospital room. I planned to tell them that Mom was staying in the hospital until they healed her. I fully intended to do those three things on Friday morning.

Thursday evening when I was reading the Bible, I kept reading through the gospels of how Jesus healed so many people. The people Jesus was healing were not even Christians. So why was my Mom, the strongest Christian I knew, suffering so badly? I laid my Bible in front of me, got on my knees, and read the Scriptures back to God the Father of how Jesus healed so many people. I read that if we had enough faith, we could speak and throw a mountain into the sea. With that same faith, we could ask for anything in prayer (cf. Matthew 21:21–22). I read to God the Scripture about the centurion and his servant. Jesus did not even need to be present with the servant for the healing. Jesus needed only to "say the word" (Matthew 8:8).

I told God that I did not understand why a Christian like Mom had to suffer like this. By now, tears were running down my face. I told God that if one Christian on the face of the earth had to suffer this badly, "Then heal my Mom and give me all of her sickness and pain." I could not bear to see her suffer anymore. I told God to "pile the pain and suffering on me." I was serious, and God knew I was serious.

When I finished praying, I got up off my knees. As I stood up, something happened. I did not understand how I knew, but I absolutely knew that God had just completely healed Mom. I walked to the alarm clock in my bedroom, and it was 10:00 p.m. I set the alarm so I could get up early Friday, and I went to bed.

As soon as I woke up Friday morning, I looked under the cover to see if I was covered with blood. I had fully expected God to give me all Mom's bleeding, pain, and suffering, because that's what I had prayed for. But there was no blood and no pain. I got up, cleaned up, and went to work.

I had told Mom I would do those three things, but I now knew there was no need. I knew she had been healed, and there was no need to take her to the hospital. All morning I waited for my telephone to ring and for Mom to tell me she had been healed.

Finally, after lunch, I couldn't take it any longer, so I called Mom. Her telephone rang and rang. She finally picked up the telephone, but she didn't say anything. I said, "Mom, it's me. What's going on?" There was no answer. Again I said, "Mom, what's going on?"

She finally answered, and her exact words were, "I don't understand what happened."

I said, "Mom, tell me what happened."

She again said, "I don't understand what happened." After she had been sick for over a year, I knew she didn't understand how this had happened. I asked her a third time, and she said, "I've been healed. It's just like I had never been sick. It's gone. I don't understand what happened."

I went by her condo after work, and Mom looked great! I asked her to tell me what had happened. She said she had been watching TV, and she was tired. She knew she couldn't lie down in bed, because lying down was too painful. She said she had gone into the bedroom and planned to just sit on the side of the bed all night and wait until morning when I would come take her to the hospital. She said she was standing in front of her dresser, looking into the mirror. Then all the pain, bleeding, and weakness just suddenly went away. She said it was like someone had flipped a light switch. She went from suffering to being totally healed in a split second.

I asked what she did then. She said, "I don't know why, but for some reason, I walked all the way around to the other side of the bed and picked up the alarm clock and looked at the time. It was 10:00 p.m." Jesus had healed Mom just as he did the centurion's servant. I had prayed for Mom at 10:00 p.m., and Jesus completely healed Mom at 10:00 p.m. This sickness never returned.

Frank Saw Demons

My wife and I were in Florida, visiting her aunt who was in a nursing home. We were at a restaurant having dinner and noticed an elderly man sitting by himself. The Lord prompted me to go over and talk with him. I told him that I was a Christian and asked if I could pray for him. Frank said he had been involved in Satan worship, and he wanted to be set free. I shared the gospel with him, and he prayed to receive Christ, but I don't think it was the real deal. I really don't know what he was up to. I think he may have just been messing with me because I told him I was a Christian.

As we talked, I learned something. This may have been why the Lord had prompted me to go talk with Frank. He mentioned that he sometimes saw demons. He said, "They look like the black shadow of a man, but no man is there. You see only the black shadow." That was news to me.

Since that time, I too have seen demons at three places: in our church, in our home, and at a church conference. Not everyone sees demons, though. Connie and I were listening to a speaker at a conference, and I saw demons moving around behind the speaker. I asked Connie if she could see them, but she could not.

A teenage girl once asked us to come to her apartment and drive out the demons. Several of us went to her apartment and prayed with her. As we prayed, she could see the demons in the room and outside her window. We could not see the demons. So, I guess, sometimes you can see demons, and sometimes you can't. Do I understand this? No. I just keep moving forward. If God wants me to see the demons, I will. If not, I won't. It's that simple. It's a "God thing." John the Baptist said it well: "A person can receive only what is given them from heaven" (John 3:27).

Demons in Me

Yes, I've had demons cast out of me. They were in me, and I didn't even know it. I went to a Christian Healing Ministries conference in Jacksonville, Florida. Francis and Judith MacNutt asked anyone who wanted prayer to come to the front of the room. I don't know about you, but I welcome all the prayer I can get. I went to the front of the room. Over fifty of us went forward for prayer.

Since this was my first time at this type of conference, I expected Francis and Judith to hit people in the head and shout, "Be healed," as I had seen others do many times on TV. Much of what I had seen on TV looked faked, and I didn't like it. I had already made up my mind that they were not going to hit me in the head and knock me to the floor. But to my surprise, they never raised their voices and never touched anyone. They simply held their hands out in submission to God and calmly prayed for each person. They prayed in their prayer language—tongues. One by one, those being prayed for fell backward to the floor. I say again, they never touched anyone. Neither did they shout, "Be healed!"

When they came to me, Judith asked, "What would you like us to pray for?"

I said, "Pray for my daughter, who is sick." I closed my eyes and heard both Francis and Judith praying in tongues. They did not touch me. Then I felt one finger touch the right side of my neck. I thought, *Where did that finger come from?* I then felt something like a huge shop-vacuum hose touch my neck. It felt like my brains and the inside of my face were being sucked out through the powerful vacuum at the point where the finger touched my neck. I felt the same sensation starting at the tips of my toes. It came up through my entire body as my insides were sucked out through the vacuum. When I opened my eyes, I was lying on the floor, staring at the ceiling.

One by one, we got up off the floor and took our seats, and the conference continued. I was greatly puzzled by what had just happened. We don't do stuff like that in our church.

One major change occurred after that prayer session. For months, I had been dead in the water. I had had no desire to read the Bible or pray. I went through the motions, but it was not real. After the MacNutts prayed over me, I again had that tremendous hunger to study God's Word and pray. But I still did not understand what had happened.

A few months later, I was studying the Bible and came across a passage that explained everything. Jesus said, "But if I drive out demons by the finger of God, then the kingdom of God has come upon you" (Luke 11:20). I immediately knew whose finger had been on my neck. It was the finger of God. It all came together. I've been told that Judith has the spiritual gift of discerning evil spirits. I don't know if Judith in her prayer was casting out the demons, or if she simply prayed and asked the Holy Spirit to do whatever work was needed. Either way, it worked. It was the demons I felt leaving my body. There was a crowd of them, and I had no idea they were even present.

Linda and Her Mom

Linda asked if we would pray with her. Jo Ann and I met with Linda, and she told us of the terrible problem she was having with her twenty-six-year-old daughter.

We each prayed, and then I asked Linda, "What's going on? Is God saying anything to you?"

Linda said, "No. I did not hear anything. But with my eyes closed, God showed me a vision. I saw the three of us walking on the beach. I knew God was telling me he sent the two of you here to help me." We continued with our prayers.

About fifteen minutes later, as we were praying, I heard God's voice. God spoke silently but as clear as a bell. He said, "It's not about her daughter. It's about her mother." We were headed in the wrong direction with our prayers, and God corrected our path. After we prayed, I said to Linda, "Tell us about your relationship with your mom."

Linda burst into tears. She said nine years before her mom had died, she and her mom had had a terrible argument. She had told her mom that she never wanted to see her again. Linda said that her mom became deathly ill. Family members called Linda and told her that her mom wanted to see her before she died, but Linda refused to go to her. Her mom had now been dead for about seven years. Linda said, "I'll never forgive myself for not swallowing my pride and going to be with my mom before she died."

> *Jesus tells us to forgive others. If we don't forgive others, all the crippling hurts and bitterness build up inside us, and we suffer. How many times have you heard someone say, "I'll never forgive you for what you did"? We must also forgive*

ourselves. In prayer sessions, we take all the hurt, pile it up, and give it to Jesus. When Jesus takes it, the person is set free. The memory is still there, but Jesus takes the sting from the memory. He replaces that sting with freedom.

We told Linda that she needed to ask God for forgiveness and even ask her mom for forgiveness. She needed to then give all the hurts and guilt to Jesus. Linda prayed and asked Jesus for forgiveness. She prayed and told her mom she was sorry. When Linda finished praying, Jo Ann and I did not say anything. Linda said, "As I prayed, I asked my mom to forgive me. Then Mom stood there before me in a vision. With my eyes closed, I saw her. She was here. She spoke to me and said she loved me and forgave me for what I had said and done to her." Jesus broke the chains of bondage and set Linda free. The memory is still there, but the "sting" is gone. Jesus took the sting away.

When you forgive someone, you set a captive free. That captive is you.

Six Years of Bitterness

Sam shared his testimony of unforgiveness with me. His wife had left him for another man, and he was so hurt that he would not forgive her. The unforgiveness turned into bitterness, and the bitterness took root. Sam said that for six years, every night when he went to bed, hatred of his wife and the other man was on his heart. When he woke up in the morning, the hatred was the first thing on his mind. It was eating him up.

One evening as Sam stood in the bathroom thinking about his ex-wife, he heard God speak out loud. God said, "Sam, you're angry with the wrong person. You're causing your own problems." He looked around, and there was no one there, but he had clearly heard God's voice. He looked in the mirror at his reflection and understood what God had just told him. He forgave his wife and the other man. God immediately broke the chains that bound Sam and set him free. That night was the first night in six years that he had a good night's sleep.

Deliverance: Wanda

At a Christian conference in North Carolina, the conference leader prayed over anyone who wanted prayer, which happened to be almost everyone in the room. We had been told earlier that during the prayer sessions, if we heard "moaning," it could be either Jesus healing a deep wound, or it could be the presence of demons. Sure enough, some people were leaning over and moaning. Others were lying on the floor, moaning. Jesus was doing his work. I personally don't have the spiritual gift of discerning evil spirits, so I couldn't tell the difference. To me, moaning is moaning.

Eventually, all the moaning stopped, except for that of one woman, Wanda, who was still lying on the floor. Most of the conference attendees had left the conference and headed home for the night. The conference staff assistant, Jan, and around ten attendees were still in the room.

I felt sorry for Wanda, who was still lying on that dirty carpet. I went over and put my hands under her arms and tried to lift her to a chair. When I lifted her up, her entire body stiffened, as straight and rigid as a two-by-twelve board. When I placed her rigid body on the chair, she simply slid back onto the carpet. There is absolutely no way Wanda, a "soft" woman around sixty-five years old, could physically do this. Even when I was in excellent physical shape, I don't think I could make my body completely stiff as she did. Through the prayers of the conference leaders, the Holy Spirit had caused the demons in her to manifest.

At that time, I had experienced demons only once. I was here at the conference to learn about spiritual warfare. As I stood there feeling sorry for Wanda, the others in the room formed a circle around her. Jan, who obviously had much experience in dealing with demons, also came over to help. She started saying, "Come on out of her, you demons. Get out of her. It's time to go home. Get out of here. I'm tired, and I want to go home."

The ten conference trainees apparently had experienced demons before, because they knew what to do. In low voices, they each started praying Scripture out loud. Demons hate the sword of the Spirit. Wanda continued to lie stiff on the floor. She could not speak. Jan kept telling the demons to "tell me your names," but the demons would only growl and mumble in response.

After several unsuccessful attempts at getting the demons' names, I asked if I could try. Jan laughed and said, "OK, see if you can get their names." I remembered how, when I cast the demons out of John, the demons mumbled at me. I knew from that experience that the demons must submit to us in the name of Jesus Christ.

I got on my knees next to Wanda's head and calmly, but in a firm voice, told the demons, "I command you to tell us your names and speak plainly and clearly so we can understand you."

The demons growled and mumbled their names. I again said, "In the name of Jesus Christ of Nazareth, I command you to speak clearly and tell us your names right now." The demons leaned Wanda up, and she looked into my eyes (the demons were controlling her movements). I saw the eyes of the demons through her eyes. Her face then distorted and squinted up around her nose. Her face and nose looked like those of a pig. I said, "You don't scare me. Tell me your names, and tell me now!"

The pig face went away, and then she opened her mouth. She stuck her tongue out at least three or four inches, way past what is normal, and her tongue turned black. Her tongue thrashed back and forth like the tongue of a snake. Again I said, "You don't scare me. Tell me your names right now. In the name of Jesus Christ, I command you to tell me your names and speak clearly so we can understand you."

The demons finally said the name, "Confusion." I bound the Spirit of Confusion and cast him out.

Wanda still could not speak. I leaned over her and said, "Wanda, can you say the name 'Jesus'?" The demons hate the name Jesus. She opened her mouth, but no words would come out. The demons still would not allow her to speak.

After a few minutes, one of the ladies standing in the circle praying and quoting Scripture said, "The Lord just gave me a word." The Holy Spirit had just given her a piece of information that was needed in casting out the demons. She said, "Wanda is choking. That's why she can't speak."

Jan said, "Wanda, are you choking?" Wanda nodded yes. Then Jan said, "With the sword of the Spirit of God, I cut you free." Wanda immediately gasped for air, but it was not over.

A man who was quoting Scripture and praying said, "God just gave me a word." Another demon spirit was cast out. More demons came out along the way.

Then the "strongman" showed up. He was stronger than the other demons. Another woman who was praying said, "God just gave me a word." She then leaned over and put her hand on Wanda's head and said, "It's not your fault." She then cast out the strongman.

I don't know if Wanda had been abused as a child or if something had happened to her later in life. Even though whatever happened to her was not her fault, it still opened a door to the demons. This strongman and the other demons had been having their way with Wanda for many years. Now they were gone. Jesus set Wanda free. The deliverance took about two hours.

Vickie, the College Student

Vickie's parents asked us to pray with Vickie. She was a senior in college. She had no problems in high school or her first three years in college. But now, she had turned into an extreme introvert. She did not want to speak up in class, and she was shying away from friends.

By the tone of Vickie's voice and the look in her eyes, we suspected there were demons present. The demons never spoke out, but we could tell they were there. Had we been working with a grown man, we might have said something like, "Hey, Bubba, I think maybe you have a few demons hanging around. Would it be OK if we run them off?" But this was a timid, young girl.

As we prayed, we said, "If there is anything here that is not of God, we command it to come out now." We prayed a few other similar prayers but never mentioned demons. Vickie asked what we were talking about. We told her that sometimes in life, we just pick up some garbage along the way and need to get rid of it. It's like when a doctor gets rid of a virus. Jesus helps us get rid of garbage. She was OK with that explanation.

After each round of prayers, Vickie would say, "Something just came out of me." We told her that it was God cleaning her up. After she said this a few more times, she asked, "What's going on? Something keeps leaving me." We told her that healing was often like peeling an onion: God does the healing in layers.

After almost two hours of prayer, Vickie started smiling and laughing. She said, "I guess God finished peeling the onion." The demons were gone. We had no idea how the demons got their hooks into Vickie, but that didn't matter. Jesus had set this young lady free. She was now back on track at college and with her friends.

Robert Exploded

Robert called and said he knew he had demons in him. We met with Robert and talked a few minutes, and then we got to work. After about fifteen minutes of prayer, Robert's face puffed up and turned red. His cheeks puffed out like he had a mouth full of marshmallows, and his mouth was about to explode. As I looked at Robert, I clearly heard God say, "Scream and get it out of your system."

I looked at Robert, but I was not about to tell him to scream and get the demons out of his system, because this man was really messed up. A few minutes passed, and then Robert exploded. He started screaming violently and swinging his arms. The demons came out screaming. After Robert calmed down, he said, "Oh, I'm so embarrassed."

I told him, "Don't be. God told me to tell you to scream and get it out of your system." I'll never forget Robert's reply.

He looked me in the eyes and said, "Then why didn't you tell me?"

That question hit me like a dagger. Why? I had heard God's voice many times before, and I knew it was God's voice. So why didn't I obey God? The answer is: because I didn't trust God. I simply did not trust what God had told me to tell Robert.

A short time later, I was reading Oswald Chambers's daily devotional book, *My Utmost for His Highest*. The March 20 devotional deals with a similar subject. Oswald says,

> To be so much in contact with God that you never need to ask Him to show you His will, is to be nearing the final stage of your discipline in the life of faith. When you are rightly related to God, it is a life of freedom and liberty and delight, and you *are* God's will, and all your common-sense decisions are His will for you unless He checks.[10]

What Chambers is telling me is that I need to be so secure in God that when I hear His voice, I respond in immediate obedience. Sometimes I don't even need to hear His voice, because if I'm that close to God, I am His voice. And, as I walk closer and closer with our Savior, His decisions, His thoughts, and His actions become my decisions, my thoughts, and my actions. In my chapter on prayer, I call this "having the mind of Christ." We know that when we're in communion with our Savior, we don't even need to ask if it's OK. We know that before we make a wrong decision, God will stop us. Or, as Chambers puts it, God will "check" us. If I should misunderstand what God says, I need to know that God will stop me, or check me, before I do the wrong thing.

I know "Satan himself masquerades as an angel of light" (2 Corinthians 11:14), but my God is far superior to Satan. My focus needs to be totally on listening and obeying. Since that time when I did not obey God in the prayer session, I have never backed off. When God speaks, I respond. God has never let me make a fool of myself.

Abortion: a Man's Guilt

Abortion is terribly wrong. The child in the mother's womb is alive. God says, "Before I formed you in the womb I knew you" (Jeremiah 1:5). I've been told that women generally feel the guilt of abortion more than men, but men do carry the guilt as well. A young man, Jimmy, from North Carolina, was vacationing in Mount Pleasant. He heard about our healing prayer ministry, and we went to his beach house to pray with him. He and his girlfriend had gotten an abortion when they were in high school, because they were too young to get married. Immediately after graduating from high school, they were married and now have five beautiful children. But Jimmy could never forgive himself for being part of killing their unborn child. His wife often blamed him for the abortion. She would never let him forget that it was his fault. He was now thirty-five years old and had carried this guilt and shame for the past twenty years.

Satan is a liar. He will encourage a person to have an abortion. He will tell you things like, "It's really not a child. It's still in the making. It's only a thing. It's OK. Go ahead and just get rid of it." Then, after the child is dead, Satan will daily accuse you of killing your unborn child of God. The Bible tells us that Satan "accuses them before our God day and night" (Revelation 12:10). After the abortion, Satan sets his hook. However, the Bible tells us, "But if anybody does sin, we have an advocate with the Father—Jesus Christ, the Righteous One.

He is the atoning sacrifice for our sins, and not only for ours but also for the sins of the whole world" (1 John 2:1–2).

Jimmy sought forgiveness, and Jesus set him free. He told me, "I know I'll see my child alive and well when I get to Heaven, and there will be no guilt; only love." I personally believe that he will, and there will be no guilt or hurt associated with the reunion. Abortion is a terrible sin, but it is no different from the millions of other sins that are out there. The blood of Christ covers all of our sins and sets us free.

Listen to Your Children

Chris is a good Christian friend who is bold in declaring his faith in Christ. His daughter told him there was "something" in their house, and she was afraid. Listen to your children when they tell you things like this. She usually kept her bedroom door closed. When she needed to go to the bathroom, she would run down the hallway to it and quickly close the door.

A friend and I met with Chris, and we started praying over the house. There was "heavy air" in a stairwell leading to an upstairs game room near the daughter's bedroom. The evil spirits were bound and commanded to leave. They left the stairwell but went to the master bedroom, which had already been prayed over and declared clean. They were again commanded to leave the house, and they finally left. We never even bothered to ask the demons their names. If your child or spouse "feels" there is something evil in your house, listen to them, because they may be right.

Demons in My House

From time to time, demons come visit our home. The first time I was aware of demons actually coming into our house was the time I broke my neck, when Satan himself showed up and tried to convince me to commit suicide.

Connie has a set of wind chimes hanging from the ceiling in our den. Sometimes when I'm reading the Bible or working on Bible study material, I will notice movement in the den. The wind chimes spin, but there is no wind in the den to spin the chimes. The demons spin the chimes just to harass us.

Out of the corner of my eye, I sometimes see the black shadow of a man walking down the hallway.

These occurrences aren't frequent, but when they happen, I just laugh and take the bottle of anointing oil and go through the house, claiming it again for Jesus. The demons leave for a while.

Once I was putting together Bible-study material on sharing the gospel. I had been using our computer for years and had never had a problem sending out an e-mail. I was trying to send one to the men in our Bible study group about the upcoming study, and it would not go through. I tried for almost thirty minutes, but it just would not send. I then tried sending an e-mail to a friend about another topic, and it went through fine. I laughed, because I knew the demons were back.

Later that same day, I had just walked through the den and returned to the computer. Connie had also just walked through the den, and everything had been fine. Then I got up from the computer and went to the kitchen. I noticed that the large stereo speaker that sat on top of the den bookshelves had fallen off the top shelf and crushed the stereo unit on a lower, extended shelf. The speaker had bounced off the stereo and landed on Connie's glass-topped table without breaking the top, but it did crush a glass jar on the table. The speaker then slid up under the table. The speaker weighed about seventy pounds and had been firmly sitting on that shelf for over thirty years.

I called Connie and asked, "When did this happen?" We had both just walked through the den, and everything had been fine. Neither of us heard any noise in the den. There should have been a huge crash, but we heard nothing. I laughed and told Connie, "They're back!" I went to the garage to get a pair of wire cutters to cut all the stereo wires. Before I could flip on the light switch, the garage lights blinked on and off by themselves at least a half dozen times. Then the lights turned off and stayed off. I turned the lights on, got a pair of pliers, and cut the stereo speaker wires. We took anointing oil and prayed over the house (and the computer) and ran the demons out of our house. I returned to the computer and sent the Bible-study e-mail without a problem.

I truly believe God is Sovereign, which to me means He causes certain things to happen and allows others to happen. He allowed the demons to mess with us for a while. Why would He let this happen? I do not know. The glass-top table has a great deal of sentimental value to Connie. How could a seventy-pound stereo speaker fall dead center on the table (again, it crushed a glass jar there) and not break the glass top? I'll tell you how: "With God all things are possible" (Matthew 19:26). He allowed Satan to mess with us but would not allow him to destroy the glass-top table that meant so much to Connie.

I've never had demons touch me in my house, but others have. A Christian friend told of how she put her children to bed, and a short time later, she heard screaming in the bedroom. She opened the bedroom door, and the beds were vibrating up and down. She screamed out to Jesus, and the bouncing beds stopped. Demons hate the name 'Jesus.' Another Christian friend shared a similar experience about her children. I expect things like this may happen more often than we realize. These two families don't go around talking about the demonic attacks. They know that Connie and I believe in spiritual warfare, and that's why they shared their experiences with us.

My wife sometimes sees angels walk down the hallway in our house. I've never seen them. She said they look like white shadows. As Connie and I work together in advancing the Kingdom of God, our differing spiritual gifts work together.

Praying over the Church: the Jezebel Spirit

I had heard of "praying over a church" before, but I really didn't have a clue what it was all about. We were told that some of the teachers at our church school, when working late into the evening, heard footsteps in the hallways. They looked down the hallway, but there was no one there. I had personally seen demons walking in the hallway (the black shadow of a man), so I knew there were demons in our church. We gathered a group of volunteers and prepared to pray over every office, every classroom, every computer, and every nook and cranny.

I was handed a bottle of anointing oil and told to go pray over the rooms on the east hallway and the rooms on the second floor of the CLC building. My good friend, William, and I began anointing classrooms, offices, computers, janitor closets, stairwells, and everything in front of us.

I really didn't know what to pray for, so as we worked through the area, I just rebuked, in the name of Jesus Christ, anything not of God and commanded it to leave. We claimed each area for Christ, anointed it with oil, and prayed the Holy Spirit would fill the area and the men, women, and children who used these areas.

Everything went well in the classroom and office areas. We then went to the second floor of the CLC. I prayed over the first room in the CLC, and as I prayed, something just didn't feel right. The next room was the men's restroom. I was about to skip over the restroom, but I remembered we had been told to pray over every room. As I prayed over the men's restroom and anointed it with oil, that uneasy feeling began to really well up in my gut. I knew something was wrong. I wet my finger with anointing oil and started to anoint the ladies' restroom door. Before I could say anything, a very strong hand grabbed my throat and squeezed it so hard I could not speak. It scared the daylights out of me. I thought that because I was a

Christian, demons shouldn't have been able to touch me, but I was wrong.

I normally would have said something like, "In the name of Jesus Christ, let go of me." But without thinking about what to say, in an extremely difficult and forceful, choking voice, I instinctively shouted, "Get out of here!" The demon immediately turned me loose and left.

William asked, "What happened?"

I told him, "Here, you take the anointing oil and pray. I'm finished." I was still shook up over what had just happened.

When our group met back together, my friend, Chris, had the same experience with a demon downstairs in the CLC. A demon had also grabbed his throat, choked him, and tried to stop him from driving out the demons in our church. Later, as I talked with God about what had happened, He revealed to me that the demon was the Jezebel Spirit, a very strong and ruthless evil spirit.

I had heard of the Jezebel Spirit, but I didn't know anything about the demon. I called a friend in Alabama that I had met at a healing prayer conference and asked her, "Have you ever heard of the Jezebel Spirit?"

She said, "Yes; she leads the choir in our church." She explained how this woman wanted to be in control of the church. She had run off many good Christian families from their church that she felt were a threat to her self-appointed authority. I asked why the pastor didn't do anything about it. She said the pastor was afraid of her. She said that this woman even put down the pastor in front of others, and he would not call her on her actions. My friend explained more to me about the Jezebel Spirit. I then bought several books on how to recognize the Jezebel Spirit and how to deal with her.

There is also a wealth of information on the Internet about the Jezebel Spirit. I encourage you to spend a few hours reading and learning how to deal with this demonic spirit. The Jezebel Spirit is a major ruling spirit and might be found in your church as well as your workplace. She normally enters a woman but will also enter a man if she finds an opening. She is a controlling spirit that wants authority and to be in control of others. She hates the authority God gave to men, and she will also attack other women she feels are a threat to her.

I have a pastor friend that I met at the healing prayer conference. He told me of how he also encountered the Jezebel Spirit. Volunteer day was approaching, and the woman in charge of the volunteers at the church came by the pastor's office. She told him, "Since Sunday is Volunteer Emphasis Day, I will lead the service, and you can take a rest. I will present the message to the congregation. I will also select all the music for the service and take care of all the other details."

The pastor stood his ground. He told her, "No. I will give you five minutes to talk about our volunteers. Then I will preach my sermon, and our music director will select the music as usual."

Jezebels hate being told no. This woman retaliated. She started telling lies about the pastor and his wife, trying to discredit and destroy them. Some people in the congregation actually believed some of her lies. She did a great deal of damage to the pastor and the church. Several months later, her hateful actions were uncovered, and she was confronted by the pastor and left the church. The pastor again stood his ground.

Curt the Alcoholic

Curt was an alcoholic, and his drinking was having a detrimental effect on his family and his job as a painter. He was about to lose his job. He tried to quit drinking but couldn't. As we prayed, I could tell that the demon spirit of alcohol came out of Curt, but he didn't say anything. Several times I asked leading questions, hoping to hear him say, "That demon just left me." Sometimes Christians who don't know what demons are will say, "Something just left me" or "Something just came out of me." They sometimes say, "Something just happened. I feel lighter."

Curt didn't say anything. I knew he had been set free, but he just wouldn't say anything to let us know that it was a done deal. I asked him if he would mind if I called him in a week or two, and he said that would be OK.

About two weeks later, I called Curt to see how he was doing. He said, "Man, I can't believe it. When we were praying, God set me free from alcohol. It was like I've had the weight of a five-gallon bucket of paint hanging around my neck for years. The weight was pulling me down and down and down. I didn't realize it until I got home. Jesus took that weight off my neck and set me free. It's gone. I'm free."

Larry, the Pastor's Son

A friend of a friend of a friend recommended that Larry, a thirteen-year-old boy from Georgia, come to us for prayer. He was in town visiting relatives. He was the son of the pastor of a church in Georgia. Larry was suicidal. He really did not want to live. Even though he had two great parents, something had happened to him. The voices, the thoughts, and the focus on death—they were constantly before him. Satan wanted him dead.

Another man and I prayed with Larry. God did not need to give us a word of knowledge. While we were praying, Jesus himself stood before Larry. Did we two prayer ministers see Jesus? No. Did Larry see Jesus? Absolutely yes! Larry said, "Jesus was here. He stood right in front of me. He placed His hand on my shoulder and said, 'You belong to me. I'll protect you.' Then Jesus left the room." Jesus set Larry free from the Spirit of Death that had been trying to kill him. Larry was all smiles. He told us what had happened, and the prayer session was over. The prayer session only lasted fifteen minutes. It was a done deal.

Right now, you may be thinking, *I don't believe Jesus can or will do that*. Jesus is God, and He can do anything He chooses. Remember, "with God all things are possible" (Matthew 19:26).

Jim and the Former Girlfriend

Jim and his wife had just recently become Christians, and they both wanted to live their lives to honor Christ. They were very young and had been married less than a year. Jim came to us for help. He had messed up. He had committed adultery. A former girlfriend had called and made an offer, and he took the bait.

> *Satan will tell you it is OK. You've been with her before, so what difference does one more time make? Then, afterward, he will accuse you before God of being a Christian who committed adultery. Satan wants to destroy you and your family with guilt and shame.*

Satan knows us—not as well as God knows us, but he knows you and me. He knows our strengths and our weaknesses. For many men, the sin is adultery with the eyes, but with other men, it is full-blown adultery. For some, the deep sin may be pornography, and for others, it may be money, a job, or a hobby. The weakness may also be pride—such as standing in front just to be applauded. Satan also knows the weaknesses of our wives and of our children. He wants to destroy our families. He wants to separate us from our home family and our church family. He wants to steal what God has rightfully given to us. The Bible says, "The thief comes only to steal and kill and destroy" (John 10:10). That's the bad news. But the good news is in the second half of that verse. Jesus says, "I have come that they may have life, and have it to the full" (John 10:10).

My friend Chris and I were praying over Jim. His body was quivering, like when you've been outside in the freezing cold too long and your inner core is quivering. Satan had his hook deep into Jim. Satan truly wanted to destroy his walk with the Lord before it even got started.

I had been praying and commanding the demons to come out, but they would not budge. Chris had been silently praying. Then, when I finally shut up, Chris said only two words. He said, "Get out." He spoke softly, but with authority. The demons heard him. When he commanded the demons to get out, they immediately left, and the quivering stopped. Jim knew they were gone and that he had been set fee. His life and marriage were back on track.

Sometimes two or three prayer ministers will pray with a person. It's been our experience that the Holy Spirit will often work through one of the prayer ministers for the healing. Sometimes He does not even work through a prayer minister at all; He just heals the person.

David: We Lost this One

David's younger brother persuaded him to come to us for prayer, so a friend and I prayed with him. From the very start, it was obvious that David did not want to be with us. He came only because his brother put a great deal of pressure on him to come. Even though his whole life was a disaster, he still did not want healing. Satan truly had a hook buried deep in this man. The entire two hours that we were with him, he never looked at us; he just stared at the floor and would hardly talk with us. After two hours, it was obvious we were getting nowhere, and we were all very tired. We discussed wrapping up the prayer session and scheduling another session in a few weeks.

After we prayed our closing prayers, David looked up for the first time in two hours. He looked directly into my eyes, and I saw the eyes of the demons. I could tell by his eyes and the expression on his face that Satan was telling me, "I beat you today," and he did. We lost this one. David left the room and never came back. I suspect he was involved in Satan worship and did not want to give it up.

I know that God can do anything. He can heal people even when they don't want healing. But in most cases, I think a person must want to be healed in order to be healed. A person must also have at least some faith in Jesus and trust Him for the healing.

Connie's Dad is Healed

Connie's elderly dad was scheduled to have a cancerous kidney removed the next morning. Connie was upset and at her wits' end. She was beside herself worrying about her dad. He was old, and she felt he might die during the surgery. I tried to talk with her and calm her, but it did no good. She was so upset that the worry brought on a migraine headache. She finally jumped up and stormed out the front door in the middle of the night. She said, "I've got to get out of here." As she walked up and down the median in front of our house, she had a talk with her Savior. When she came back into the house, she was completely at peace. She had finally given the surgery and the worry to the Lord.

The next morning at the hospital, the doctors decided to do one more CAT scan before the surgery. The cancer was completely gone, and the surgery was canceled. Jesus had already healed her dad.

My Painful Back

I've had a bad back for forty years. If I'm careful, I can go months with no problem. But when I mess up and lift something too heavy, my back goes out and I have a great deal of pain. I know for a fact that when I ask my wife to pray over my painful back, God will take away the pain. But I usually just put up with it for two or three days. My wife says I'm hardheaded. Then, when the pain is unbearable, I'll ask my wife to lay hands on me and pray for my back. We both kneel, she'll put her hand on my back, and she prays a simple healing prayer for about five minutes. When she says "Amen," the pain is either completely gone, or it will be completely gone in an hour or so. It works every time.

All Christians Can Pray for Healing

I could share many, many more testimonies. But I think by now you get the point: Jesus is still healing people today. It's not necessary to have a great deal of training to pray for someone. All Christians can pray for healing. When someone asks for prayer, simply place your hand on his or her head or shoulder (if the person is OK with this) and pray and ask Jesus to heal the person. If, during the prayer, you hear the voice of God, obey and do what He says.

Once we were praying over a young lady, and Chris heard the Lord speak. The Lord told Chris, "Get on your knees and pray over her feet." Chris got on his knees, placed his hands on her feet and prayed. We don't always understand what God's doing; we are to simply obey.

Not All Bad Stuff Is from Satan

Not all bad things that happen to us are caused by demons. As a matter of fact, I suspect we cause a lot of the bad stuff ourselves. If we eat too much greasy food, we'll probably get indigestion. If we flunk a test at school, it's probably because we didn't study enough. We sometimes tend to blame Satan for our own actions.

When you get the flu, you go to a doctor. When you get a demon, I hope you will go to Christian friends and let them cast out the demon. Most of the demons I've dealt with have been light work and come out relatively easily. Most of our prayer sessions last around an hour or two. My good Christian friend, Brian, helps set people free from Satan worship and the occult, and his deliverance sessions sometimes last a day or two or even longer.

The bottom line is this: Jesus said, "I have given you authority to trample on snakes and scorpions and to overcome all the power of the enemy; nothing will harm you" (Luke 10:19).

CHAPTER 18

Near-Death Encounters

Before becoming a Christian at age forty-four, I had my share of close calls with death. After becoming a Christian, I continue to have close calls. Many of them amount to one second, twelve inches, a fraction of an inch, or downright miracles. In the Bible, God says, "For he will command his angels concerning you to guard you in all your ways" (Psalm 91:11).

The Bicycle Crash

One evening when I was a child, I was riding my bike home just before dark and running late. I needed to get home in a hurry. As I rode down the side street by the Methodist Church, I didn't bother to stop at the stop sign. A car was zooming down the cross street, and I slammed into its left front fender. I was banged up, and the bicycle was bent up, but I walked away from the accident. Had I arrived at that intersection one second earlier, I would have been run over.

Lightning and a Pine Tree

I had my special deer hunting tree in the Francis Marion National Forest. It was a very tall pine tree. I could use a climber-stand, climb fifty feet high, and look out over a large area of the forest. I hunted rain or shine, because deer move just as well in the rain as they do when it's dry. My hunting buddies would tell me I was crazy for hunting in the rain. They said my metal tree stand and my metal rifle were like lightning rods. I would say, "There are billions and billions of trees here in the forest. What are the odds of lightning hitting the one tree I'm using?"

I had planned to take off work Friday and go deer hunting even though it was raining, but something came up, and I couldn't go. Saturday, I did go hunting. When I got to my special tree, it was in shambles. Lightning had picked out my one tree and blown it to pieces. Had I been in the tree and hunting Friday morning, I would have looked like a burnt marshmallow on the end of a stick. I took that as a sign from God—I no longer hunt in the rain.

The Barge

I used to love deer hunting on Bull Island, which is about fifteen miles north of Mount Pleasant. I normally camped on the island all week and hunted, but sometimes that did not work out. In those cases, I would make day-trips to the island to hunt. I would take my fourteen-foot Jon boat to the Isle of Palms and launch it into the Atlantic Intracoastal Waterway. I would make the run to Bull Island in the dark, hunt during the day, and make the return run home after dark.

One of those early mornings, it was extremely foggy, and I could hardly see my hand in front of my face. A spotlight is useless in heavy fog, but I was so familiar with the night run that I could make it in the dark with no spotlight. As I headed up the Intracoastal Waterway, I heard a loud, roaring noise that seemed to be getting closer and closer. I couldn't figure out what it was. It sounded like a freight train.

Then I came to a very small opening in the fog. Suddenly, there before me was a huge, ten-foot-high black wall, and the wall was plowing through the water directly toward me. I immediately swerved the boat to the right. By only a few feet, I escaped having a huge, saltwater barge run over me. If there had not been that one small break in the fog, I would have been run over by the barge and ground to pieces in the barge's prop.

Almost Electrocuted

At our hunt club, we had an old mobile home we used as a bunk house. One day, the water pump quit working, and I suspected a loose connection or corroded contacts on the pump's pressure switch. The well and well pump were at the edge of a swamp. I was standing in about three inches of water when I pulled the cover off the pressure switch. I used a voltage meter to confirm that there was no power on any of the wires, and I knew it was OK to work on the switch.

As I started to place my screwdriver on the first screw, I heard God's voice. He said, "Treat it like it's hot." I knew it was God's voice, so I did as He said. I switched to an insulated screwdriver to free the wires. I was careful not to touch any of the wires even though I knew they were not electrified. After I had loosened all four wires, I checked them again with the voltage meter, and there was no current. Then I questioned God, asking, "Why did you tell me to 'treat it like it's hot'?" God did not answer. I took the screwdriver and swiped the blade across the wires, and 220 volts of fire flew everywhere. The wires *were* hot! Had I not obeyed when God spoke, I would have been electrocuted.

After I finished working on the pressure switch, I went back to the mobile home. I used the voltage meter and checked an electrical outlet inside the trailer. The meter showed 120 volts. The meter again worked fine.

Move Out from under It

On another day at the hunt club, I was going to put some corn in a deer feeder. I had built a homemade angle-iron bracket with a metal pulley and attached the bracket about twenty-five feet up on a tree using a strong chain and hardened bolts. I used a thousand-pound boat trailer winch and a wire cable run through a pulley to lift the two-hundred-pound metal barrel of corn and battery-operated feeder. I had been using feeders in this fashion for years and had never had a problem. I always "over engineered" the metal brackets, bolts, and pulleys.

I was cranking the winch handle with my right hand, and the barrel was headed up the tree. As I cranked, I was standing directly under the barrel. When the barrel was only a few inches from the top, I heard the Lord's voice. He said, "Get out from under it." I only needed to make two more turns on the winch handle, and I'd be finished. But I've learned to obey God. I moved over to my right, out from under the barrel, and started making the last two turns of the winch handle using my left hand. I made one turn of the winch handle and then BAM! Bolts on the bracket sheared off, and everything came crashing to the ground. The weight of the corn drove the feeder motor all the way into the ground. Again, if I had I not obeyed God, I would not be here, because the metal barrel would have crushed my skull.

Lightning and Fishing

One afternoon, Connie and I were fishing for redfish at our favorite spot on Schooner Creek at Capers Island. A power line runs through the marsh, across Capers to Bull Island. At one point, the power line runs close to Schooner Creek. There were rain squalls on the mainland about ten miles away. I could see the squalls and a few bolts of lightning. Connie, of course, wanted to head home, but I kept telling her the rain was moving from west to east and would miss us. "Don't worry," I kept telling her. She kept bugging me about leaving, and I kept ignoring her because I wanted to fish. Then, all of a sudden, BOOM! A bolt of lightning hit the power pole near our boat. We were not hit, but it sure made our hair stand up.

Connie threw her rod down and started pulling up the anchor. She said, "I don't know about your end of the boat, but this end of the boat is leaving!" It was time to head home.

Almost Electrocuted Again

I wanted to share the gospel with a young friend named Tim. One day as we talked, he asked me if I wanted to work a "side job" with him wiring a house. I knew it would take three days to rough in the wiring, and there would be an opportunity to share the gospel. Sure enough, it worked out that way. The second day, I shared the gospel with Tim, and he accepted Jesus as his Lord and Savior.

A month or so later, Tim and I needed to return to the house and do the finish work on the wiring job. We did the inside work first, assuming we would have good weather all three days. On the third day, we planned to complete the outside work, and it started pouring rain. Tim and I did not want to come back the next day, so I told Tim, "You finish up inside, and I'll do the outside work in the rain." I had a towel and spare clothes in my truck.

I killed the breakers to the outside lights and then stood on a ladder in the rain, wiring all the outside light fixtures. I then killed the breaker for the heat pump so I could install a disconnect switch on the outside of the house. I was kneeling in a puddle of water as it poured rain. I knew the power was off because I had killed the breaker myself. I took a pair of uninsulated pliers and started cutting one of the cables. I remember feeling the first *sting* of electricity hitting my hands, and then *someone* kicked the pliers out of my hands. The force of the kick was so great that it threw me backward, and the pliers landed in the water about ten feet to my right.

When you cut into a hot wire with uninsulated pliers, as soon as the electricity in the wire hits your hands, the muscles in your hands immediately cramp. Your fingers cramp and grip the pliers even tighter, and it's all but impossible to turn the pliers loose, even though you're being electrocuted. For you to be freed, someone must quickly kick the pliers out of your hands.

I had obviously killed the wrong breaker. The heat pump lines were still hot, and I should have been electrocuted. I should be dead. I looked to see who had kicked the pliers out of my hands, but there was no one there. However, my God and His angels said, "Not today!"

The Broken Neck

I mentioned in chapter 14 that I broke my neck in a four-wheeler accident. Here are the details. One afternoon in October 1998, I was deer hunting on Mr. Tisdale's farm. I was riding my four-wheeler around the edge of an overgrown field, looking to my left for deer trails. Just as I turned my head to the front, there before me was a drainage ditch. I did not even have time to apply the brakes. The last thing I remember was feeling the sensation of the four-wheeler dropping out from under me, and then everything went black.

When I regained consciousness, I was lying spread-eagled on the other side of the ditch, looking up into the sky. I was paralyzed. I could not move. I had been thrown over the handlebar, landed on my head, and broken five of the seven cervical vertebrae in my neck. The first thought that came to my mind was, *Boy, you really messed up this time.* Then I thought, *Man, I only had six more months to work, and I could have retired and hunted and fished every day of the rest of my life.* Then, I thought about my wife, who would now have to push me around in a wheelchair, spoon-feed me, and change my diaper for the rest of my life. I truly felt sorry for bringing this burden on her.

Then I came to grips with the reality of being paralyzed. I told God, "I know you are Sovereign. You cause things to happen, and you allow things to happen. If you want me in a wheelchair the rest of my life, that's OK with me. I'll be the best witness for Christ from a wheelchair that you've ever had. I'm not going to let being paralyzed stop me from telling others about Jesus. I'll still live out every day of the rest of my life for you, even from a wheelchair." I meant what I said as I lay there praising God. His peace engulfed me. God is Sovereign, and I totally trust Him.

After an hour or so, the temperature started dropping, and it was going to be dark soon. Buzzards were circling overhead. I knew I was in trouble. I again talked with my God and said, "Lord, we need to be doing something right away, or I'll die tonight lying on the cold ground." I still could not move any part of my body—I was paralyzed. Then, after a few minutes, out of the corner of my eye, I saw the index finger on my right hand move. I was not moving it; God was. I lay there and praised God. Then another finger moved, and another. Then the fingers on my left hand started moving. Gradually, my hands, arms, and legs were moving. I was not moving them; God was moving them for me. God was bringing life back into my paralyzed body.

Some might say I was only in shock, but I know that I was paralyzed. I truly believe that if I had lain there and whined and complained to God, I would still be paralyzed today. Instead, I did what came natural: I praised God. I just lay there and praised my God.

Looking back on it now, I remember how Job dealt with tragedy. He was a hundred times worse off than me. Job's wife told him to just "Curse God and die!" (Job 2:9). Job's reply was, "Shall we accept good from God, and not trouble?" (Job 2:10).

I certainly was not thinking of Job when I was lying paralyzed on the ground. I just absolutely trust God, because I belong to Him. I was bought and paid for at the cross. I belong to my Savior, and I'll praise him no matter what comes my way. Now God began to work his miracles. His angels were with me. At least seven miracles followed:

1. I got to my feet and looked around. There were huge fire-ant mounds all around me. I had landed on the ground between them. Had I landed paralyzed and unconscious on top of one of them, the ants would have eaten me alive.

2. I picked up my rifle, thinking I might need to fire three shots in the air to get help. I wasn't sure I'd be able to walk out of the overgrown field. I did not realize it at the time, but when the four-wheeler hit the side of the ditch, so did my rifle. The barrel was full of mud. If I had tried to fire the rifle to call for help, it would have exploded in my face. God saw to it that I would not need to fire the rifle.

3. I could see a power line over the tops of the six-foot-tall weeds, and I knew there was a dirt road under the power line. I was very weak and in a great deal of pain. I didn't know if I could make it to the road, but if I could make it that far, at least I would die where someone would find my body. As I broke through the tall brush and stepped out onto the dirt road, at that very second, Mr. Tisdale just happened to drive by. He gave me a ride out of the woods.

4. Mr. Tisdale drove me to his house, where I got out of his truck and lay on the ground. He asked if I wanted him to call 911, and I said I thought I'd be OK. He asked if I thought my neck was broken, and I told him I didn't think so. With my hand, I moved my head from side to side, which should have severed my spinal cord. In the army, I learned how to break an enemy soldier's neck so that he immediately died. I wasn't dead, so I figured I must have just "sprained" my neck.

5. I drove my truck sixty miles to my house. I held my head up with my left hand to take some pressure off my neck, and I steered the truck with my right hand. Halfway home, I stopped and called my wife on my cell phone. I told her I had been in an accident and hurt my neck. I needed her to call the doctor and find out where they wanted to examine me: at the emergency room or at the Family Practice Center. I told her to come to the house and pick me up, because I did not want to try to drive in the downtown Charleston traffic.

6. Connie was at the house waiting for me. She was told to take me to the Family Practice Center, and when we arrived, the doctor saw me right away. Since I could walk and drive, the doctor thought my injuries must not be too serious, and I was sent to a room for X-rays. A sweet, young lady told me, "Mr. Kelly, I need you to stand next to that wall and look straight at me." I stood there, and she took an X-ray. Then she said, "Now I need you to turn your head to the right," and I turned my whole body to the right. She said, "No, face me, and then just turn your head to the right."

   I said, "I can't do that. It's too painful. That's why I'm here. My neck is busted."

   She smiled and said, "You have to turn your head. I need to get another X-ray."

   I said, "No, you'll have to find another way to get your X-ray. I can't turn my head."

   The sweet young lady walked over to me and smiled. Then she put one hand on the top of my head and one hand on my chin and jerked my head 90 degrees to the right. I let out a scream that could be heard all over the building. I should have dropped dead in my tracks, but my Lord was with me. She apologized, and I went back to the exam room.

In a few minutes, the doctor came in and said, "Keep standing there. Don't move. EMS is on the way. We're sending you to the emergency room." He said that the X-ray had shown two vertebrae that were broken, and he suspected others may also be broken. The EMS technicians placed a foam collar around my neck, strapped me to a gurney, and drove me to the emergency room.

7. The emergency-room doctors were waiting. They immediately slid me off the gurney onto a CAT scan table and took a few pictures. As they tried to slide the table out of the CAT scan machine, the foam collar around my neck caught on something inside the machine. The two technicians operating it started pulling hard on the table. As they pulled and jerked the table, my head and neck twisted around, and I yelled, "Stop, stop!"

   One technician said, "Hang on, the table's stuck, we'll get you out." They pulled even harder and twisted my neck and head even more. Out of the corner of my eye, I saw a nurse look inside the opening in the CAT scan machine. She saw my head being twisted around and screamed for the men to stop. They should have pulled a dead man out of the CAT scan machine, but my Lord was with me. The CAT scan showed the two broken vertebrae that the X-ray had shown, plus three more that were split in half. The doctors installed a "halo" brace on my head and upper body and placed me in a bed in a patient room. Shortly after that, a concussion set in, and I did not remember anything for the next seven days.

At a follow-up visit, I asked the doctor if I could see the CAT scan pictures. He pulled them up on his computer. He started with C-7, the vertebra that attaches to the shoulders. He shook his head as he looked at the damage to each of the five broken vertebrae. When we were looking at the C-1 vertebra, which he said is the most critical, he could not explain how it had broken the way it did without cutting my spinal cord and critical nerves. He said, "You should be dead."

I told the doctor, "God held his finger right here and protected my spinal cord." I held my finger to the CAT picture. He nodded yes, because he had no other explanation. I should be dead.

Three and a half months later, the halo brace was removed. Our God completely healed my broken neck. I still enjoy riding the four-wheeler today.

Baby Back Ribs

This story is not about something life threatening, but it's interesting. Connie was cooking baby back ribs in a large pan covered with aluminum foil. The ribs had been cooking at 250 degrees for several hours. She asked me to take them out of the oven and see if they were tender. I took two hot pads, opened the oven door, and carefully lifted the pan out of the oven. It was extremely hot, and it was burning my hands through the two hot pads.

As I moved over toward the counter, the pan tipped. The pan was full of 250-degree water and fat drippings, and it all poured out and drenched my legs and feet. I was wearing shorts and flip-flops. Connie saw what happened and screamed, "Get in the shower, and I'll run cold water on you!" I stood there looking at my legs and feet and expected them to immediately burst into huge water blisters. So did Connie. But nothing happened. I touched my legs, and the liquid was cold. There were no burns or even redness, only a mess on the floor..

The Appointed Time

I could share many more testimonies of how my God has kept me alive. I truly believe that there is an appointed time when you and I are to die. That date has been set for us, and that is when we will die, unless we deliberately choose to disobey God and do something foolish to end our lives sooner. Here are several Bible verses that relate to our deaths:

> "All the days ordained for me were written in your book before one of them came to be" (Psalm139:16).

> "A person's days are determined; you have decreed the number of his months and have set limits he cannot exceed" (Job 14:5).

> "No one has power over the time of their death" (Ecclesiastes 8:8).

> "Just as people are destined to die once, and after that to face judgment" (Hebrews 9:27).

It's not a matter of when we die. It's a matter of what happens next?

CHAPTER 19

America, a Christian Nation?

"Blessed is the nation whose God is the Lord" (Psalm 33:12).
Every ten years, our government takes a census. One of the questions on the 2010 census was about our religion. I personally don't have a religion; I'm a Christian. But I knew what the question was looking for, so I responded as a Southern Baptist.

I found the following statistics regarding the religion question on the Association of Religion Data Archives website.[11] Other sites also report data from the census. Listed under "Religious Traditions, 2010," they report some interesting statistics (the following numbers are rounded).

They report that there were 309 million people in America in 2010. Of these, when asked about their religion, 158 million responded "none." In the report, they are referred to as the "unclaimed." This 51 percent of Americans say they have no religion at all. The remaining 151 million Americans, or 49 percent, claim to be affiliated with one of the religious organizations (both Christian and non-Christian) included in the data.

There are many definitions of a Christian. My short definition is "a person who is saved by the grace of God by placing his or her faith in the atoning work of Jesus Christ (without works)." After subtracting out what I consider the non-Christian doctrine groups, and reviewing data from various other Internet sites, my guesstimate of people in America who attend a Christian church (both members and non-members) would be around twenty-five percent.

Franklin Graham asked, "Could it be true that half of the people sitting in Protestant churches on Sunday morning have doubts about how to get to Heaven?"[12]

I am also concerned that many of our church members may not be Christians. I know, because for thirty years, I was a non-Christian church member. Billy Graham said,

> Millions of professing Christians are only just that—"professing." They have never possessed Christ. They live lives characterized by the flesh. Tens of thousands have never been born again. They will go into eternity lost—while thinking they are saved because they belong to the church, or were baptized, and so on.[13]

Where Are We Headed?

In an article by Carol Pipes at LifeWay.com about Thom Rainer, president of LifeWay, she notes that

> Nine out of 10 churches in America are declining or growing at a pace slower than the rate of their communities. Churches limp along as members drift out the proverbial back door.[14]

Why are so many of our Christian churches declining and even closing? I personally believe it is because we no longer share our faith in Christ with people in our communities and invite them to worship with us. I came across an article in the *Baptist Courier* that said, "Statistics show 93 percent of people polled would go to church if asked, but only 16 percent report being invited."[15]

Jesus told us, "Go out quickly into the streets and alleys of the town and bring in the poor, the crippled, the blind and the lame. 'Sir, the servant said, what you ordered has been done, but there is still room.' Then the master told his servant, 'Go out to the roads and country lanes and compel them to come in, so that my house will be full'" (Luke 14:21–23).

So why don't we "Go out to the roads and country lanes and compel them to come in?" I've heard many answers. The most popular answer is, "We don't want to impose on our neighbors." For our neighbors, which is worse: to be imposed on today, or to spend eternity in Hell?

Various data presented on the Internet indicate that while many Protestant churches are declining, the Mormons and Jehovah's Witnesses (JWs) are substantially growing. We often see the Mormons and JWs going door-to-door inviting our neighbors to their churches.

We need to check the numbers for our own particular denominations. Where are we headed? If our churches are declining, what can we do to reverse the declining trends?

A friend of mine who believes in telling others about Christ said, "If you knew the pilings under the highway bridge had buckled and the bridge was about to collapse, wouldn't you warn others?"

We need to share the good news of the gospel of Jesus Christ with as many people as will listen to us. We need to invite them to worship with us. We also need to warn those who reject Jesus Christ about the coming judgment that awaits them. (cf. Revelation 20:11–15).

CHAPTER 20

In Conclusion

How does it all end? It doesn't end. Because of our ongoing relationship with our Savior, our lives and our testimonies will be an ongoing, never-ending story. Our God is not somewhere far off. He is here with us and longs for us to have a personal relationship with Him right now.

We are to take a stand for Christ, but we're not to stand still. There's work to be done. The work lies ahead of each one of us—one day at a time.

Don't live in the past. Live in *the today* and *the tomorrow*. This book of testimonies and ramblings is a work in progress. Even as I write, more testimonies and ramblings are being put together.

Every day is an adventure, because we don't know where our Lord will lead us and where He will use us for His glory. Then, when our Savior returns for His church, the most glorious adventure of all time will begin.

Thanks for listening to the testimonies and ramblings of a redneck disciple of Jesus Christ.

I pray you will choose to be a disciple of Jesus Christ. Don't turn back.

To God be all the praise, honor, and glory!

[1] Billy Graham, Christ Has Conquered Death, *Decision Magazine* (April 2014): 9.
[2] Billy Graham, The Reason for My Hope: Salvation, *Decision Magazine* (November 2013): 12.
[3] Roberts Liardon, *God's Generals, Why They Succeeded and Why Some Failed,* (New Kensington, PA: Whitaker House, 1996), 48. Liardon's quote came from Wayne E. Warner, "Neglect Not the Gift That Is in Thee," Etter Sermon from *The Woman Evangelist* (Metuchen, NJ and London: Scarecrow Press, 1986), 307, Appendix C.
[4] Oswald Chambers, "July 17th devotional," in *My Utmost for His Highest* (Westwood, NJ: Barbour), 144–145.
[5] "Prayer in Silence," *Healing Line* (September/October 2005): 4.
[6] Billy Graham, How to Be Sure You're Saved, *Decision Magazine* (September 2012): 18.
[7] Billy Graham, The Problem with Our World, *Decision Magazine* (September 2013): 2.
[8] Warren W. Wiersbe, *The Strategy of Satan: How to Detect and Defeat Him* (Carol Stream, IL: Tyndale House), 127.
[9] Billy Graham, The Problem with Our World, *Decision Magazine* (September 2013): 4–5.
[10] "March 20th devotional," in Chambers, *My Utmost*, 57.
[11] http://www.thearda.com/rcms2010/r/u/rcms2010_99_US_name_2010.asp
[12] Franklin Graham, A World in Desperate Need of the Truth, *Decision Magazine* (June 2012): 40.
[13] Billy Graham, *The Holy Spirit: Activating God's Power in Your Life* (W Publishing Group), 111.
[14] Carol Pipes, "Rainer: Church Membership About Service, Not Privilege." LifeWay, May 1, 2013, http://www.lifeway.com/article/news-rainer-book-church-membership-service-privilege. The article references Thom Rainer's book, *I Am a Church Member* (B&H Publishing Group).
[15] Joni Hannigan, "Florida Baptist Witness, Rainer: People need to be reaching lost." *Baptist Courier* (January 2, 2003): 13.

15388700R00193

Made in the USA
Middletown, DE
05 November 2014